THE 97% FACTOR™

The 97% Factor moves leaders in business and other institutions off well-traveled data-paved roads of process and performance improvement into the richer territory beyond the Pavement Ends sign. None other than Dr. W. Edwards Deming, the father of the whole data-driven, quality movement, warned leaders:

The 3% we can measure misses the 97% that matters.

The 3% misses the devastating effects of problems without solutions, implementations that bog down, projects that languish and die, broken promises to customers and each other, and all the other hard-to-quantify human factors that leave everyone scrambling for sanity, survival, and leadership. Here in 97% Territory lay the big gains awaiting discovery. And here also are:

The 10 Principles of No Fail Leadership
Delivering results that matter where results matter most

ISBN: 978-1479306312
Printed in the United States of America.

THE 97% FACTOR

DRIVING SUCCESS BEYOND
THE DATA-PAVED 3%
THAT MANAGEMENT CAN MEASURE

10 PRINCIPLES OF NO FAIL LEADERSHIP

NIEL K KLEIN

NKK BOOKS

*To my wife, our four children and their spouses,
and our eight grandchildren.*

CONTENTS

PART 1: NO FAIL?

A Brush with Failure /   11

The 10 Principals of No Fail Leadership /   18

Postmortem of the Near-death Experience /   19

Wanted: More Mass Casualty Incidents /   27

No Fail Leadership's Vision, Mission and Way /   33

PART 2: PAVEMENT ENDS

Assumptions /   51

Processes on the Loose /   69

PART 3: DETACHING BELIEVERS FROM THEIR BELIEFS

Principle 1
*All problems stem from conflicts of belief
about what's true* /   85

Fear, conflict, consequences and Principle 1 /   109

Principle 2
*Nothing is ever what it seems.
The truth lies elsewhere* /   133

PART 4: GETTING THE TRUTH ON THE TABLE

Principle 3
The truth is always positive, even when it's painful /   173

Principle 4
Make it 100% safe to tell the truth /   191

Principle 5
No blame, no excuses /   215

PART 5: FROM INPUT TO UNDERSTANDING

Principle 6
Work from facts first, opinions later /   245

Principle 7
*Get input from frontline people before
making decisions they must implement, not after* /   261

PART 6: FROM SOLUTIONS TO IMPLEMENTATION

Principle 8
*Only make promises we can keep,
and keep all the promises we make* /   277

Principle 9
Etch all decisions in jell /   305

Principle 10
Implementation is never a "no-brainer" /   323

Looking ahead /   351

Acknowledgments /   361
Index /
About the Author /   368

PART 1

NO FAIL?

A BRUSH WITH FAILURE

The Mass Casualty Incident

High school football. The Bulldogs' school bus was packed with jocks and cheerleaders along with coaches and parents trying to keep everyone in their seats.

Forty miles of two-laners wound through dense, upper Great Lakes forest separating the Bulldogs from their rivals. The fall's vanguard maples had already turned brilliant red-orange or yellow. One, its leaves caught between green and yellow, glowed translucent chartreuse in the afternoon's slanting sun. Every bend in the road turned a new page of blazing color.

School busses aren't Porsches on winding roads, but they stand tall and aren't to be messed with. The oncoming SUV tracked normally as the bus driver watched it round the sweeping left-hand curve ahead. It wandered briefly onto the center stripes and then safely back. The motorist seemed absorbed with something in his lap. His passenger, horrified, grabbed for the steering wheel.

The SUV crossed its lane and slammed full speed into the left front wheel of the bus, making it ricochet toward the ditch. The bus driver stomped on the brakes and yanked the wheel left to steer back onto the road, but the rear broke loose, kicking up gravel on the shoulder. He had no choice but try to drive the ditch to stay upright. Not a chance. The bus bounded over something that tossed it onto its right side, sending twenty tons of screaming metal, kids, parents and coaches to a halt.

Hotel conference room: 8 a.m. the next day

I'd just spent nearly two weeks of mornings as a management consultant leading a joint, offsite workgroup intent on rebuilding the relationship between EMS Ambulance's paramedics and the emergency room staff at Our Lady Hospital. The aftershocks from yesterday's school bus accident nearly toppled everything we had built.

We had come far, considering how long the tension had gone on. For years, the paramedics had criticized Our Lady Hospital as disorganized and slow attending to incoming patients. The medics especially bristled at the disrespectful, "Oh, not another one" attitude when the ER was under pressure. Downtown Medical Center, Our Lady's regional competitor, didn't treat incoming patients that way, and the medics openly said so.

That frustrated and angered Our Lady's ER nurses and doctors no end. They believed that the medics, given a choice, favored Downtown's ER when transporting patients. They also considered the attitude of some of the medics less than professional.

But both groups sensibly agreed that the community needed two first-class, hospital ERs for everyone's benefit. And that meant honestly nailing down critical problems underlying the patient handoff process at Our Lady and fixing them. In fact, just the previous morning the group had finally—and together—employed No Fail Leadership's principles to solve the first piece of the handoff problem and looked forward to the newfound camaraderie in upcoming sessions.

Then, late that afternoon, the SUV rammed into the school bus.

Our Lady's ER clinical director, who was on duty that shift, heard "Mass Casualty Incident" (MCI) over the 911 radio and saw an opportunity to show the ER's stuff. She invoked Code MCI, scrambled a team of doctors, nurses and support people, and went all out to be ready for a major influx of patients.

The hours crawled by. Per radio traffic, they learned that the EMS paramedics on site directed ten victims to a rural county hospital and twenty-three to Downtown Medical Center. Only five showed up at Our Lady, none seriously injured.

Our Lady's ER staff was furious. So were the doctors, radiologists and other Code MCI conscripts waiting in the staging area with nothing to do. How, they demanded, could EMS's medics show such blatant preference—in the midst of an ongoing workgroup aimed at improving their interactions—for Downtown Medical Center!

The fireworks began the next morning the moment the joint workgroup assembled. Our Lady's ER head and clinical leader confessed to wondering how to convey the anger that their ER staff felt toward EMS without losing their cool themselves. They adamantly stated that unless the issue was resolved satisfactorily, they saw no point in the workgroup going forward. Positive achievements would not survive. And the team from the paramedic operation feared the same.

To all, this couldn't come at a worse moment.

Cooling down the meltdown

I was speechless listening to the accusations, finger pointing, defensiveness and guilt. Collapse seemed imminent, and I found myself buying into that fear. My sanity finally returned long enough to ask if I could see this differently.

"Time out," I interrupted. "This could not have come up at a better time. In fact, the timing is perfect." A dazzling array of "you've got to be out of your mind" looks shot my way. No one spoke.

"What would have happened if this Mass Casualty Incident had occurred six months ago?" I asked. "You'd each have stayed in your respective dens, licking your wounds and building up a world of hurt feelings with no release or recourse. Here you have an instant forum. Everyone assumes that medic bias determined how many patients went where. Maybe so, maybe not. Nothing is ever what it seems. How can we find out?"

"The radio tapes," suggested a paramedic.

Without dissent, everyone pledged to put opinions, blaming and excuses on hold while we played the tapes. We listened to every transmission, sequentially, between the medics, hospitals, fire and police departments and others responding to the MCI. Then we read the transcripts. We pored over every event from the 911 dispatchers' initial alerts through every on-scene decision, including those about ER destinations.

Clearly, nothing was even remotely what it seemed. The truth lay in an "elsewhere" bordering on the truly bizarre.

First, the SUV driver wasn't distracted and didn't die from the collision. His passengers nearly died from the collision. He was already dead at the wheel from heart failure.

Second, the accident occurred at the boundary between two counties, each with its own 911 radio frequencies and dispatchers. The bus came to a halt in one, the SUV fifty yards away in the other. The bus's 911 calls routed automatically to EMS Ambulance's dispatchers and vehicles in the city. The SUV's routed to the 911 dispatcher in the adjacent rural county, home of a small hospital and its volunteer emergency responders. Both dispatchers sent vehicles. Neither of them coordinated the response or jurisdictions with the other.

Third, the accident never should have been declared a Mass Casualty Incident at all. By protocol only medics on the scene can declare an MCI. To do so, they must run up against a greater number of serious casualties than they can tend to and transport. The dispatcher then calls in paramedic, fire, and other units from nearby areas to assist. The MCI label got slapped on before any ambulances arrived on the scene. When the EMS medics got there, they found one fatality, two other men from the SUV with serious injuries, and thirty-five bus riders sitting on the side of the road with bumps, bruises, and one broken arm. Two ambulances could handle the two serious injuries.

So who designated the incident an MCI? Formally, no one. The medics in transit from the rural hospital heard about the high school football team on the bus and speculated about a potential "Mass Casualty Incident" over the emergency radio. Our Lady's clinical director heard the speculation on the monitor and assumed that an MCI was in effect.

How come the rural hospital got ten patients, Downtown Medical Center twenty-three and Our Lady only five? Different reasons. The rural ER was closest and could only handle ten. Downtown got twenty-three because the bus dispatched for the students only seated twenty-three, none seriously injured. They just needed to be checked and released to their parents. Why Downtown instead of Our Lady? Parental choice. Downtown was closer to home. Our Lady ended up with the five that wouldn't fit on the bus, including the student with the broken arm.

Conclusion: medic preference clearly played no role.

And neither did promises that Our Lady presumed were forthcoming from EMS. By protocol medics transport to the nearest hospital or to the one the patient requests. A promise of preference would have been worse than inappropriate. Our Lady misread the situation up front, prompting it to declare Code MCI. Indeed, Our Lady feathered its cap by responding more professionally than Downtown's ER, which did nothing to prepare. But Our Lady acted on assumptions based upon some en-route ambulance's speculations, not fact. In fact, EMS medics never uttered "Mass Casualty Incident." Nor did Our Lady ask for clarification. Had it done so, it could have called off Code MCI and sent its people home.

To our astonishment, we also learned that no one—neither medics nor ER staff region-wide—had adhered strictly to the formal MCI protocols for years. No one even knew what they were. Protocols had been replaced by workarounds-of-the-moment that over time people hardwired into standard operating procedures. The pressure of this MCI exposed the flaws and scared everyone.

The two groups took immediate action. They hosted a conference of emergency and medical services region-wide to review, update and reassert the protocols. All emergency personnel underwent retraining.

At the end, I admonished the workgroup with this:

"Suppose this group had dissolved earlier in anger, ignorant of what really happened. No one would have heard the 911 tapes and the truth. Facts—painful and embarrassing but enormously positive—would never have silenced opinions that turned out to be wrong. No one would have learned anything. Hard feelings, blaming, and excuse-making would have gone on as always. Bottom line, we'd have had a leadership failure across the board. And the Mass Casualty mishap this time would have set us up for a Mass Casualty meltdown the next.

"Now that would have been a leadership catastrophe."

The 10 Principles of No Fail Leadership™

1. All problems stem from conflicts of belief about what's true.

2. Nothing is ever what it seems. The truth lies elsewhere.

3. The truth is always positive, even when it's painful.

4. Make it 100% safe to tell the truth.

5. No blame, no excuses.

6. Work from facts first, opinions later.

7. Get input from frontline people before making decisions they must implement, not after.

8. Only make promises we can keep, and keep all the promises we make.

9. Etch all decisions in jell.

10. Implementation is never a "no brainer."

POSTMORTEM OF THE NEAR-DEATH EXPERIENCE

A TRAINED PSYCHOLOGIST in a client organization, after witnessing No Fail Leadership's 10 Principles in action, described them as "diagnostic, prescriptive and predictive—diagnostic of what's wrong, prescriptive of the cure, and predictive of success if followed and failure if not."

Let's apply them to the Mass Casualty Incident meltdown, focusing on diagnosis. If worth their salt, the 10 Principles should stand on their own when applied and begin contributing to a solution. Let's test them.

Mass Casualty Meltdown: diagnosis using the 10 Principles

- *Principal 1. All problems stem from conflicts of belief about what's true.*

If so, who believed what?

The past. Based upon long experience, EMS medics believed that Our Lady's emergency room staff was slow and disorganized, compromising patient care, and treated medics with disrespect.

Our Lady's ER staff believed that EMS medics complained too much, lacked professionalism and transported too many emergency victims to its competitor, Downtown Medical Center.

The accident. Our Lady's clinical leader concluded—based upon a premature comment from a rural medic who hadn't even arrived at the accident scene—that a Mass Casualty Incident was underway and declared Code MCI.

The EMS medics onsite knew firsthand that the incident was not an MCI. They simply did what they were trained to do and what the circumstances warranted.

The conflict. When only five accident victims showed up at Our Lady's doorstep compared with twenty-three at Downtown's, the ER staff besieged its clinical leader with complaints that the EMS medics were guilty of bias-as-usual in the midst of a joint workgroup where bias, if any, ought to tip their way for a change.

Our Lady's leaders, convinced that they were in the right, arrived at the next morning's workgroup angling for a confession and contriteness from the EMS people as the price of continuing to work together. The EMS leaders, caught off guard, didn't know *what* to believe.

- *Principal 2. Nothing is ever what it seems. The truth lies elsewhere.*

What Our Lady's leaders assumed had happened had *not* happened, in any way. Nothing *was* what it seemed. The truth lay distantly elsewhere. If EMS had conceded the plausibility of Our Lady's initial accusation of bias, would the workgroup have survived long enough to even look?

- *Principal 3. The truth is always positive, even when it's painful.*

Our Lady made a mistake declaring Code MCI. It made another one accusing the EMS medics of bias, which proved untrue. Those mistakes, painful and embarrassing as they were, illuminated life threatening breakdowns in MCI protocols. Greatly worried, participants banded together to disarm this ticking bomb.

- *Principal 4. Make it 100% safe to tell the truth.*

Initially, was anyone even interested in hearing the truth and dealing with it? Our Lady's leaders—on the attack first thing the morning after the collision—felt safe to vent, because they believed they had been wronged. But what about the EMS people—the accused? Did they feel informed and safe enough to resist? Not on the spur of the moment.

The time out and the radio tapes staved off a kangaroo court. People recognized the tapes as evidence that could cut either way and agreed to the wisdom of creating a "100% safe" zone to listen to them before rendering a verdict.

- *Principal 5. No blame, no excuses.*

The blaming began the previous night at Our Lady's ER when only five patients showed up. The accusations of medic bias fell upon the medics the following morning. EMS's people were so taken aback that they couldn't immediately respond. Had they countered with excuses instead of radio tapes and an invitation to seek out the truth, the joint effort could have come unglued then and there.

- *Principal 6. Work from facts first, opinions later.*

Had people long-jumped to conclusions? Without a doubt. Fortunately, the facts so quickly muted the early opinions that later on, no one even admitted to having expressed them.

- *Principal 7. Get input from frontline people before making decisions they must implement, not after.*

By the time the last radio tape played, we had extraordinarily rich input about what happened and didn't happen in the field. Without that input, the workgroup would have missed the underlying protocol breakdowns altogether.

- *Principal 8. Only make promises we can keep, and keep all the promises we make.*

Did EMS make promises of preferential treatment to Our Lady for its workgroup participation, implied or otherwise? Both sides expected evidence of improvements in the patient handoff process, which ultimately occurred. But Our Lady believed that a promise of preference was implied by agreeing to workgroup participation, further proof that its people had lost touch with the formal protocols. By protocol, medics transport to the nearest hospital or to the one the patient requests, leaving little room for medic choice. A promise of preference would have been cause for disciplinary action.

- *Principal 9. Etch all decisions in jell.*

Our Lady's ER clinical leader etched Code MCI in stone, not jell. She focused so singlemindedly on superior execution, that she neither sought nor picked up on radio reports that cast doubt on the MCI designation. Had she deliberately etched that first decision in jell, she would have alerted the ER nurses to report game-changing updates from the field.

- *Principal 10. Implementation is never a "no-brainer."*
  - *The simple is never simple.*
  - *Telling people once is never enough.*

Once upon a time, although no one could remember just when, both EMS medics and Our Lady ER staff must have understood the protocols, because medic and ER nurse training included them. But recall fades, despite management assumptions to the contrary. Currency of knowledge can fall far behind too, when management vigilance wanes about taking refresher courses and when updating skills defaults to on-the-job coaching by regulars that have their own way of doing things. All this happened here. The two groups had not paid attention to crumbling standards nor kept up the pressure to learn.

Implementation is never a "no-brainer." The simple is never simple, and telling people once is never enough.

Coroner's Report

The workgroup hadn't even made it to Principle 1. Start with Our Lady's long-standing resentment about the EMS criticisms of their performance compared with Downtown Medical Center. To that add their belief that medics chose to divert business to their competitor. Our Lady was primed to assume that medic bias drove decisions made at the accident scene that Our Lady didn't like. It had not occurred to them that, according to Principle 2, "nothing is ever what it seems, the truth lies elsewhere."

Weren't all the Principles they hadn't followed "diagnostic" of their brush with failure—even "predictive" of it? And didn't a strong dose of Principle 2 jump-start the "cure?"

Troublingly, this workgroup had used these principles success-fully for two weeks. In the heat of the moment, they forgot everything they learned—forcefully reminding me that Principle 10 "Implementation is never a 'no-brainer,'" applies to me too.

The Leadership Journey

If, in your estimation, No Fail Leadership's 10 Principles passed the diagnostic test of the workgroup's near-death experience, then you can look forward to using them to tackle an actual problem within your own organization. The No Fail Leadership Test in the next chapter opens that door, giving you an opportunity to learn the 10 Principles by testing them on your own case history. As the postmortem of the Mass Casualty Incident demonstrates, you can start applying each Principle as you encounter it. Each builds upon the ones that came before, stepping stones to No Fail Leadership and from there to No Fail solutions and implementations. Once you understand and internalize the 10 Principles, you will find yourself applying them more routinely, confidently, and effectively as needs arise.

As a leader, you will be more fully equipped to:

- *Understand the dynamics driving your organization.* Together, we will penetrate the inner workings of organizations, specifically, how people get things done and what stands in the way when action bogs down.

- *Stay centered.* When tension escalates around you and everything seems to be falling apart, thinking clearly makes you a stabilizing influence and a leader others gravitate to and respect.

- *Spot and diagnose problems fast and accurately.* When a problem surfaces, you will learn to ask which of the 10 Principles of No Fail Leadership haven't been honored. The answer often and instantly reveals why the problem exists and why it persists.

- *Solve problems more unerringly and completely.* You will be confident that you have:

    - Targeted the right problem rather than the surface problem.

    - Partnered with multilevel people who can solve it comprehensively, with authority to approve the solution.

    - Developed a plan that the people who must implement it can buy into.

- *Succeed.* You will be able to craft and carry out No Fail implementations, where things get done faithfully from the outset. If implementation needs correction based upon early feedback, you can adjust so quickly that success doesn't stand in doubt.

As a leader under a leader, you will be a more valuable contributor. Almost every leader reports to someone higher up, including outsiders. To excel, good leaders require good followers as much as good followers require good leaders.

No Fail Leadership teaches and trains us to be proficient in both roles. When leaders and followers operate from the same philosophy and playbook, they get more accomplished quicker and better than ever before, with widespread buy-in. And through their successes they become magnets and role models for others.

WANTED: MORE MASS CASUALTY INCIDENTS

YOU MUST KNOW FIRSTHAND of organizational breakdowns as exasperating as the Mass Casualty Incident I just shared that have you, your coworkers, and the enterprise itself scrambling for sanity, survival, and leadership. Take the No Fail Leadership Test coming up. Its questions—and your answers—exemplify the difficult, ubiquitous problems No Fail Leadership and No Fail leaders tackle, delivering results in the 97% Territory.

Create a case history

Use your answers to target problems within your organization that let you put No Fail Leadership to work immediately as the 10 Principles unfold.

It's a simple yes-no test I have given in client organizations three ways:

- An all-employee survey to take anonymously and return to me

- The same survey filled out and handed to me when we meet

◉   The same survey filled out in my presence before an
    interview starts

Everyone answers the same questions, from CEOs down to
employees on the front line and production line, with anonymity
guaranteed.

In every case, I have cleared the twelve questions with the CEO,
because they look for red flags and wave them. Never once has
one been changed or eliminated. Top leaders wanted answers,
truthful answers, not gold stars.

The breakdowns in performance that the test highlights reflect
fundamental breakdowns in the values, beliefs and behavior pervading the organizational culture and its leaders, pointing out
what's wrong that must be fixed to leverage the 97% Factor.

Case History Start-Up

To take the test and create your Case History, follow these instructions:

1. **Pick an organization you know well,** either your current one (to maximize the practical value of time spent with this book) or a past one.

2. **Study the 12 breakdowns on the Leadership Test with care. Grade sternly.** A weakness does not have to happen all the time or everywhere. If it shows up often enough to impede performance or happens rarely but must be dealt with, check the box.

3. **Write down the specific problems or events that came to mind when deciding to check a box.** Be brief: one sentence per problem. Details will pile up as we proceed.

4. **Of the problems you have identified, pick one you want most of all to work on.** Then pick a couple runners-up to keep track of in case you change your mind.

These recollections constitute the substance of the Case History you will work on throughout this book.

Leadership Test

How many of these 12 breakdowns in
97% Territory undermine your organization?

Solving problems and implementing plans

☐ 1. Implementation plans lose momentum and bog down.

☐ 2. Problems, even urgent ones, pile up without action, and some never get solved or resolved at all.

☐ 3. Out of expediency, problems are worked around instead of solved, creating more problems downstream.

Accountability and culture

☐ 4. People dismiss or block critical new ideas claiming, "My plate's too full" or, "Been there, done that, won't work."

☐ 5. Management isn't clear when things go wrong, or why.

☐ 6. Too often, people accept responsibility but duck accountability, blaming others and making excuses.

☐ 7. Frontline problems are often covered up as people seek safety in silence.

Workforce interactions

☐ 8. Communication is great within groups but weak overall.

☐ 9. Departments, levels and individuals don't respond to each other's needs and disagree on roles and responsibilities.

☐ 10. We're weak at recruiting, mentoring and keeping good employees.

Customer-perceived value

☐ 11. Customer expectations aren't always understood or met, let alone exceeded, hurting satisfaction, trust and retention.

☐ 12. We make too many promises we can't keep and/or don't keep all the promises we're capable of keeping.

You're in good company

Leadership Test takers usually mark six to nine of the twelve breakdowns as ongoing problems within their organization. Generally speaking, the higher placed the test taker, the more severe the critique.

A few people have actually checked all twelve. In follow-up interviews, almost all test takers have bared their souls. When people know that top leadership has commissioned someone pledging anonymity of source to search deeply for the truth to make things better, they don't hold back.

As leadership traits go, fearlessness about getting to the truth and making it 100% safe for truth-tellers to speak frankly spreads messages of trust and empowerment throughout a workforce.

What's the business payoff?

A more valuable "you."

Through your case history work, you will have identified and diagnosed a Leadership Test problem that demands attention. You will have pre-tested a new competency for solving it and be prepared to jumpstart and lead an in-house effort to deliver a solution.

Over the long haul, as you grow into a savvier leader and problem solver, you also grow in value as an asset to your organization in your current role and potentially beyond it, even if you are the only one that grasps and uses the No Fail Leadership 10 Principles.

Roadmap

You've seen the 10 Principles in action and have identified problems No Fail Leadership can help you solve. It's time to start unfolding the No Fail Leadership roadmap and step into the territory where human thinking, behavior and action govern the 97% of business activities you can't measure or predict. The next chapter covers what No Fail leaders do, what No Fail Leadership strives to accomplish with leaders, its strategy for building them, and its means for making this happen.

No Fail Leadership Vision, Mission and Way

PEOPLE WANT AND NEED GOOD LEADERS and leadership and lament the lack of them. Employees can go through a whole career without ever experiencing the thrill of planning and executing something together really well. That's because their leaders have never had that experience either.

How good a leader can such leaders be? And what kind of leadership can they teach? Do as I do?

Learn to lead by learning to succeed

People do not learn to lead others by coming up short every time they try. Instead, they learn through tangible successes, minor and major. The more successes they accumulate, the better they get at orchestrating them—basic training for leadership.

They also attract and keep the high-caliber followers they need in order to lead. And as leaders rise, the smart ones leave behind a crack corps of followers mentored and trained in leading. Weak leaders don't. They collect losses and losers, driving good people away. Good people's to-do lists are too long to bog down in non-accomplishment and their days and careers and lives are too short to tolerate this.

WHAT NO FAIL LEADERS DO

—The Goal—
Inspire and mobilize the heroic effort to fulfill
the purpose and promise of performance enshrined
in a powerful mission.

Implicit in a mission is a promise to perform on behalf of its beneficiaries. Leading to achieve a lofty, measureable purpose is only Part One, such as getting subsidies to double the number of college graduates. Implicit in such a purpose is Part Two, the promise and expectation of institutional performance, like educating the students to earn their degree, not just conferring it for being enrolled. All too often people assume that achieving Part One achieves Part Two.

The No Fail view of leadership elevates Part Two—delivery of the mission's promise of performance—into a leader's explicit marching orders, backed by a powerful, common cause. Doing so unites thinking, resources and action, reducing untold waste. The order also enlists leaders at all levels to champion the cause and mobilize the heroic workforce efforts to realize its aims.

NO FAIL LEADERSHIP'S VISION

—The Goal—
No Fail leaders at all levels who
deliver when others don't.

What does "No Fail" mean?

Setbacks aren't failures: they're input.

Everything we do in life is a pilot test. Top-notch experiment-ers—and leaders—do not expect perfect success on each try. They expect the unexpected and look for it, including disasters in the making. They learn lessons that others don't, build upon them and accomplish feats others never dream of. *They do not fail.* When results fall short, they find out why, adapt, try harder or try something else.

Not everyone relishes challenges. Many people would rather space them out as far as possible. Others like to play hero, acting and reacting with zest as crises crop up. They believe that apply-ing a tourniquet constitutes the epitome of success. They lack the curiosity to explore the deeper lessons about why the crisis arose in the first place.

Not learning is failure. So is not trying. People and enterprises that try, learn, retry, and learn even more push the limits of what's possible. They venture together into new territory boldly and in-telligently with their eyes open. They do not fail.

Why do so many ambitious attempts to improve performance fall so short?

"…because the innovator has for enemies all those who have done well under the old conditions, and lukewarm defenders in those who may do well under the new."
—Machiavelli, The Prince, *1513*

Machiavelli's 500-year-old voice still speaks clearly to captains of process improvement who have braved the turbulent waters. Nei-ther coddling nor kicking ass seems to work over the long haul. Attempts to impose process change and coax employees to ac-cept it can spark a mutiny. People see it as too disruptive, labor-intensive and threatening no matter how well intentioned it may be and no matter how many high-profile Fortune 500 pioneers made the journey successfully before.

Peter Pande, Robert Neuman and Roland Cavanaugh, in their how-to book *The Six Sigma Way*, noted that while 90% efficiency is common in manufacturing activities, "most non-manufacturing activities are only about 70% effective (if that)."[1] I'd put it at 50-70% in manufacturing, worse in service. The promised returns in financial performance, efficiency, productivity and customer kudos rarely showed up in service industries except at Disney and a few other like-minded icons.

And even in these, dysfunction lived a life of its own behind the scenes. Excellence serving customers didn't always translate into excellence serving colleagues.

Is it any wonder? Think of the serious obstacles—Leadership Test obstacles—standing in the way of success. No practical solutions or answers seem to exist. The problems reflect people problems far more than process problems, and attempts to impose Six Sigma, "lean" and other production bred, metric heavy methodologies meet with stiff resistance from Machiavelli's "enemies of change" and "lukewarm defenders" of it.

Truth is:

> *No process or performance improvement methodology will work unless employees at all levels want it to work. Creating a culture and environment that motivate people to want it to work is a leadership responsibility.*

NO FAIL LEADERSHIP'S MISSION

—The Goal—
Move leaders beyond the 3% they can measure
and into the 97% that matters.

For decades, business leaders have been trying to solve non-manufacturing, service intensive Leadership Test problems using metric-driven methodologies that worked eliminating waste and raising quality on production lines.

---

1 Peter S. Pande, Robert P. Neuman and Rolande R. Cavanaugh, *The Six Sigma Way* (New York; McGraw-Hill, 2000), xiii.

The ancestor of today's methodologies, perfected by Dr. W. Edwards Deming, was "statistical process control," which American industry employed during World War II to manufacture and distribute instruments of land, sea and air warfare. Statistical process control vastly reduced defects, delays and rework by segmenting the manufacturing process, measuring accuracy at each step, identifying problems where they occur, and then adjusting the processes and hardware to fix them. Accuracy shot up as defects went down. Tolerances exceeded expectations. In net, quality soared.

Shortsightedly, America abandoned Deming's methods in the post-war rush to satisfy domestic and world demand for U.S. products, especially cars. Detroit's Big Three wouldn't even take Deming seriously. So, in 1950, he introduced statistical process control to Japanese businessmen. The Japanese latched onto it because it delivered higher quality and lower cost, objectives that American producers considered mutually exclusive. Quality circles popped up everywhere. Japan even established a prize in Deming's honor to encourage achievement. The quality of Japanese cars, consumer electronics, machinery and high-tech products soon eclipsed our own. Caught napping, U.S. manufacturers fell behind, merged, went out of business, or produced offshore.

American industry finally woke up to the quality revolution in the 1970s and 1980s. Over the years, "Statistical process control" metamorphosed into TQM (Total Quality Management), CQI (Continuous Quality Improvement), The Toyota Way, Six Sigma, "lean" manufacturing, Lean Six Sigma, and other, niche makes and models. Industry management soon tried to apply manufacturing's managing-through-measuring methodologies to their service and support activities. Whole service industries like banking, hospitality and healthcare soon followed suit—without, as *The Six Sigma Way* acknowledged, comparably good results.

Measuring how well machines behave doing their job is one thing. Measuring how well people behave doing their job is another matter altogether.

Right from the beginning, Dr. Deming, the father of the data-driven, quality movement, recognized the seductiveness and danger awaiting executives who put their trust in numbers rather than people. In his last book, *The New Economics (Second Edition)*, published in 1994 just after his death, Deming cited Dr. Edward M. Baker's work during the war at Ford Motor Company, which concluded that "unique (manufacturing) processes that produce figures" apply to only 3% of a business's activity. "Anyone," Deming continued, "can be 100% successful with the 3%, and find himself out of business."[2]

The 97% falls directly into management's lap—namely, the responsibility for business strategies, planning, companywide systems, and managing people. "Here are the big gains, 97%, waiting." ... "The results of most activities of management cannot be measured," he stated, and "the magnitudes of the most important losses from action or inaction by management are unknowable." Paraphrased, Deming's conclusions distill into this:

The 3% we can measure misses the 97% that matters.

Why, then, would leaders delegate leadership to metric men who worship Dr. Deming and his descendants but don't believe or heed his warning?

Because management thinks there's safety in numbers

Management can quantify, fix and track progress solving problems on the production line and in heavily repetitive activities like shipping, record keeping, flight reservations, and retail and Internet purchases. But Leadership Test problems elude quantification.

Such problems, CEOs complain, are too ... human, too ongoing, too hard to measure and too stubborn and costly to attack directly. "There is always room for improvement," they confess, "but the process improvement teams are getting better at working together, and that's good enough."

Well that's not good enough. Why, one might ask, would management relentlessly squeeze every ounce of waste out of high-volume production and transactional activities, yet tolerate as

---

2 W. Edwards Deming, *The New Economics: For industry, government, education*, 2nd Ed. (Cambridge, MA; MIT Press, 1994), p. 37.

much waste in work that is service intensive and can spell the difference between customers coming back or taking their business elsewhere? And why would service-based departments and businesses tolerate it at all? Here's what I hear:

- ☉ *"The waste isn't tangible enough to grasp in service activities."* Hidden waste takes so many forms and spreads so wide that there's no one mosquito to see and swat.

- ☉ *"Tackling such waste may be right to do but it's not worth the effort."* The results resist quantification and don't show a clear, quick return. "We've got a plateful of hard, immediate problems to work on first."

- ☉ *"We all waste time, but in the end the work gets done, so why bother?"* To quote Leo Tolstoy, "Everyone thinks of changing the world, but no one thinks of changing himself."

Too many people in leadership roles venture no deeper than formal processes. The deeper problems seem too amorphous to solve, too "up close and personal." What leaders have learned and applied to date may not be equal to the job. They don't know how to succeed, and they lose their appetite for trying. It's too thankless. So they make excuses for doing little or nothing other than demanding performance.

Yet as leaders, we must deal with these problems successfully. What happens informally behind the scenes undermines formal efforts to improve productivity. People disengage. Mediocrity prevails. We cannot allow self-deception and apathy to continue in the face of dysfunction and waste of talent, even though the problems and solutions seem hard to measure.

Faced with such problems, there's no safety in numbers.

Dysfunction-as-usual costs a fortune

Any Leadership Test boxes you checked, even if only one or two, signal a need for action. And the checkmarks reflect only your assessment. Frontline and support people will check different boxes than top execs because they compete from the playing field, not from the upper deck. The list gets longer fast when we add in the problems outsiders see, even in companies that think themselves well run and successful.

The resultant waste of money, manpower, customers, opportunity, agility, competitiveness and profitability can rise to staggering heights.

Do the math

Think of the vast amounts of time people waste each day doing unnecessary work or the wrong work. Or working around queues, delays, miscommunication and other systemic dysfunction. Based upon my observations and the anecdotal comments of managers and employees, the time wasted averages from 1½ to 3 hours a day. That's roughly one-to-two days a week, up to 96 days in a 48-week year and 20-40% of the payroll!

What's your total payroll? Do the math.

And what about the opportunities and profits we lose because everything takes too long? Or because we put off fixing things we do poorly? Or because we lose mishandled clients? And our competitive edge? And our best employees? The grand total quantifies leadership performance.

Solutions-as-usual cost another fortune

The People's Choice: workarounds. Get the job done any way we can to meet the deadline. That may take extra money, manpower and overtime. But we'll worry about the inefficiency and chaos later … when time permits.

Management's Choice: do-it-yourself fixes. After all, that's why we build a workforce.

Management's Fall-back: The Gods. When all else fails or falls short (as Leadership Test answers concede), we can always hire consultants. They offer specialized solutions to specific problems such as OSHA compliance or selecting business insurance); technological solutions that, for example, standardize, computerize and integrate business systems, and generalized solutions that institute "lean" Six Sigma models the consultants admit work better in high-volume production than in service.

According to Jeffrey Liker, Ph.D., in *The Toyota Way*, far fewer than 1% of U.S. companies that pursue "lean" understand it. Leaders experiment with left-brain "lean" methods, often with good results. But they don't institute "lean thinking" beyond the pilot test. The benefits dissipate and die.

The good news: Creating major competitive advantage doesn't come easily

We cannot solve the frustrating, costly problems pervading the 97% overnight, all at once, or once and for all. But the hard work works to our advantage. Competitors face the same challenges we do. If we overcome them first, masterfully, we leave competitors in the dust, playing catch-up.

Consider No Fail Leadership's vision of leadership and what the program seeks to accomplish with people in leadership roles or aspiring to them.

- A corps of top-flight leaders of a top-flight workforce

- An enterprise that delivers

And as the 10 Principles of The No Fail Way demonstrate, this vision is backed by the means to achieve it.

THE NO FAIL WAY

Consider the 10 Principles a new core competency. They evolved from the need to move beyond the Leadership Test problems that trap leaders in bad dreams, running hard in slow motion. They offer a comprehensive, no-nonsense way to surmount such problems from the executive suite all the way down to micro cultures and individuals. And they work especially well in service, support, and customer-intensive activities, where "low hanging fruit" awaits plucking for big cost savings and competitive advantage.

I have arranged the 10 Principles in the order I employ them in problem-solving sessions, privately in our head and openly with others. They progress through stages we know—information gathering, analysis, planning, implementation and feedback. But the specific principles involve more overlap and back-and-forth movement than lockstep methodologies we may be used to.

Principles 1 through 4 set the mental stage for tackling problems intelligently, honestly, with clarity of sight and without fear, denial or wishful thinking. Principles 5 and 6 provide a roadmap for getting to the truth. Principle 7 urges problem solvers to involve frontline people as partners in decision making—it's the only way to succeed. Principles 8 and 9 guide strategy and planning, and Principle 10 opens the way to No Fail implementation.

The 10 Principles of No Fail Leadership™

1. All problems stem from conflicts of belief about what's true.

2. Nothing is ever what it seems. The truth lies elsewhere.

3. The truth is always positive, even when it's painful.

4. Make it 100% safe to tell the truth.

5. No blame, no excuses.

6. Work from facts first, opinions later.

7. Get input from frontline people before making decisions they must implement, not after.

8. Only make promises we can keep, and keep all the promises we make.

9. Etch all decisions in jell.

10. Implementation is never a "no-brainer."

Three-Percenters, take heart

No Fail Leadership does not scrap what works in "the 3% we can measure." In fact, it solves problems in "the 97% that matters" utilizing many of the same process and performance improvement techniques many of you have already learned through special training or on the job, only it puts those production-bred skills to work in new ways. Meanwhile, No Fail Leadership adds competencies to master the human interaction problems that frustrate our best-laid plans, skills that make the difference between keeping promises and customers—and employees—or not keeping promises and driving business away.

The journey begins

As soon as we venture beyond the Pavement Ends sign, we're in 97% Territory, fraught with ruts and road hazards like "Assumptions" and "Processes on the Loose" that can launch us where we might not want to go. Let's deal with these before delving into the individual principles of No Fail Leadership.

From this point onward the dominant pronouns will be "we" and "us," not "you." We're in this together.

ORIGIN AND EVOLUTION: THE 10 PRINCIPLES

The 10 Principles

Once there were only two: Principles 4, *Make it 100% safe to tell the truth* and 5, *No blame, no excuses*, a principle I adopted from Dr. Leonard Bertain, an early colleague, who introduced me to it through his book *The New Turnaround* and our work together. The initial two expanded to ten as I encountered issues that the first two didn't address. The final ten have now withstood more than a decade of hard use.

No Fail Leadership did not begin with internal process and performance improvement or business leadership in mind. Early on, I was focused on external performance improvement—on the universe of markets, competitors, products and services, and on ways to attract and accumulate high-value business. My professional need to make sure that clients kept the promises they made took me deeper into their operations, ultimately and intimately into the whole issue of leadership itself.

Those of you schooled at work in heavyweight process and performance improvement methodologies know that the No Fail Principles do not tread the well-worn path of Total Quality Management, Six Sigma, and "lean." No Fail strikes off into areas that process improvement practitioners tend to downplay or avoid—namely, the human dynamics underlying the performance breakdowns highlighted by the Leadership Test. How and why my path diverged helps explain the uniqueness of the principles that evolved.

Outside looking in

Talk about being an outsider!

Consider my first full-time job in product management at Procter & Gamble in Cincinnati. My qualifications going in were a B.A. in creative writing and an M.A. in music composition. When I accepted P&G's job offer on the spot, the executive who offered it said, "With a background as strange as yours, we were wondering if you could make a decision."

P&G taught us all how to think strategically, outside in instead of inside out, focusing on the marketplace, customers and competitors first instead of on production, processes, sales goals and profits. We viewed satisfying customers as a critical goal, not a cost to contain. This outside-in strategic mindset coupled with fact-driven decision making and unrelenting insistence on thoroughness figured importantly in the evolution of No Fail Leadership's mission, vision, objectives, and its 10 Principles.

My next stop was Doyle Dane Bernbach Advertising. DDB revolutionized advertising in the 1960s with the Volkswagen Beetle magazine ads. "Think Small" and "Lemon" (which showed a Beetle with a flat tire, its only defect) made fun of the cars, a first and a no-no in an auto industry that glorified size, power, fins and status and flooded our TV screens with claims of competitive superiority for each and every model. But not VW. Or Avis, another DDB client. Avis, a distant second in the rental car market, chased down Hertz and bit serious chunks out of its hide with DDB's campaign "We're only number 2. We try harder."

DDB hired me because a major new client needed someone at DDB that spoke Procter & Gamblese. I showed up as the P&G fox in the DDB chicken coop. DDB detested P&G's formulaic TV ads—slice-of-life skits stuffed with must-have copy points and superiority claims that left little room for the creativity that made DDB "DDB." Over the years the creative people and I developed mutual respect, taught each other enough to meld the best of both worlds, and produced DDB-quality work that succeeded in highly competitive marketplaces.

I learned three lessons about frontline involvement, truth, honesty, and promise keeping from all this that eventually inspired Principle 8, *Only make promises we can keep, and keep all the promises we make*:

- ⊚ Honesty in advertising trumps over-enthusiasm.

- ⊚ Honest promises, brilliantly executed, can inspire an advertiser's employees, literally and voluntarily, to "try harder."

- ⊚ An agile David with a tiny budget, P&G caliber marketing and a great campaign can give Goliath one helluva headache.

When I opened my own marketing and advertising firm in 1975, our output sprang from this strategic, customer- and message-driven, outside-in mindset. We got really good at striking marketplace gold in hills that competitors tromped over unsuspectingly.

We mined it first through cagy marketing thinking and innovative, strategically solid creative work that exploited the existing advantages of the client's product or service.

Second, we never allowed clients to make promises they couldn't keep, despite the protests of some who thought that puffery was standard ad procedure. Customers found the honesty so refreshing that more of them knocked on our clients' doors than anyone expected, sometimes in numbers that overloaded the system. The trouble was that we had no influence over what happened to lookers once they became buyers.

That created two Principle-8 "promise" problems. First, we could not insure that a promise made was consistently kept. Second, our upfront strategic and market investigations often unearthed a "stretch" promise that could be game changing if our client could deliver, because it was a promise that competitors couldn't make or hadn't even thought of. If top management became intrigued with its potential, we would ask what adjustments employees would have to make to keep it on and behind the frontlines. Usually very few. We also volunteered to work shoulder to shoulder with employees to insure that execution went as intended ("implementation never being a no-brainer").

Inside looking around and out

Over time I backtracked promise-keeping activities deeper into our client's operations until our group wound up helping to up-grade service, support, products and other components through-out the promise-keeping drive train. I quickly found myself im-mersed in the world of process and quality improvement to which I had been only lightly exposed at the time. My training ground was a client that had twice won the Deming Award for manufac-turing excellence. My testing ground was a string of clients that kept throwing new predicaments at the evolving Principles then in effect.

As an ex-Procter guy, the numbers approach to process and performance improvement certainly caught my fancy. But I soon witnessed that while Total Quality Management, Six Sigma, Lean Six Sigma and the like worked great for the GEs, Toyotas and Motorolas that pioneered them, companies that tried to replicate them within their own organizations often struggled and failed. And the setbacks occurred not as much on the production line and elsewhere in the 3% we can measure. They occurred in the tough-to-manage, service-intensive interactions, internally and with customers, *that can occupy half a workforce* even in manu-facturing.

PART 2

PAVEMENT ENDS

ASSUMPTIONS

What's a product?

Envision the opening session of a twenty-person workgroup of leaders, managers and employees from an enterprise that markets some product or service and has an ongoing operational problem the CEO wants solved.

To get the discussion going, I ask, "What's a product?" with my dry-marker poised to write their answers on the whiteboard until it is black and blue and red all over and people have run out of things to add.

Specifics of the list will vary with the client's industry and products, but the entries invariably get into products versus services; fulfillment of customer needs and wants; features and benefits; accessories, warranties and other add-ons; brand names, style, reputation and other image issues; pricing and value; quality and performance; pre-and-post-sale customer care; and all the other attributes that impact on sellers, intermediaries and end users ... most of which you've probably heard before.

Then, I find or create an empty space on the whiteboard or an easel chart and write down my own definition of a "product," reading it out loud as I write:

"A product (or service) ... is a bundle of assumptions ...
we believe—not know— ... we can sell profitably
... to someone else."

A former colleague of mine, consultant Len Bertain, recently surprised me by revealing that he has asked my "What's-a-prod-uct?" question at client meetings for years. People who answer never drift closer to my definition because they focus on attributes. Then he shares my definition, word for word. People sit in stunned silence, the same reaction I've experienced. The mental leap from "attributes" to "a bundle of assumptions" is so alien that even though participants are exhilarated by the levitation, they're not sure where they have landed, and the new place seems a bit unsettling, even magical.

But once the "bundle of assumptions" concept sinks in, they confess that they had never thought of attributes in this larger context. They had taken attributes as givens to work with, not question. And they acknowledge openly that no product will ever seem the same again.

Never underestimate the power of assumptions

Assumptions play an overwhelming role in the short and long-term conduct and success of the business. They drive the creation and execution of formal processes in the 3% we can measure, and they advance or undermine what happens in the 97% that really matters. They underlie every one of the problems and conflicts that the Leadership Test raises and the 10 Principles try to address. If even one assumption goes awry, the whole project, pro-gram or enterprise can collapse. And if we don't know the as-sumptions upon which these efforts stand, we will never know what accounts for their success or lack of it.

The danger of assumptions on the loose takes on more impor-tance as we discuss the first four Principles—on belief, truth and conflict, what seems versus what is, plus the essential need for truth and a safe harbor for people who tell it.

As this chapter proceeds, you will begin diagnosing your Leadership Test case history's issues as assumptions and outcomes. You will:

- *Identify* the specific assumptions underlying the thinking, behavior and action that manifested as your case history unfolded. Why did people do what they did? Based upon what criteria and evidence? What obstacles emerged and what broke down? With what effects?

- *Assess* which assumptions proved to be off the mark.

- *Ask*, did people get into each predicament with both eyes open or were they led around by assumptions they never fully understood or challenged?

I want to talk about what led up to that early definition of product as a bundle of assumptions and how it evolved. Once you understand how the assumptions motif applies to specifics like products and services, you will quickly grasp how it scales up to processes and to the human interactions that animate the enterprise as a whole.

I hope you'll learn not to demand or expect the certainty of 2 + 2 equaling 4 in human endeavor. It's not available. Things people do don't always add up. The 10 Principles help you do your best to back up new assumptions with knowledge and facts and quantify the effects of the old ones. But insisting upon certainty of outcome up front stifles experimentation. Experimentation generates the knowledge leaders need to solve problems and adapt, prerequisites for growth.

"Product" as "assumptions"

At Procter & Gamble, marketing plans didn't just lay out a plan of action. They also documented the assumptions behind the recommendations, not only to justify the proposal, but also to preserve a record of the underlying thinking. This enabled the product group, even when the initial thinkers had moved on, to compare expectations against marketplace reality and figure out which assumptions—which beliefs—proved correct and which ones didn't.

Many decision makers I've encountered elsewhere never even think to resurrect the original plan, if they can find it ... if there was one. They merely look at the current problems and try to fix what they see. Expedience and impatience can cost dearly. A lot of soldiers have lost their lives in wartime charging a hill without bothering or being able to talk with the troops who charged up the hill before them.

I spent my post-P&G decade developing and executing marketing and strategic plans that were detailed beyond most clients' patience. The experiences reinforced the belief that exploring the initial assumptions before being lured down their seductive path can open unexplored avenues to paradigm shifts and incredible riches. We start questioning the original assumptions far earlier than before. We entertain others and probe where they might lead before committing to any one of them.

The "assumptions" motif seeding my field of thought bloomed into this definition of a "product" or "service" that I introduced up front:

A product (or service) is a bundle of assumptions we believe—not know—we can sell profitably to someone else.

I urge you to understand this definition and use it. Unlike the usual definitions, this one contains two implicit calls to action:

- ⊚ Track down and validate all existing product and service assumptions before it's too late to adapt.

- ⊚ Keep a close eye on the most risky ones as time and the marketplace puts them to the test.

I also urge you to memorize it. Remembering it when things are going well will scare you off the path of complacency and procrastination and send you exploring hills others haven't climbed in order to protect your lead. Remembering it when things go wrong will speed you along the path to recovery.

Let's take this definition apart

⊚ *"A bundle of assumptions ..."*

Most people think of a product as something we can see, hear, touch, taste, smell, hold, use and experience. For services, add the people who deliver them, how they deliver them and how well. But beneath all the sensory input lies a bundle of assumptions that ultimately can make the difference between whether the product or service succeeds or fails.

The bundle includes assumptions about the relative superiority of one product or service over another, or about its superiority versus other alternatives, such as buying one of several new cars or keeping the old one and buying a good bike. A wrong product or marketing or after-sale service assumption anywhere along the line can severely limit success and even kill the product.

Consider Stardust, a mid-1960s dry bleach that P&G hoped might carve out a segment of the huge liquid bleach market, 95% dominated by Clorox. Its dry formulation took out tougher stains than Clorox, and unlike liquid bleaches, it contained brighteners that made colors look richer, not bleached out. Consumers who home-tested the product during its development phase clearly recognized its performance superiority. So, P&G named it Stardust in honor of the brightness advantage and opened its test markets by sending sample boxes to upscale households. While that generated instant trial, Stardust's purchase and repurchase activity fell short of expectations. Follow-up research revealed that the brand had a light-duty image, contradicting earlier blind tests. How could that be?

Because, Stardust stepped into the big leagues with three strikes already against it.

Strike 1: Its cost. It cost twice as much to use per load as titan Clorox.

Strike 2: Its powder form. The heaviest hitter in powder bleaches at the time was Snowy Bleach, a light duty competitor promising color safety more than whitening, no match for Clorox. To overcome its price negatives and unpromising "Snowy" incarnation, Stardust needed to look like the home-run threat that its product performance showed it to be.

Strike 3: Its name. (Announcer) "On deck, about to make his first appearance in the big leagues against Clorox, let's hear it for…Stardust!"

Would Stardust's fortunes have been different if P&G had picked a different name? P&G owned options that hadn't been marketed at the time. One was Bold. Enough for a home run? Probably not, but maybe enough for a single, getting the brand on base with a chance to score.

Or, consider a happier case history—Lestoil, the first liquid floor cleaner. During that same era, P&G's Mr. Clean and Top Job and Colgate's Ajax were killing it in the supermarkets. Lestoil smelled awful. It was packaged in clear glass that showcased its anemic amber color and looked old-fashioned against competitors sporting unbreakable plastic. Also, like Stardust, Lestoil was considered light-duty.

So what did Lestoil do? What it didn't do was change its formula, smell or color. Instead, it repackaged itself in a miniature, army-green drum, renamed itself Janitor in a Drum, and jumped back into the fray as an institutional-strength cleaner. The strategy worked. Share of market shot up, and housewives considered it the heaviest-duty liquid cleaner of all.

Ah, the power of a name and package, two assumption in a bundle of equally critical assumptions!

Unless we understand and document all the assumptions underlying our product or service we will not be able to identify and evaluate what's working and what isn't. Lacking that, how do we know which elements to spend more on to compete effectively and profitably and which ones to cut back on or eliminate?

Documentation really helps when our product limps along and we're not sure why, or when deciding whether to invest more or scrap it. Reviewing the original assumptions can provide clues. We don't want to continue investing in a marginally successful product with a subtle, but fatal flaw. Nor do we want to scrap a product with a hidden kink we can easily straighten out.

- *"... you believe, not know ..."*

No certainty exists in the promotion and sale of a bundle of assumptions. What we believe is a winner may fail miserably, shocking us. Wishful thinking suckers us into waiting too long to act, to react, to change, buy or sell, embrace or cut loose. We've all made such mistakes.

Belief is not knowledge. Do not confuse the two.

- *"... you can sell profitably ..."*

We may have the greatest product or service in the world, but we have to sell it at a profit or the return doesn't justify investment in time, money, and effort. Others bet on our survival too—workers for their paychecks; suppliers for payment; and customers and sellers for quality plus after-sale support and ongoing improvements.

This return-on-investment imperative applies to philanthropic activities, too. Even if beneficiaries pay nothing for the service, we must convince donors of its value or they won't donate. Value means worth doing, and worth doing means a benefit that exceeds the cost. Poorly run philanthropies expect angels to bail them out. They forget that large, sophisticated donors view donations as investments. Dysfunctional or failing philanthropies don't top donor lists.

- *"... to someone else."*

We do not sell our product or service to ourselves. We sell it to others, who may not think our baby is as cute as we do.

Time after time we encounter companies whose leadership preaches—and whose employees believe—that their products and services outclass all competitors. Meanwhile potential and current customers rate them quite differently. We see this delusion in the marketing and sales departments as commonly as in the CEO's office.

Improvement in performance plateaus when company leaders and employees don't think they have problems any more serious than the ones they solve daily doing business as usual. They camp in the paradise between internal perception and external reality, willing away their borrowed time, ignorant of their vulnerability.

Customers inevitably detect underperformance, usually sooner than later. They stop buying or buy elsewhere. We've seen leaders and employees actually get angry and hurt that customers switch brands because they no longer share employees' belief in their product's or company's excellence. And when a customer or outsider points out specific shortcomings, I have also heard employees snap back, "I'm tired of always hearing about how ABC does it better. I don't want to hear about it anymore!" (Echoes of an 11-year-old's outburst when Mom compares him to a better behaved sibling?)

We don't sell to ourselves.
We sell to savvy buyers with need and money.

If customers don't buy because they believe one thing and we believe another, their belief trumps ours. Denial will not change that.

97% Factors

Product / service assumptions

Accept in principle that our products/services really are a "bundle of assumptions we believe—not know—we can sell profitably to someone else."

How highly do we believe our products and services stack up versus competition?

How highly do people we sell to and who use our products and services rate them?

What do we believe that they don't?

The intangibility of all products

Some fifteen years after moving on from P&G I came upon a 1981 Harvard Business Review (HBR) article by Professor Theodore Levitt at the Harvard Business School. His insights validated and extended my existing thinking about the role that hidden assumptions play in the marketplace and the workplace. Titled, "Marketing intangible products and product intangibles," it has held an enduring place on the magazine's list of HBR Classics. I urge you to order a reprint from HBR.

All products are basically intangible, Levitt argued, whether they are hair dryers or hospitals, soaps or schools. That's because we can rarely try out products in advance. Even test-driving a new car doesn't really tell us how well it will perform or how high the cost of upkeep will be once the excitement of buying it wears off and we settle into ownership.

Marketers of tangible products go to great lengths to manage intangibles. Levitt cites package detergents. Tide's detergent beads were white. Cheer-with-bleach had blue beads to signify whitening. Bold added green beads to the white and blue ones to communicate three-way cleaning—dirt removal, bleaching, and color brightening. In side-by-side comparisons of competitive products, users could detect the cleaning, bleaching, and brightening benefits versus less well-endowed competitors. But these subtle differences needed reinforcement through powerful intangibles—i.e. promises of cleaner, whiter, brighter clothes.

The whole product branding, naming, package design, advertising and marketing industries exist to add intangible benefits to tangible products—fame, fortune, health, beauty, status, youth, maturity, tradition, avant-garde-ness, peer acceptance, self-acceptance, sexiness, nerdiness, machoness, and on and on. Faced with a choice of two boxes with hidden, free goodies inside, one marked Apple and the other not marked, which do you pick?

Most people swear that the car, clothes, cleaners and other purchases they take home are tangibles, not intangibles. But people readily accept the intangibility of services, such as counseling, public transportation, healthcare and education.

Consider our local hospital. How much did we really know about the quality of medical care we'd get before we checked in?

We bought promises based upon reputation, size, status, and the hospital's gleaming, modern buildings. We bought based upon the number of medical specialists or the emergency room team or the testimonials of doctors and patients. Or upon our first impressions of the people who greeted and registered us.

In fact, the first impressions we accumulate from packaging and promises are the institution in our minds. And impressions can change in an instant. If we get wind of problems in service delivery, service quality, general stability or philosophy of care or education, we'll look elsewhere. Why risk our welfare, time and money on intangibles that make us uncomfortable?

Procter & Gamble markets products such as Tide laundry detergent on intangible promises too. But P&G controls its products and promises from conception through production, distribution and advertising all the way to our washing machine. Buyers get pretty much what they expect.

Not so for services, Levitt argued. Services are people-intensive in both production and delivery. That can cause enormous ongoing quality control problems. People forget, make mistakes, are bureaucratic, uncaring or can't relate. In fact, in service settings such as hospitals I've mentioned, we cannot distinguish production from delivery. We assemble the "product" in our mind over time as we migrate from person to person, from experience to experience. We create it bit by bit with each hour of exposure, and no one samples the identical product. We could have our surgery and return home thrilled with the professionalism and tenderness of care, while the patient in the next room could be furious enough to sue. We could love our alma mater and donate heavily while another graduate wishes he'd gone elsewhere.

To make matters even more precarious for services, Levitt continued, we can easily un-sell customers we've sold by under-filling expectations. Unless we routinely sell and resell customers on the value of what they buy, one bad experience or a competitor's blandishments can lure them away for good. So now tangibility cuts both ways:

- ⊚ The more intangible the product is, in this case a "service," the more important the tangibles are, such as the people and setting, because the tangibles convey the promises in a way people can relate to, internalize and remember.

- ⊚ The more tangible the product, such as a laundry detergent, the more important the intangibles are—the promises of satisfaction.

This interplay of tangibles and intangibles clarified in my mind the mechanism through which beliefs and their underlying assumptions exert their influence. It plays out not just in the marketplace. It also impacts the growth and persistence of problems and conflicts between a company and its customers, employees, suppliers and middlemen.

97% Factors

Tangibles and intangibles

What tangibles convey the promises of satisfaction about your product and service?

What intangibles?

What role do they play in your own Case History problems?

From "product" to "processes"

Processes are just as much a "bundle of assumptions" as everything else. And they are just as intangible, even though in the quest for tangible structure and control, management may try to choreograph them as carefully as ice dances in the Olympics.

Unfortunately for us enterprising business people, the ice in the skating rink is far more predictable than the torn-up turf in our arena. And we don't have the arena all to ourselves. Like gladiators, we share it with existing and upcoming competitors, including some outside our industry with revolutionary ideas that can make our industry obsolete. We also have to contend with political and economic uncertainties here and globally, plus governmental and other regulatory bodies that keep changing the rules. And, like top skaters, we face the subjectivity and fickleness of the judges, our "customers."

We also have to contend with ourselves and each other as we interact with processes.

Formal and informal processes

The assumptions that underlie processes may seem particularly elusive. The formal processes we think people follow are often overridden by the informal processes people devise and use to deal with workload, predicaments, and expectations under pressure. The informal processes can range from brilliantly innovative to rigidly self-serving and dismissive of the impact they have on customers and coworkers.

Furthermore, the assumptions underlying informal processes operate in secrecy, sometimes unwittingly, sometimes intentionally. If we authored them, we may want secrecy as an instrument of control, of self-protection. Or we may naively think that our assumptions are the same as everyone else's and not worth mentioning.

We might not even be aware of our assumptions at all. When I ask people about the assumptions behind why they do something a certain way, I commonly get blank stares, or improvised explanations, or justifications based upon buzzwords and business-as-usual, like "it works" or "that's the way we do it (or I want it)." But once the archaeological dig into assumptions begins, people generally get caught up in the discovery, even embarrassment, of how long those long-buried, untenable assumptions have been misleading us around by the nose.

97% Factors

Dysfunctional processes

Think of one or more Case History processes that don't work as intended.

What did the processes attempt to accomplish?

What assumptions led people to believe they would work?

Were these old processes in place for years, upgraded periodically; new processes created ad hoc to meet an urgent need; new processes designed with foresight; new processes imported from outside vendors?

Do people follow them or go their own way?

Do the processes still make good sense, or have they created or worsened Case History problems?

An enterprise as "assumptions"

An enterprise is as much a bundle of assumptions as a product, service or process. Indeed, it includes all these bundles and more. "More" starts with the mission and vision bundle, then drills down into bundles detailing assumptions about the who, what, where, when, why and way business gets done—a potpourri of customers, value, design, funding, supply chains, production, marketing and sales, meeting deadlines, controlling costs, improving processes, leading people, expanding and growing.

Document critical assumptions

Stakeholders, current and future, need to know the premises upon which the enterprise bases its activities. Assumptions fill people's heads—from the CEO to the clerk—as they solve problems and make and implement decisions. If the assumptions are flawed, so are the efforts. All too often, flawed assumptions go unnoticed because no one goes diving for them. They lurk beneath the surface, nibbling us to death or striking disastrously when we least expect it, potentially eating us alive. (US automakers' early dismissal of Japanese competition comes to mind, plus IBM's early dismissal of personal computer clones.)

Enterprise assumptions vs. business assumptions

At its inception an enterprise exudes newness, purpose, adventure, energy and risk, where assumptions play an upfront, unmistakable role. The assumptions skew as much toward strategic as tactical issues—such as the product premise, the value customers place on it, the marketplace and competition, the business model, the return on investment, etc. People know that these critical assumptions are being tested and are expected to evolve. They think about them, get involved, watch them for signs of miscalculation, and lose sleep over them.

As the enterprise matures, it tends to metamorphose into an ant hill—a well-established business with workers industriously bustling about, armed with an address, offices, plants, equipment, an SIC code, an organization chart, processes and routines, inputs and outputs, a website and an annual report. All are very tangible. In short:

A "business" is what an enterprise tends to settle
into once it begins to thrive.

Business assumptions gradually skew toward short-term tactical matters. Tactical assumptions accumulate as the list of people, projects and tasks grows and diversifies. Enterprise assumptions become footnotes.

Why bedrock assumptions get paved over

◆   *The passion drifts from purpose to productivity.*

Workers and managers, who may not have been around from the beginning, become more intent on how efficiently things are undertaken (the source of their pay) than the purpose of the whole undertaking. When today's imperatives inevitably throw some of yesterday's assumptions into question, people adjust the business to the need of the moment with barely a backward glance.

◆   *Historical continuity and memory fade.*

Old, company-wide assumptions get superseded by new ones to fix problems-of-the-moment that get superseded by even newer assumptions fixing newer problems without top management realizing that the "fixes" have permanently deconstructed and altered the fundamental way we conduct business. No one remembers why we did what we did. All "history" becomes short term, teaching few lessons. Strategic missteps multiply, hard to retrace and redirect. The trail is too cold.

- *Unity of purpose and action erodes across departments.*

Departments, or functions within them, go their own problem-solving way, unaware of the problems that their narrow assumptions and self-serving solutions create for colleagues upstream and downstream. Before long, departments that ought to work in sync operate at cross-purposes, separated by conflicting assumptions, ends, means and rewards.

Eventually the tactical assumptions can so supersede the strategic assumptions that strategic issues end up relegated to quarterly and annual planning retreats. The big ideas and assumptions that inspired the enterprise may no longer drive it. The distance between the inspiration and the reality is too vast.

Keep in mind that the people who keep the wheels turning may be uninformed, but they think on their feet and make the best judgments they can under pressure given business needs, the information at hand and the reward criteria. They can devise quite ingenious solutions, no doubt about it. But the solutions can be seriously ill-advised due to faulty or forgotten assumptions.

I've created this picture to get your attention. I want to sensitize you to the persistence and power of assumptions strategically and tactically as we go about our daily lives at work or at home—especially the assumptions we've forgotten. The "assumptions" theme figures importantly in No Fail Leadership.

97% Factors

Strategic assumptions

Think of the strategic assumptions that drove the founding of
your enterprise and the operational area within which
you work. (The mission and vision statements may help.)

Have tactical assumptions overshadowed strategic assumptions
and vision?

Is the Case History a manifestation of "losing our way?"

Coming up: From "product" to "process"
to "enterprise" to "people"

Let's take a look at the informal processes that people institute out
of necessity to get their job done. Then we will be fully prepped to
plunge into the 10 Principles of No Fail Leadership.

Processes on the Loose

INDIVIDUALS AND MICROCULTURES institute informal processes to get work done when formal processes fall short. People devise new ones ad hoc, often on the spot, as they struggle to perform in the face of a unique, fluid mix of people, beliefs and behaviors that can change daily. It's a mix that they must work with, work through and work around.

Informal processes are powerful and largely self-serving. Some work better than the formal processes they override; some don't. Whether better or worse, they often conflict—with both existing formal processes and the informal processes created by others.

They also operate beneath management's radar until sparks fly.

Fundamentally all processes begin as informal processes

Formal processes evolve from informal processes through trial and error. They jell into narrowly focused procedures at the task level that string together into an overall, beginning-to-end process for accomplishing something.

Processes that work command increased authority with repetition and codification. Man's early processes passed from generation to generation, little changed over the eons—like processes for hunting, gathering, building shelters and cities, farming, making clothing, producing tools, maintaining social order, preserving cultural and artistic conventions, conducting warfare and appeasing the gods.

Eventually process authority outlasts the viability of the processes themselves. The shopworn old ways cannot go on. The unlimited mileage warranty on processes we rely on can expire at any time. Rapid growth or rapid decline can void the warranty. So can new technology. Or a David that achieves better results faster and cheaper than our Goliath. So can new rules imposed by judicial, regulatory and legislative bodies bent upon righting some wrong. Or a frustrated CEO who scraps current processes and replaces them with an off-the-shelf package of "best practices" assembled elsewhere. Any of these developments can make current processes ineffectual or obsolete.

Even tactically appropriate processes can become tactically inappropriate if the situation morphs into something unanticipated. A department upstream, for instance, could have adapted its formal processes for its own purposes without consulting colleagues downstream, who still follow existing processes and wonder why work that once flowed smoothly along no longer does.

Don't get overly enamored with or intimidated by elaborate, colorful, official looking process maps, workflow charts, etc. They can make action appear more under control than it really is. Maps give us a visual picture of steps to getting something done, and we benefit from that picture. But it's just a start, not the end. The maps map one way we process or presumably process things, not the only current way, or the best current way, or the best future way. Too many people independently follow their own processes that formal maps usually don't reveal. That leaves management standing in the dark wondering what to do with the maps once it has drawn them, particularly in service intensive industries and activities where rote, rigid processes deal poorly with ambiguity and surprises.

The right and wrong of reasonable

Some informal processes prove genuinely helpful and some prove genuinely not. But they all seem right and reasonable at the time. They range from very right to very wrong, as does the thinking of the people who create them. When existing processes fail the effectiveness test for whatever reason, workarounds proliferate to keep the business moving. The managers who birth them may not even tell anyone beyond their inner circle. They consider disclosure to be unimportant, inappropriate, or somehow not in their best interests.

Processes on the loose can paralyze an organization's ability to function and adapt. They're usually not fully thought out. They're created to handle some parochial mess, often insensitive to unintended, broader consequences.

The processes go astray because no one documents them, making them hard to round up and corral. No user manual exists, or if one does, no one keeps it current. People who do what they're told may not understand the rationale or value of such workarounds or who plays what role implementing them or what management expects of implementers and how it will measure their performance. Employees, especially new ones, hear different stories from different supervisors and coworkers, who have a hard time keeping current. Who even knows what "current" is? Leaders have trouble pinpointing what's going on or the implications, if they even sense rogue processes overtaking the organization.

And the undertow can drag us right out to sea before we know we're in danger.

Processes on the loose

⊚   *Some get the job done despite limitations.*

These processes may be keepers. They fill holes in the formal processes. We want to know about them early on, follow their progress and incorporate the best of them into the formal processes. Colleagues upstream and downstream need to know about them too and give feedback, because changes can impact their work directly. For experimenters to open up, they have to feel safe and welcomed doing so.

    ⊚   *Some help short term but may not adapt long term.*

People cobble together workarounds and informal processes to handle new or evolving challenges—especially Leadership Test challenges—that render existing processes unfit for duty.

But makeshift solutions that bail us out short term may not work or adapt for the long haul. Mid-level managers and front line employees who create workarounds may not think cross-departmentally and cross-functionally. What helps one group may hurt others. Departments evolve separately, their processes at odds. Their drawbridges may be down and their gates open for day-to-day interchange, but moats clearly surround their bulwarks.

Unwisely, top management leaves people alone because the job gets done. The hands-off mentality, trusting as it may be, can have downsides. The colonies run the realm without oversight. Conflicts of beliefs, objectives, agendas and priorities go unattended. Individuals, teams and whole departments barely understand or appreciate the larger picture, the cross functional links, or the problems employees cause one another by following their own self-defined processes.

Don't accept informal processes as solutions simply because they "work" now. Chaos may be their unintended consequence.

    ⊚   *Some fail the acid test: performance under pressure.*

Processes, both informal and formal, can become albatrosses around the organization's neck when work slows way down to maintain process integrity, or people abbreviate them to get the work out, hoping to pick up the pieces later … if there's time.

Performance under pressure: an opportunity to evaluate abbreviated processes

People improvise. They take shortcuts, skipping over some of the formal and informal process steps altogether. That triggers an unscheduled pilot-test of the process, providing answers to such question as these:

- ⊚ Did we really need all those old steps if we can complete the work without them?

- ⊚ Did some steps we skipped prove so crucial to performance that we piled up errors, extra work and expense that we could have avoided?

We may find that the processes were wrong all along, because of bad assumptions, bad design or both.

⊚ *Bad assumptions.*

The working assumptions about predicaments and process purposes could have been wrong from the outset. Process designers may not have agreed on objectives and priorities. Was upfront data inadequate or misleading? Were expectations unrealistic?

For example, I have found unrealistic expectations built into customer contact processes. Management demands more structure than the unpredictable variables dealing directly with customers will allow. To keep customers happy, employees follow steps they like and quietly alter or sidestep those they don't.

⊚ *Bad design.*

Through bad design, processes, formal and informal, can end up too complicated to use faithfully or too stripped down to do the job. Complicated processes do everything but do nothing easily. Stripped down processes don't do the heavy lifting. They leave too much work undone and may not interface well with other processes and people upstream or downstream.

The dangers of over-complexity and over-simplicity exist whether we develop the processes ourselves or adopt someone else's. Six Sigma and lean manufacturing and off-the-shelf processes have existed for a long time. None carry a guarantee of success, especially in service activities that aren't repetitive or rote, where unusual, unexpected situations are the norm and employees consider production-bred processes unworkable.

Designed to fail

Badly designed business processes have a parallel in the badly designed products that are supposed to make our lives easier but bushwhack us on the trail to getting something done, like phones, microwave ovens and computers. Please bear with this side trip, because it explores eye-opening territory that very few business people I've met know much about. It leads to deeper understanding of the human dynamic in process improvement and how enlisting it, rather than fighting it, can help perfect processes before committing to them.

Back in 1980 Don Norman, retired professor at Northwestern University, wrote *The Design of Everyday Things*. People, he noted, quite reflexively blame themselves when they can't understand how to make an everyday object work. Their ego and experience say it ought to be a no-brainer.

Norman compared yesterday's simple push-button desk phones with today's multifunction systems sporting multifunction keypads that double-dare us to dial it right the first time. Unable to figure out how to dial despite detailed instructions, we get frustrated and feel guilty. The same goes for using our home appliance touchpads or mastering our feature-heavy sound system.

Or opening doors. Their sole function (when unlocked) is to open and close without requiring much thought about whether we should push it or pull it (on the left or right), swing it or slide it, lift it up or pull it down, or rotate or fold it, correct?

Now, envision an architecturally dazzling office skyscraper with an inside and outside bank of elegantly minimalist glass doors. Have you ever found yourself trapped between banks, pushing on doors, looking like mime Marcel Marceau doing his "caught in an invisible box" routine?

What's the matter with us? Are we stupid? Not necessarily.

You and I are not the problem. The problem is bad design, concocted by highly educated people with ingenuity, good intentions, plus a misguided belief that everybody can think like them and intolerance for those who don't. What they think ought to work doesn't always work in the real world. And the design problem compounds when humans interact with technology like computer hardware and software, and it compounds geometrically when interacting with still more complex things like processes. And each other.

Norman's insights in the 1980s built upon those of other interdisciplinary pioneers from the 1960s onward and birthed a new academic and practical discipline called Human Computer Interaction (HCI). It's new enough that even Information Technology people aren't universally familiar with it. But Microsoft is. And Google and NASA.

HCI's mission is to make the human interface with hardware, software and other technology so simple and intuitive that anyone can master it with ease. How does it do this?

- *HCI experts bring multiple disciplines to bear on the problem*—psychology, sociology, computer science, graphic design and human factors, among others.

- *They involve end users very early in the design process.*

- *Above all, they conduct extensive usability testing of prototypes.* Typical end users try out design after design, revision after revision, until the prototype passes the simplicity and intuitiveness test.

- *They don't go "live" with the final version before pilot testing* with more users against its "simple and intuitive" design objectives. Only then, do they move the design into production.

Consider for a moment how much money, manpower and time HCI people can save their companies by "getting it right the first time" (or as close to right as possible). Not having to start all over saves a bundle. So does not diverting resources to deal with errors, delays, re-do's, returns, refunds, and endless after-sale service.

There is no process without people

As Deming cautioned, when processes break down, the processes themselves—the steps that process-mappers map out in great detail—usually explain only 3% of what matters. The more service-intensive the activity, the truer this is. What overwhelmingly matters in the other 97% is the interaction between the processes and the people who must implement them.

Almost every process improvement guru from Deming forward has warned against over-focusing on "process" in process improvement. But the more distant the disciples and practitioners wander from the fountainhead, the more they fixate on the mantra, "All problems fundamentally are process problems," and launch into Lean Six Sigma and other metrics-heavy solutions.

CEOs, CFOs and boards of directors attach to these methods because they have scored high-profile successes in production environments, and because they stress data heavily in measuring performance and accountability. Emboldened in-house practitioners, many of whom came out of manufacturing industries as certified Lean Six Sigma trainers, see no reason why what worked in production won't work as brilliantly in service activities, like human resources, marketing, sales, and customer relations. So, with management's blessing, these advocates resolve to transplant it faithfully despite resistance from employees in service roles, confident that over time they too will see the light. All the momentum is in the direction of processes, not people.

Unfortunately, relying chiefly on processes and metrics to solve the Leadership Test's all-too-human problems doesn't work very well.

*Keep in mind: The interaction between people and process
counts far more than the process itself. There is no
process without people. If the people aren't willing,
process implementation will flounder.*

An uneasy coexistence

While top and middle management quests for certainty, compliance and control, the workforce looks for leadership and latitude. Distrust coupled with fear fogs the gap between management's wants and employees' needs.

Management witnesses dysfunction and waste and institutes new processes to tighten order and accountability. Employees in service roles already distrust such methodologies based upon past botched encounters. They regard imposing them without frontline input as a forced march into an unknown that's long on intellect, statistics and control and short on heart, soul and the enabling competencies—and freedom—needed to succeed. True to form, the new processes seem out of sync with what's really right and wrong, creating unnecessary work and adding responsibilities without new authority to fulfill them.

Truth is, people on the frontline usually know what goes on more intimately than anyone. Why, employees ask, weren't they invited to contribute up front? They may already have come up with workarounds and informal processes that work well or that deserve airing, evaluating, keeping or tossing. Not getting their detailed input "before making decisions they must implement" violates Principle 7. Without facts, top-down solutions can miss the mark and jeopardize performance, a truth that managers may not want to hear or do anything about.

Worse yet, eschewing input from frontline people sends a terrible message: managers think; workers do. That does nothing to promote trust or engagement. It also drives deeper issues underground. The whole system can be suffering from Leadership Test flaws in the interaction between people and processes, flaws that set everyone up for failures that management can't undo or prevent with further layers of iron-handed structure and control.

*Practitioners who quest for certainty in human endeavor
are misguided enough. Those who believe that certainty
is achievable are even more misguided.*

So are the extremes these believers will go to achieve it.

Employees run for cover. The result? Less input. More work-arounds. More processes on the loose.

People Process Interaction

No Fail Leadership evolved its methods to make problem solving and solution implementation simpler and more intuitive, both for people on the frontline and for management. It's the organization-wide dynamic I've been calling "People Process Interaction" (imitation being the sincerest form of plagiarism).

People-process interactions deserve to be equally simple and intuitive, but they aren't. They bog down in complexity, dysfunction, informal processes and other workarounds. Control comes not through self-evident logic and design validated by end-user input and pre-testing. It comes instead through top-down obedience training, short leashes and stern judges who probe and measure everything.

Even in corporate Information Technology departments, I find few software developers who know HCI except in name only. None I've encountered so far have HCI specialists. Their IT developers say that they informally try out new software on a few users and adjust accordingly. But they rely heavily on intensive user training, not intuitive design. They find themselves puzzled and frustrated when users have trouble following their instructions. Six Sigma and other process improvement designers these companies use, in-house or out-of-house, seem to suffer from the same mindset.

The HCI experience provides precedent and practical methods for elevating human factors to their rightful role alongside metrics when improving people-process interactions. No Fail Leadership strives to do likewise as people interface with each other solving Leadership Test problems and implementing solutions in the "97% that matters."

- *No Fail Leadership brings multiple disciplines to bear—* people with input, ideas and a stake in the outcome, from top management to employees on the front line, across and within departments (and, selectively, suppliers, buyers and users). Principles 1 through 6 come into play here as we set aside blaming and opinions and get to the facts and truth behind what's going on.

- *Its principles involve end users very early.* For solving problems and implementing solutions, our "end users" would heavily include frontlsine implementers plus their customers, who could be internal colleagues or customers in the traditional sense. As Principle 7 advocates: *Get input from frontline people before making decisions they must implement, not after.*

- *We conduct extensive "user testing."* As Principle 8 advises, *only make promises you can keep, and keep all the promises you make.* Trying out possible solutions to Leadership Test problems on stakeholders ups the odds that the solution we pick will deliver what it promises. The same applies to promises we make to customers externally.

- *We don't go "live" broadly until users find usage as "simple and intuitive" as design objectives intend.* User-test the details before pilot testing implementations ("etching all decisions in jell," Principle 9) and then pilot test implementations before going "live" (because "implementation is never a no-brainer," Principle 10).

Bad design can be caught before it metastasizes if we take the time to investigate thoroughly up front, plan carefully, and don't "go live" before running the old and new processes independently, in parallel, during the transition. Impatience bred of ego and arrogance sunk the Titanic, and it also can sink an enterprise that hasn't the patience to do something right.

Who would have expected that software designers and pro-grammers—the reputed geekiest loners of modern times—would, in concert with web designers, be at the forefront of honoring human behavior and interaction in what they design? And teaching lessons that business people can adapt and adopt?

97% Factors

Informal processes on the loose

Did informal processes contribute to your Case History's breakdowns? If so, how and to what effect?

Were any of them "user-tested" before going live? If so, superficially? Thoroughly?

Formal processes on overload from emergencies or other pressures

What steps were short-circuited or cut?

What steps proved too indispensable to eliminate?

Were all the original steps really necessary?

PART 3

DETACHING BELIEVERS

FROM THEIR BELIEFS

PRINCIPLE 1

All problems stem from conflicts of belief about what's true.

THE BELIEFS WE CARRY WITH US—today's unique, intensely personal beliefs—reflect an accumulation of our best thinking, perceptions and assumptions about the reality we have encountered and experienced along life's way and about our expectations for the future.

We think we possess and control our beliefs and fears. In truth, they usually possess and control us. They lead us around by the nose in many ways and directions day in and day out just as mysteriously as magnetism controlled the lodestone compasses of ancient mariners.

Clashes of belief, from minor to mortal, underlie all problems with other people, other ideas, other interests, organizations and cultures and other ways of doing business. We believe one thing to be true; others believe something else. We even clash with ourselves, when our accumulated beliefs about what's true for us conflict with each day's new reality. Examples abound:

⊚ The teenager believes his room is clean; Mom doesn't.

- The salesperson believes the service department can deliver and install the machine in three days; the service manager believes two weeks is more realistic.

- The computer user believes the software is the problem; the software developer believes it's the user.

- One manager believes in intuition and quick action to seize opportunities; another believes in deliberate action to avoid the chaos and cost of hasty decisions.

- The teachers believe that parents aren't parenting; the parents believe the teachers aren't teaching. The students believe that the A's and B's they received to promote self-esteem will translate into A's and B's on job performance reviews later on. Working people know different.

- The supplier believes the extra charge for the client's revisions was reasonable; the client believes that the bid covered such changes.

- The legislature believes the new law will end abuse; the industry believes the law penalizes law-abiders with suffocating paperwork that abusers can circumvent.

- Department A believes that Department B isn't cooperating; Department B believes that Department A's procedures are out of date, making matters worse.

- Management believes that the new process improvement initiative will work; the people on the frontline believe that it's dead on arrival ("Been there, done that") even though they know nothing about it.

TWO TRUTHS ABOUT OUR BELIEFS

1. We see the present through lenses thickly coated with the past

Beliefs are mysterious in origin. Some develop based upon very recent experiences, emotionally or intellectually charged and consequential in the moment. Other beliefs evolve over the course of a career as we accumulate lessons from mentors and mismanagers, successes and failures. Still others predate the current job by decades of other jobs, other experiences, other relationships, other life lessons, other childhoods.

The past plays an overpowering role in each day's decisions, a role that so far exceeds its validity that it's a wonder anything ever changes—despite the adage, "the only constant is change." Consider how easily we attach to a persuasive but one-sided argument advanced by a family member, friend, co-activist, business associate or authority figure. Consider how often we witness ourselves or others rush to judgments based upon one or two powerful experiences that may be totally inapplicable elsewhere.

When we interact with people, ideas and things, we think we stand fully in the moment, seeing and responding to what unfolds in front of us. In truth, we don't. When we look at the present, we look through lenses heavily coated with the past, difficult as that may be to accept.

In fact, the accumulation of personal experiences, prejudices, prejudgments and fears so thickly overlay the present that each person at the table operates in a different reality. We talk at each other, not with each other. And we can't believe that what seems obvious to us eludes others completely, despite common input.

2. The stronger the belief, the weaker the evidence that supports it ... and the likelier it is to be wrong

Consider the extreme: a mob, pumped to a self-righteous frenzy by a rabble-rouser adrenalized with perceived injustices, half-truths, accusations, demands for satisfaction and a hidden agenda—acquisition of power. No information or intelligence exists within the mob, just ignorance and emotion.

Research by professors Frank R. Kardes (marketing, University of Cincinnati) and David M. Sanbonmatsu (psychology, University of Utah) on strong beliefs[1] uncovered that, first, nearly all evidence we get is limited, incomplete or fragmentary, and a lot of it comes from "clearly partisan sources." Second, people willingly make decisions based on "scraps of information" using whatever presenters present, insensitive to what's omitted. As a result we form strong beliefs based on weak evidence. Third, the less we know or remember, the stronger our belief.

Kardes and Sanbonmatsu dubbed it:

"THE PARADOX OF STRONG BELIEFS"

*"People are often most confident
when they are most wrong."*

Principle 1 detaches believers from beliefs long enough to get to the truth

We cannot solve a problem we cannot see clearly, and we cannot illuminate it with truth through windows shuttered tightly with beliefs. Principle 1 gently pries open the shutters by getting antagonists to agree that their "problems stem from conflicts of belief about what's true" and that to resolve their conflict they must set aside beliefs and jointly seek a fuller understanding of "what's true."

What's "the truth?"

*In No Fail Leadership, "truth" and "true" mean
in accordance with fact or reality: accurate, correct, avoiding
error, misrepresentation, or falsehood.*

This is the common-sense definition science uses to pin down truth. So do Total Quality Management, Six Sigma and the like. They all emphasize experimentation, plus measuring and tracking errors, defects, delays, successes and failures of all kinds in the 3% we can measure.

No Fail Leadership goes further. It digs into the 97% caldron brimming with Leadership Test problems that put organizations on the sick list. Beliefs and behavior rule action here, making "truth" harder to figure out, let alone quantify, a reality that leaders must learn how to deal with.

BELIEFS:
RESISTANCE, FEAR AND THE CALL FOR HELP

Beliefs matter

⊚ *Beliefs allow us to accept or reject something new with little thought.*

Like "been there, done that, won't work" or "if it ain't broke, don't fix it." Beliefs harden into stereotypes and biases that stand at-the-ready to shoo away or swat annoying ideas that get too close.

⊚ *Beliefs define our world so that we know where we stand.*

The unique accumulation of personal beliefs puts us in league with some people and ideas while at odds with others. And the more rigidly we believe our beliefs of the moment, the more we limit our objectivity.

⊚ *Beliefs act as mission control for our interests, choices, efforts and attitudes.*

Like a compass, our beliefs help us set and stay our course through life. They can also autopilot us into thunderheads.

⊚   *Inspired beliefs help us convert nonbelievers into advocates.*

A lone believer surrounded by hostiles needs converts, quick. Just ask any new leader presenting a new vision of the company to a skeptical board of directors or to a skeptical workforce. But over time a leader with a wise, attractive package of beliefs can inspire superior performance among a formidable cadre of followers capable of defending and spreading the word. Lincoln, Gandhi, and Churchill come easily to mind, plus business legends like Henry Ford, Microsoft's Bill Gates, and GE's Jack Welch.

Beliefs isolate believers

And that's intentional, although many would vigorously claim otherwise. Believers look for comfort and safety in likeminded groups. The optimum size can vary from one other person, to the family or clan, an ethnic, religious or affinity group up to a nation or even group of nations. Believers safely reside in the inner circle. To believers, that's inclusion, not isolation.

But believers treat outsiders with suspicion bred of fear. The "ins" exclude the "outs" and want it that way. Like it or not, the "outs" find themselves isolated from the "ins."

Isolationist thinking creates silos separating one department from another, hierarchies separating management from the people who report to them, and rigidly structured work rules that separate management and labor.

A confederation of individual and clannish special interests tied together by rules or paychecks lacks unity of purpose and agility. It cannot respond effectively over the long haul to pressures to adapt internally or in the marketplace.

Red flags

⊚   *"I am what I believe."*

We tend to see ourselves as the sum of beliefs we think underpin our identity and self-image. We can misconstrue a challenge to our beliefs and opinions in business settings as an attack on our identity, triggering unhelpful confrontation. And changing the beliefs we share with cliquemates can smack of disloyalty or weakness of our conviction. No wonder people defend their beliefs tenaciously.

But the belief that "you are what you believe" cannot be accurate. Think of Saul's epiphany on the road to Damascus. He could not have switched abruptly from Christian persecutor to Christian missionary unless some fundamental goodness in his makeup existed that Jesus was able to awaken. Something deeper existed before the transformation and may have triggered it. Whatever it was, it sustained him through difficult times.

⊚   *The testier the defense, the louder the call for help.*

The more we fear that a challenge to our beliefs might succeed, the more aggressively we defend them, seething internally if not reacting visibly. And the more we feel out of control and in danger of rejection, the more desperately we look for friendly reinforcements to help restore order and put the threat to rest.

If this is as true for you as it is for me, expect others to feel the same way.

Make no mistake: beliefs isolate and exclude

The earlier we detach people from them, the quicker we can diagnose problems together and find solutions worthy of united support.

BELIEFS AND THE TYRANNY OF THE PAST

We all value experience—our own and others'—relevant to an issue at hand. It pilots our decision making and helps us avoid repeating costly mistakes. We find comfort when we have it and feel naked and vulnerable when we don't.

Nonetheless, we insist that we can come to a meeting with an open mind and resent any suggestion to the contrary.

Don't kid yourself, we aren't neutral about anything

Beliefs are powerful, personal. We aren't neutral about our beliefs. In fact, we often defend them beyond good sense. We're not neutral about:

- The enterprise we work for—its leaders, employees, mission and purpose, products and services, and even its customers. Our perception and enthusiasm motivate or demotivate everything we do, all day.

- People who cross our path routinely, rarely or by repute. Instant impressions can last for years.

- Meetings we attend. We judge both the participants and outcomes as worthy or unworthy.

- Facts we gather, analyze, report, accept and reject to suit our beliefs and intentions.

- Plans we labor to create and the ideas and inspirations that go into them. We don't much appreciate critiquing that goes beyond tweaking.

- Our expectations of others and their expectations of us, be they managers or employees, customers or suppliers, board members or the governmental agencies we deal with.

- Promises made and promises kept—ours to someone else or theirs to us. We forgive our lapses while chastising others for theirs.

We're not even neutral about the clock on the wall. It's either for us or against us. We're especially un-neutral about our ideas and beliefs despite their consequences. We created them. We aren't neutral about things we create.

Old ideas are hard to dislodge

One of my favorite stories about such resistance to new ideas came out of a book called *Lean Thinking*[2] by James Womack and Daniel Jones out of the Massachusetts Institute of Technology. The story also testifies to the coerciveness of the good old ways.

For decades Porsche's product engineers designed and produced superlative sports cars with casual disregard for the high price that buyers had to pay for the thrill of driving one and the prestige of parking it at their city's hottest nightspot. The shop floor craftsmen had little input into design, but they prided themselves in finding a way to turn designer fantasy into road reality. Even if they spotted a serious design problem, frontline suggestions to correct it ran the uphill grind of *gruppen meisters* to *meisters* to *obermeisters* to production managers to production directors to the executive VP—hardly a formula for racing suggestions to the finish line. Porsche's 950 suppliers, meanwhile, delivered 10,000 defects per million parts, leaving responsibility for inspection to Porsche. Porsche maintained huge inventories of parts to guard against disruptions and relied on end-of-line inspections to catch defects, which skilled troubleshooters reworked.

Porsche's sales and production tumbled by half from 1986 to 1988 and almost half again by 1992, thanks to lack of demand. Thirty-eight-year-old Wendelin Wiedeking took over in 1991 and soon eliminated the *obermeisters* and *gruppen meisters*, leaving just *meisters*. He also instituted a *kaizen* (continuous improvement) program to lower defects and costs and to raise the quality, throughput and motivation. But that wasn't enough. The waste—the *muda* in Japanese—was still crushing. Porsche craftsmen needed a totally new way of thinking and doing. So Wiedeking brought in a Japanese *Sensei*, a Toyota-seasoned master of lean thinking.

Chihiro Nakao, accompanied by Wiedeking, walked into the assembly plant, spied all the eight-foot shelves of parts inventory, then loudly asked, "Where's the factory? This is a warehouse."

When informed that this was indeed the factory, he announced in front of the workforce to the head of production (a PhD engineer) that change must begin at once. The gall of Nakao's effrontery was unheard of and met with shock and resentment. At Porsche, employees didn't "just do it." They had to "negotiate it."

The first priority was to cut inventory in half and "treasure hunting for parts." The Porsche *meisters* thought the task was outrageous, but if someone had to do it, they would salute and do it without the help of an irreverent outside consultant. So they unofficially challenged the *Sensei* to a duel and dove into furious planning. The *Sensei*, meanwhile, simply dressed Wiedeking in a blue jumpsuit, handed him a circular saw, and told him to saw the top four feet off of every eight-foot shelf. Weideking did. The job was done in a week. That cut the parts inventory in half and led to other innovations that cut it essentially to zero. The Porsche team gave up, stunned. The *Sensei* won.

Even superior new ideas get tossed aside, or worse

Galileo paid dearly for proving through telescopic observations that the earth revolves around the sun as Copernicus had theorized, and hence the earth could not occupy the center of the universe. The Inquisitors in Rome, ecclesiastically threatened by anything other than an earth-centered cosmos, put Galileo on trial for blasphemy. They ordered him to recant. He spent his last eight years of life under house arrest for having challenged orthodoxy.

What do you do with a new idea of yours that those in authority aren't ready or willing to hear? How many times will you, like Galileo, put your wellbeing in jeopardy by coming forward? At what point do you shelve it, scrap it, or quit and start a new company, as many frustrated innovators before you have done?

New ideas have a knack of popping up at the most inconvenient, disruptive times, like when our new idea lands on someone who feels content with the way things are done and going, or when he has created a brilliant solution that our idea leapfrogs over. As recommenders or decision makers, what do we do, especially if the new idea comes from an unexpected or unlikely source such as another department or an employee way down the ladder?

Evaluate it on its own merits, blind to its source? Brush it quickly aside (considering the "source") and move on? Consign it to a list for future consideration with no serious intent of doing so?

Why do old ideas refuse to die?

Back to Machiavelli:

> *"... because the innovator has for enemies all those who have done well under the old conditions and lukewarm defenders in those who may do well under the new."*

The enemies of innovation don't realize that they are self-destructing. The more they disengage, the quicker their talents and skills atrophy. That in turn accelerates their irrelevance. Instead of securing their place in the organization by growing and contributing, they paint themselves into a very lonely corner shared by complainers and obstructionists that coworkers avoid. Eventually, management ushers internal enemies like these out the door.

THE PROBLEM WITH TRUTH

I have been struck by the number of definitions in which truth means truth that people accept uncritically or cannot verify. Two overall problems with "truth" throw even our primary definition—accords with fact or reality—into question:

We can't really trust our senses

An oar in the water looks bent, but we know it's not. The sun looks no bigger than a pencil eraser held at arm's length, but we know it's vastly bigger than that. We can turn our head toward sounds that emanate from the opposite direction or arrive so late that the source has vanished over the horizon. Our senses of touch, taste and smell aren't reliable either.

Maybe combining input from all the senses and applying reason can get perception in sync with fact or reality, right? Don't bet on it. Try getting ten on-the-scene statements that agree from ten witnesses to the same crime. Or agreement among participants in a highly charged business meeting about who said what to whom when, why, and with what results. Complicate that with lapses of memory, attention or judgment compounded by misunderstandings, prior preconceptions and misconceptions, misuse of numbers, naiveté and ignorance. We begin to question whether facts and reality that people can agree upon exist at all.

We can't really know what someone else is thinking

"Who knows what evil lurks in the hearts of men?" sayeth the Shadow, the 1930's radio crime fighter. People can say one thing and think something entirely different. We routinely misinterpret each other, bristling at assumed slights or assuming agreement that isn't there. We mislead, exaggerate and make honest mistakes. We report our perceptions selectively and deceptively instead of telling the truth, the whole truth and nothing but the truth.

We can't really know what someone else is thinking unless they want us to know. And if telling the truth seems unsafe, we'll never learn the facts or what's really going on.

Where does that leave "the truth?" Out there, but elusive. We have to probe to find it.

The truth, like beliefs, takes many forms

No Fail Leadership's definition of truth—"in accordance with fact or reality"—isn't the only one. It helps to understand the others, because several could pop up in a single discussion or debate, muddying the affair no end. If we can quickly identify which form we are encountering, then we can deal with it effectively, moving with it, through it, or past it instead of bogging down in it.

People's judgment, opinion or idea—their "truth"—may have little to do with facts or reality, but it seems true to them because it:

- *Agrees with their personal experience.*

  - A one-time, powerful experience, good or bad, can lead us to expect a repeat performance, such as making a record-high sale with our first customer, or failing on our first try at entrepreneurship.

  - Repeated successes or setbacks can make us conclude we are uniquely invincible, inferior, or a lousy judge of marriage partners.

  - A career's worth of consistent but narrow experiences can jell into expectations, such as an undercover cop becoming cynical about humanity compared with a medical researcher with a history of breakthroughs.

  - Most stubbornly, prejudices ingrained culturally over a lifetime can feed the roots of entitlement thinking, class and race conflict, and lawsuits galore.

- *Seems logical to them.*

Think of the one-sided arguments advanced by politicians, activists or deceptive ads that lead to only one conclusion—theirs.

Hold your adrenalized urge to side with one-sided cases advanced by articulate, passionate people within your own organization, because there's a good chance that a one-sided argument is truly one-sided.

- *Seems intuitively right.*

Forty-five percent of corporate executives "rely more on instinct than on facts and figures in running their businesses," per a May 2002 survey by Christian & Timbers cited by consultant Eric Bonabeau[3]. Doing so is "romantic," elevating business to an "art form." In effect it simplifies business complexities by tuning them out. It "makes us feel special. ... What better way to justify a high status—and a huge salary—than to claim the superhuman power of exceptional instinct?" Trouble is, we remember the jackpots we hit but forget all the money we lost hitting one.

Deferring to intuition without examination, ours or someone else's, constitutes a high risk gamble worth avoiding. Facts and "fine distinctions" matter because "often, they're precisely what separate success from failure." Leaders need to litmus-test their personal chemistry. Does it favor instinct or information?

- *Applies established truths.*

Such as, 2 + 2 = 4. Unfortunately, mathematically accurate numbers can add up to totally irresponsible untruths. Proponents selectively omit numbers that contradict their conclusion or include numbers that mislead. Even established truths destabilize in the face of new thinking.

Consider how Einstein's theories about the physics of the universe irreversibly bent the daily Newtonian reality we once took for granted. Yet even Einstein failed to formulate a theory connecting the physics of the universally large with the physics of the irreducibly small. Forging the link may require ideas even more counterintuitive than Einstein's.

- *Is widely accepted but liable to be proven false.*

Such as bloodletting to cure disease, or a flat earth, or any assertion prefaced by "we always ..." or "everybody knows that ..." Consider our post-World-War-II belief in the unchallengeable superiority of American industry. Its leaders brushed off W. Edwards Deming and his revolutionary methods for Statistical Process Control. So he presented them to the Japanese, who adopted them, built products outclassing and outlasting our own, and left U.S. manufacturing scrambling for survival to this day.

- *Rests upon spiritual reality that people accept but cannot verify scientifically.*

In short, their truth rests upon beliefs. In analyzing and solving problems advocated in this book, we urge getting beyond beliefs and into verifiable facts and reality. But that does not preclude elevating transcendent values. The values embedded in the 10 Principles of No Fail Leadership play powerful roles enabling people to set aside their distrust and fear and unite behind leaders and solutions that deliver.

That's what the 10 Principles are for. All have proved their practicality in application. Pragmatists will appreciate that. And people who value spirituality will appreciate the Principles' ability to turn abstract, higher values—like honesty, integrity, promise-keeping, open-mindedness and brotherhood—into concrete realities we wish were more systemic in business environments.

USING PRINCIPLE 1

—The Goal—
Detach believers from beliefs
long enough to get to the truth

Beliefs can be powder kegs

Beliefs enable or disable the best-laid plans, from the simplest no-brainers to the most mission-critical, life-or-death endeavors. Beliefs separate Machiavelli's "enemies" and "lukewarm defenders" from the strong advocates we need to improve performance. What we presume drives individual beliefs can differ markedly from reality.

Do not disregard or dismiss beliefs you disagree with, consider inconvenient, naïve, or misguided, obstructive or even flat-out wrong. We make our beliefs in private and reveal them selectively. We believe in our beliefs and fiercely protect them. If mishandled, they can ignite instant conflict.

When we dismiss another's beliefs with a wave of the hand or feigned interest heavy with prejudgment, particularly in front of others, we dismiss and demean the believer. And we have no idea what lies at the other end of the fuse we may have lit.

Identify what each side believes to be true about the situation

The numbers that come out of the 3% we can measure shed little-to-no light on the beliefs busily at work in the 97% that matters, beliefs that people keep to themselves. Their concerns can range from thoughtful and legitimate to fear-based non-issues that they may never have put into words before or felt safe to express. But asking people what they believe to be true—with emphasis on true—about a problem they face, its consequences, and its downside if not fixed begins drawing out these beliefs so that we can deal with them.

Beware of strong beliefs

Strong beliefs, whether they come out of our mouth or another's signal beliefs that very likely rise from weak foundations, a red flag not to ignore. We may also be dealing with a believer strongly attached to his belief who will defend it passionately and view its undoing as a personal attack. Consider yourself forewarned. Acknowledge that a conflict of belief exists and mutually agree to suspend commitment to any belief until we have all the facts. Remember: People are more than the sum of their current beliefs. Beliefs change.

Don't give a strong belief a free pass

Giving in may seem the best way to avert a scene and speed things along. But bad decisions cost too much to let them slip through in the interest of peace keeping. How can we learn what lies behind the call for help unless we probe? Besides, follow the No Fail Leadership principles, and confrontation gains no foothold.

Talk about the "paradox of strong beliefs"

The paradox may offend some people. But simply knowing that "the stronger the belief the more likely it is to be wrong" helps keep the passion out of the moment. Knowing stops heated attacks. It reminds us to honestly assess our own strong beliefs and the evidence supporting them before trampling the beliefs of coworkers with less authority or sway. Knowing also makes us less opinionated in expressing our own beliefs and more open to discussion.

Don't bet on neutrality

We can't be truly neutral about anything at all. The more strongly that past beliefs dominate the present, the more strongly they subvert neutrality.

Keep this lack of neutrality firmly in mind when solving problems or listening to well-reasoned sober arguments pro and con. Logic isn't self-evidently neutral. The less neutral we are, the harder we have to work to gain the trust of others and the harder for them to gain our trust when their neutrality is in doubt.

Principle 1 removes both the myth and the mask of neutrality by getting the beliefs and biases out into the open without threatening the believers. Again, the key word is "true." Ask someone what facts led to their point of view. We learn the truth behind what they see. And what they see others may not—valuable and unique input for any intelligent solution to emerge. Honoring that input honors the belief-holder.

Leaders do that.

Don't make it safe to play it to safe

When assessing the cultural dynamics of an organization, I ask employees at all levels whether they feel comfortable bringing new ideas to the attention of their superiors and peers and whether the right people will seriously consider them. The responses almost always lean towards the negative side no matter how ardently management claims to want new ideas and honest feedback ... or how accessible the suggestion boxes.

Sadly and all too often, expressing new ideas isn't safe. New ideas that bypass immediate superiors earn us no gold stars. Nor do new ideas that challenge established thinking and established people. Implementation and follow-through can impact directly on many other people without their input or consent, causing resentment. The originator can feel isolated and personally endangered by the resistance, especially if he or she has shied away from submitting ideas in the first place.

Leaders must want new ideas, encourage and welcome them. Ideas don't have to be perfect, just really good. Don't make it safe to play it safe.

You do not have to cling to a bad or obsolete idea

As one adventurous CEO said about a major effort that didn't work, "Well, that didn't work!"

People expect politicians and issue advocates to freeze their position on an issue and allow no melting whatsoever. We never hear proponents say, "Well, that didn't work," even when reality and results argue for serious reappraisal. Any change of position meets with charges of waffling, weakness and abandonment by zealous supporters. So the problem persists without resolution or solution until some third party—like the courts or an army or a new leader—steps in and imposes a solution. That usually means that the winner takes all, when a blended solution might have been far better.

Defenders of business-as-usual have always amazed me for their shortsightedness. Business-as-they-know-it only applies to the business where they work. They can't take it with them. One might ask what will change their life more: helping the business adapt, or getting fired and having to adapt to a brand new employer's version of business-as-usual, which could be totally antithetical to everything the brand new employee believes to be true?

Don't automatically count out people who foolishly believe that dog paddling in a sea of past thinking represents safety. "Dog paddling is a pilot test of going nowhere," I remind dog paddlers. "So how's it working for you?" A sudden gulp of that reality precipitates a stunning shift of perspective about merely staying afloat: it's of no value and no fun. They're ripe for change. They just have no idea how to do it or trust it.

Enemies of change need to realize the fulfillment that awaits them if they set aside the past, immerse themselves in the challenges of the present, and embrace intelligent change for the future. They will become more a part of the team, more valuable, more stable and more at peace. Not less.

Some become leaders.

Don't be a bureaucracy of one

A "bureaucracy of one" is a person who thinks like a bureaucrat even though the company may have virtually no bureaucracy at all. Such people can, out of fear, allow no idea through their gate. They discourage ideas from everyone under them or above them. You can be a bureaucracy of one; I can be one. We can be one most of the time, sometimes, or rarely. We can be one once and only once at the worst possible time, when we desperately need a new idea, but we feel too threatened to entertain it or too complacent to recognize the danger we're in or too arrogant to reach out or too tempted to procrastinate.

Obviously, not all ideas merit being chased down until captured and examined. Some jump up as inspirations of the moment, without merit. Other ideas emerge fuzzily and narrowly focused, victims of ideation myopia.

But others arise from a confluence of input, experience and insight and illuminate new paths worth exploring seriously, even if briefly. They expand thinking and understanding. Formal brainstorming sessions tend to be idea friendly; the problem comes when we get caught off guard, perceive a threat, and counterattack before knowing if the threat is real.

Most of us like to think we welcome ideas from others. I like to think that of myself. After all, my role is to enable the people who care most about the business to birth productive ideas and bring them to fruition. Nonetheless, I freely confess that I have reflexively closed down on good ideas from others. It has happened professionally, at home, in formal and informal interactions with everyone from family to friends to casual associates and business acquaintances. It happens less now than before, but it still happens.

The remedy takes a bit of practice in instant self-censorship and self-control, but it is not difficult. Curb the impulse to attack. Stop the knee before it jerks. That done, ask:

"What sparked your idea? Let's compare notes."

The foundational facts may be accurate and the insight on the way to being profound even if the idea isn't quite right. Maybe it's worth adjusting. Maybe our idea is worth adjusting before it leads the company astray. New ideas don't necessarily threaten our own. They may extend and enrich them. On the other hand, we may learn that the idea lacks substance or traction. So what? Accept and evaluate the idea-giver's gift quickly, objectively, and kindly. Mentor the employee in why some ideas move forward and others don't. The next gift may be a keeper.

Intervene early

We can detach people easier up front than later, when opposing sides have delivered speeches, recruited kindred spirits and sparked confrontation.

Early intervention challenges us, but it's not as difficult as we might think. State the obvious: "You believe one thing, others believe something else. Let's get to the bottom of it." That's a legitimate goal. People will accept it. Besides, we are not asking people to give up their beliefs, just not jump to conclusions and into battle.

Here's what we don't want to happen. One hospital engaged the consulting arm of a Fortune-100 Six-Sigma manufacturer to increase throughput in its emergency room. After many weeks and countless thousands of dollars, the consultants presented their design for a more production-oriented ER. It looked promising to management. But when the CEO unveiled it to the ER staff, the doctors and nurses told management to take their "production line" and stuff it. Not one recommendation was implemented.

Right from the outset, the staff believed that processes developed outside the healthcare industry did not apply inside of it. At the time, attempts were few and successes fewer. Management had not acknowledged or addressed the beliefs and fears at the headwaters, sparking a rebellion downstream.

Educate even earlier

The more stubborn the beliefs are, the more stubborn the problems. The better everyone understands this before the problems heat up, the more capably we can define the real problem and solve it. Getting past the conceptual discussions up front, particularly about the Paradox of Strong Beliefs, largely prevents derailment of the deliberations later on.

97% Factors

Strong beliefs

What strong beliefs surfaced and what supported them:
evidence, advocacy, rank, group-think, fear of change, other?

New ideas

What new ideas were floated? If few or none, why?

Who were the advocates, "enemies" and
"lukewarm defenders?"

Were good ideas seriously entertained?

Were old ideas hard to dislodge?

Conflicting beliefs

Were they about the real problem?

The solution and expected outcomes?

The implementation's execution and success?

Fear of loss

Try to remember who believed what and what each side was afraid of losing. Was any of this really clear?

Fear, conflict, consequences

and PRINCIPLE 1

Fear: the hidden hand behind the waste

Like a puppeteer, fear pulls our strings in the 97% that matters, a far bigger theater for bad actors and performances than the theater starring the 3% we can measure. The concept of "waste" is heavily used in business, but not the concept of fear as the root cause.

Fear influences our thinking and decision-making far more than we dare to acknowledge. It plays a major, controlling role behind the scenes even when we swear on a stack of Bibles that our deliberations are models of objectivity and logic. Unless we get the fear out of the way, too much of what we say and do will be myopically self-serving.

Fear has no place in a business setting. It's not productively motivational, wise or necessary. It stands squarely in the way of truth-telling. It debilitates decision-making. It destroys creativity. It intimidates, disempowers and paralyzes those in its grip. It creates dysfunction everywhere it creeps in. It manifests in conflicts of belief about what's true from which problems stem, per Principle 1.

We're dogged by enough fear just going about our lives without someone trying to herd us with a stick. Fear nibbles away at us daily as we worry about mistakes we've made, situations we're afraid we can't handle and things that might go wrong. We fret about what someone might think or say. We stress out about decisions we've made or still have to make. About power, status, friends, health or time slipping away. About the loss of things we hold dear. About change. About the loss of control.

These fears are primal. They churn deep in our psyche. Like molten mantle beneath the continental plates, they stress our fault lines until our volcano erupts or an earthquake shakes our very foundations, professionally or personally. And we bring all those fears to work with us every day.

The result? Conflict.

Our brains and fear

Medical researchers, psychologists and others who have studied the brain have vastly enriched our understanding of the biological basis for how we feel, think and act. Their discoveries help explain what governs behavior within organizations.

They tell us that humans have three brains that evolved in succession, each enveloping and remaining connected to the old one, not replacing it.

The first is our reptilian brain. Ancient, primitive instincts hardwire us for survival—fight or flee, hunt and kill, court and reproduce, dominate physically and defend our territory. In humans these instincts drive individual, family, tribal, national and even international behavior. They show up equally powerfully in business and non-business organizations of all descriptions. Obsessions with power, acquisition, expansion, authority, one-upmanship, tradition, ritual, status symbols and the status quo all emanate from these deep-seated impulses. Fear underlies all of these obsessions—fear of losing or not having something needed for survival.

Our second oldest brain is our mammalian, or limbic, brain, which wraps around the reptilian brain. It registers and stores memories of rewards, punishments and other experiences that allow us to recognize and react to more subtle and complex dangers. Our emotions developed and reside here, along with the dawning sense of self-awareness.

Our modern human brain—the neocortex that Hercule Poirot calls his "little gray cells"—enwraps both of the older brains. It expanded so massively over time that today it occupies 85% of the total.

As infants our reptilian brain rules our lives. As pubescent teenagers, our mammalian brain runs amok, leaving us awash in irrational loves, hates, fears and mood swings we barely control. As adults, powerful fears and emotions continue to influence reason, often superseding it in ways so subtle we think we're making rational decisions when we're not.

Together, like the powers behind the throne, these brains can quite adeptly manipulate the intent and content of the most logical, creative recommendations and decisions, even urging the higher brain to deceive by selecting convenient details and omitting others.

Marketing, advertising and sales people have long exploited our fears of isolation, lack or loss. They lure us with promises of inclusion, plentitude and one-upmanship. And they link us with their products and services through the emotional drawing power of reputation, image, metaphors, and satisfaction of basic needs and wants.

Modern marketers aren't the only manipulators. Our ancestors employed such techniques for millennia building clans, cities and states, and ethnic and religious groups that kept us together in a hostile world. Our business leaders, managers and coworkers do likewise when they try to march us in the same direction. Theirs.

No one is immune to fear. But we don't have to succumb to it either, especially not in the business world. We're not helpless. We have that choice, thanks to our "little gray cells."

We can say no

Many people ardently believe that peace is the absence of war or conflict, and will go to extraordinary lengths to avoid both at all costs.

Peace is not the absence of war or conflict.
Peace is the absence of fear.
Avoiding conflict does not eliminate fear.
View attack as input and confront the fears that fuel it.

Say no to management by fear

A totalitarian regime may rule its subjects with little or no armed conflict—no "war"—but its people live in fear. They experience no peace. And neither does the tyrant, whose fear of being overthrown precludes trusting even those in his inner circle.

In business settings, even renowned ones, some people with power act like tyrants, employing fear and intimidation deliberately to get underlings, peers and even superiors to do their bidding. They prowl and scowl, even when they smile. They're rarely happy with anything and clearly dissatisfied with most everything. Employees don't know where they stand. They're praised one minute and chewed out the next.

Some perpetrators actually take pleasure creating a culture of performance driven by fear, where failure (as they opportunistically define it) isn't an option. They brag about their eminence among outside peers. They equate iron rule with "leadership," the kind they think the board of directors and shareholders admire because it gets "results."

Yes, it's true that at times complacency imperils and debilitates successful organizations and individuals, and an abrupt wakeup call may be in order. Threats usually spur individuals to work harder in the short run to keep their job—"harder" meaning working longer or doing things the same old way, but faster.

Losing their job isn't the only loss people fear. When a manager whips people to row the boat, the message is, "You're a bunch of slackers incapable of meeting expectations any other way." That's abuse. People lose faith in their ability to deliver under pressure. They lose their incentive to excel, especially top innovators and producers. They know that moving two steps forward often starts with one step backward. When management tolerates no backward steps, why risk it?

Injecting fear or guilt, even in legitimate crisis when success demands the utmost from everyone, stimulates nothing. As with any other drug, the injection of fear soon wears off, requiring another. Administering fear in multiple injections or drip doses over time cures nothing either. It creates drug tolerance. Over time, employees don't believe management is serious unless the fear exceeds some rising threshold requiring higher doses, creating ever-greater resistance.

One way or another, employees eventually shut down or rebel, even the most loyal ones. Some underutilized, over-pissed employees make their discontent known. Others, discouraged, learn to mosey along anonymously at some minimally acceptable level, a power trip for the unempowered, until pressed to pacify management with a new burst of serious rowing. Still others simply stop functioning, paralyzed by insecurity.

Is the response I've described any different than the response we get from our kids when we threaten them? Or the response we gave our parents when they tried to corral us with threats? The lesson at home or office is this: over the long haul, fear...does...not...work!

Many of us are parents, and we all were kids once. We teach the lessons we've been taught. When we teach others, intentionally or not, that we have little faith in their initiative and integrity, they may eventually come to accept our assessment and act accordingly. I'm not advocating inflating people's self-esteem. That's manipulative and dishonest. It backfires. I'm advocating that leaders not let their own fears of inadequacy corrupt their assessment and expectations of others.

> *Tyrants need to step back and ask themselves,*
> *"Is this tyrant really me?"*

A person cannot honor his own integrity while dishonoring the integrity of others. He honors his own by honoring theirs.

Say no to bullies

Bullies incarnate in many forms, including petty tyrants, jerks, creeps, abusers, tormentors and more. Bullies shut down the productive exchange of viewpoints and ideas. They fear that an opposing belief, clearly stated, will give it a foothold and undermine their own argument.

The worst bullies are chronic "assholes," whom Stanford professor Dr. Robert Sutton defrocks unceremoniously in his landmark book *The No Asshole Rule*. He distinguishes "temporary assholes," that any of us can be on occasion, from "certified assholes." Certified assholes "persistently leave others feeling demeaned and de-energized" and torment victims that "usually have less power and social standing than their tormentors." As Sutton concludes, "The difference between how a person treats the powerless versus the powerful is as good a measure of human character as I know."[1]

Bullies, like world class tyrants, cost far more than they're worth. Sutton cited U.K. research calculating the costs where 15% of the workforce was bullied and 30% were bystanders. One in 4 of the targets left the organization, and so did 1 in 5 of the bystanders, a total of 100 employees out of 1000. The replacement cost? $20,000 per person, $2 million in total. In Silicon Valley, management tracked the annual waste generated by a top-performing, certified-asshole salesman. When it tallied the hours and cost of time spent by his direct manager, HR professionals, senior execs, outside employment counsel, recruiting and training a new secretary, overtime costs due to last-minute demands, and anger management training, the bill totaled $160,000. They sat him down with the numbers and deducted $96,000 from his year-end sales bonus.[2] They were kind. They'd probably have been better off deducting him from the workforce.

Say "no" to assholes and bullies whether they sit in high places, in the conference room, or the next cubicle. Steamrollers do not honor the terrain. They flatten everything that stands in their way and pave it all over with blacktop. Then they paint white stripes

---

1 Robert Sutton, PhD, *The No Asshole Rule* (New York; Warner Business Books, 2007), 25.

telling people where they can and cannot park. An enterprise is not a parking lot.

Do not permit such behavior. It is not leadership. Employees do not achieve peace by being a doormat for others to clean their shoes on. That's just as true handling relationships between two people as it is between departments, organizations, interest groups and nations.

Say no to victimhood

Consciously or subconsciously, victims don the mantle of victimhood to duck responsibility for their behavior and welfare. Bullies make it easier for people to play the victim role, but in their own way …

Victims are another form of bully.

Victimhood enables the abused to abuse those they perceive as abusers, whether the perception is accurate or illusory. It excuses uninvolvement, inaction, parasitic behavior, mediocrity and fierce defense of gross incompetence.

Even in the best-run, employee-centered companies people abound who find power in victimhood. They take without giving back. And what they take comes at the expense of their leaders and coworkers, of company productivity and agility, customer goodwill and the health of the business overall. They wear blinders to everything and everyone but themselves. They avoid truth that's inconvenient and penalize those who see things differently. They confuse opinion with fact. They deflect responsibility through finger pointing and blaming and want input from no one other than those who agree with them. They resist any change they don't initiate, and they do not care about the costs and consequences that their demands impose on others.

In short, victims see the world as hostile, and they live in constant fear and isolation. They drag down their coworkers and the company. They cannot be tolerated. They, like aggressive bullies, must change or go.

The victim mentality

At one time or another each of us has probably denied the painful reality of situations we cannot avoid or felt victimized by forces we believe lie outside our control. Fortunately, most of us get over it. Others may not. Alcoholics and drug abusers represent extreme examples. Possessed and dispossessed, they blame internal devils and anything other than themselves for their plight.

But you don't have to be hooked on substances to be hooked on victimhood. Victims bitch endlessly about too much pressure, too much work, too little appreciation, unfriendly coworkers, bad management, bad home life, and an insensitive, politically incorrect world. In the context of Principle 1, victims represent a huge conflict of belief with everyone else about what's true, no less than bullies.

At work, they thrive on chaos. It validates their importance and indispensability. It justifies their plea that management scale back its expectations. It distances them from their failures to perform. Even when overwhelmed by their workload, they avoid asking for help and resist accepting it, finding fault with every suggestion that comes their way. To accept help admits inadequacy, invalidating their indispensability.

Heavy-laden with self-pity, they retaliate by abusing not only themselves, but the people around them. And whether they admit it or not, they thrive on victimhood.

They get at least partial fulfillment of four out of five of Maslow's hierarchy of needs. They get their basic needs for food and shelter taken care of by the company (Maslow #1), which often faces high hurdles trying to fire them. They often find help, safety and security (#2) through job, societal and governmental entitlements. They can find some social satisfaction (#3) as they connect with other victims, misery loving company. And in the esteem category (#4), they gain attention and even status and validation as their plight attracts attention and sympathy within their company, family, city or on some broader stage.

But in Maslow's hierarchy they do not achieve self-respect and self-esteem (more of #4) or self-actualization, self-fulfillment and realizing one's full potential (#5).

De-victimize the victims

We are not responsible for saving them, and we do them no favor by trying. We don't even have the power to do that. Only they have it. They park and shut off their engine because they like where they're at, their denials notwithstanding. And only they can move their parked car. That's true for individuals acting alone or collectively. For a business to change, individuals must commit to change, one at a time, until they collectively overcome inertia and build momentum.

Further, even if we could bus victims to the Promised Land, we shouldn't. They'd look back and know deep down that they do not belong there because they didn't get there on their own power. Despite our good intentions, we would have sent a terrible message—namely, that we believed them unworthy of undertaking and completing the journey on their own.

People who have bought into victimhood do not benefit from our pity or us helping them be victims, hard-hearted as this may seem. Do you know families with an adult son or daughter who sits around, claiming to look for a job but rejecting the available jobs as unworthy, meanwhile leveraging parental guilt to leech away the family's resources to finance his or her indolence? The more responsibility we try to shoulder for victims' welfare, the more we reinforce their attachment to the victim mentality, behavior, and addiction to the belief that they are entitled to other people's money.

We may have reason to salvage them to protect the viability of a team. That's a business issue. Redemption isn't, and we shouldn't pat ourselves on the back for trying to make it one. We need to check out our motives. The guilt we may feel for not being in their shoes just reinforces their feelings of helplessness and unworthiness. We may indeed view such victims as incapable of acting on their own behalf, but we run the risk of fixing their problems to inflate our own self-worth more than build theirs.

Instead, don't buy in to victims' theatrics or dependency or our own impulse to act as savior. Remind them that they are better than the identity they have created for themselves and that they have the wherewithal to thrive. Once they stop getting attention for their victimhood, they experience an isolation that no longer delivers safety or sympathy. The payoff ends. Eventually the situation gets too uncomfortable to endure. They are ripe for change.

97% Factors

Bullies and victims

Who are the bullies and victims in your Leadership Test Case History or histories?

What has been their effect on the morale and productivity of the people around them?

What other problems have they caused or made worse?

Did anyone ever tell them "no?"

View conflict as input and confront the fears that fuel it

Letting conflict smolder unconfronted burns up acres of manpower, time and money. Facing it squarely can yield huge gains in input, understanding, ideas and ultimate buy-in to the solutions that grow out of it.

Conflict manifests visibly through attack, whether overt or subtle, through words or deeds, or threatening bedfellows or attachment to a point of view at odds with our own. The attack can be immediate and direct, well-orchestrated and deliberate. Or, it can be sneaky and passive-aggressive, through an exchange of words or looks or documents—you name it. Management-by-fear, bullying and victimhood incarnate the most insidious forms.

View attack of any kind as input. Never lose sight that it stems from fear. And the fears may prove groundless. We fear losing something we believe we must protect, or we fear we lack something we believe we need. The greater our fear, the more we latch onto facts that validate our preconceptions and dismiss those that don't, guaranteeing conflict.

We dare not attach early to the logic or righteousness of one side or the other or be bullied into accepting forceful arguments without examining them. Instead, search collegially for truth, together. That diffuses conflict immediately. Draw out the perceived fears on both sides. Examine the evidence and instincts that support them.

Then deal with them. Until we do, no solution will get the buy-in needed for successful implementation. Half-solved problems often cost more than no solution at all. Right from the start, problem solvers individually and as a group need to get their fears and their egos out of the way. The more dispassionate and genuinely fraternal the deliberations are, the bigger the gains in understanding and ideas and the quicker, better and less costly the solution.

If "steamrollers" refuse to stop even after understanding their negative impact on coworkers and productivity, consider delivering an ultimatum to change for the better or be sent packing.

The secret life of attack

+ *Attack admits to our vulnerability.*

If we believed we were truly invulnerable, then assaults coming our way, even physical ones, would bounce off of us so harmlessly that initiating attack would never cross our mind. We don't deck a two-year-old that has a tantrum and kicks our shin. We give him a timeout.

Attack betrays and acknowledges our vulnerability. The more vulnerable we feel, the quicker we attack, be it with words, aggressive action or passive stonewalling.

+ *When we attack others, we attack ourselves first.*

Attack pumps adrenaline, accelerating our heartbeat, raising blood pressure and doing all the other things fight-or-flight demands. Meanwhile, our target nonchalantly ambles on. We're pumped; he's not. Smoldering worry and stress can be worse. They take a slower toll, but they have been implicated in all sorts of mental and physical disorders.

Now, multiply one person by the number of angry, frustrated people in an organization, waiting to attack whoever and whatever causes them grief. Walk into some companies, and you can almost smell the adrenaline.

Rumbling in the ranks or in our stomach sends signals that we leaders should not ignore or dismiss as normal and inconsequential. Employees may be telling us something we need to know in the only way they know how.

+ *Even the first attack on others is counterattack.*

It is our preemptive self-defense, a counterattack based upon fears and "what if" speculations about what might happen if we don't attack before someone attacks us. Our goal: disable the enemy before it disables us.

Siblings let their vulnerability hang out, uncensored. Any real or imagined slight can trigger countless rounds of accusation, denial and counterpunches, all for mommy's benefit and to secure footing within the family. At work, the child in us counterattacks in ways not so different:

- Arrogance, complacency, and procrastination

- Gossip

- Finger pointing and blaming

- Angry confrontation

- Ducking responsibility

- Accepting responsibility but ducking accountability

- Resisting performance improvement or change of any kind

Whenever we see "attacks" like these, think "counterattack." Ask what fears and vulnerabilities drive the controversies playing out in front of us or inside of us.

A personal confrontation with attack

An advertising client some years ago agreed to experiment with radio advertising. The plan tested a handful of news and music formats targeted at the same audience. Most responses and business came from two news stations and very little from the music stations. The next media flight's money went to the news stations.

The relatively junior sales rep from one music station protested loudly, attacking out of fear of being squeezed out, even after I fully shared the responses, results and rationale with her, the logic of which only increased her sense of vulnerability. She counterattacked by taking her case directly to the client, who was not a media expert. I considered that act a threat to the client-agency relationship, exposing my own fear of loss, plus on her part a breach of protocol I could have brought to the attention of her boss, doing her no good.

The client called to tell me about the meeting. My own fears of loss welled up thinking that she had prevailed, undermining the agency's credibility. She hadn't. Her aggressive attack on my choice of stations surprised him and made him uncomfortable. He didn't like being asked to take sides on an issue outside his area of expertise, which made him feel vulnerable. So, he politely told her that the agency's advice held sway, which did not sit well with her, exacerbating her own fear of loss.

My first impulse was to report the incident to her boss, whom I knew. But complaining behind her back was no better than her complaining behind mine. I would have confronted her quickly in person, which would have been another point of attack at some level, but we had no business reason for further contact. (To be continued.)

♦   *Attack is a call for help.*

Attackers believe that attack makes the vulnerability, fears, and hunger go away. The more determined the attack, the louder the plea for help.

One hears managers bemoan breakdowns in internal communication, cooperation, creativity, accountability, customer sensitivity, buy-in to carefully laid plans, et al. We can complain about the people all we want, but the plea underlies clashes of wills and interests and ideas. And the more commonly such attacks occur and the greater the number of different individuals who participate, the more desperately employees subconsciously pray for management or someone to lead them out of the wilderness.

♦   *Don't get suckered in.*

Our kids want us to pick sides, their side. So do our employees. They want us to do something, now. And some managers take the ego bait. They pride themselves on their prowess in sizing up situations and making quick decisions. So they try to settle the matter on the spot without full knowledge of the issues on both sides.

I've had tempers flare in problem-solving sessions when one side thinks the other is being obstructive or close-minded or playing favorites. Instead of aligning with one side or getting embroiled in the drama of it all, view attack as "input" about the attackers and the situation even if the attack seems targeted at you directly. When we say to ourselves, "It's input," we pause to ask, "What's really going on here?" instead of accepting what we see at face value, like a member of a lynch mob.

Confrontation, continued

Fast-forward several years. Different client. More radio. Different stations. I requested proposals, and the same young lady showed up, now experienced and working for a different station. The surprise of recognition nonplussed her momentarily, reviving her memories of the last encounter and mine too, but I didn't react. We went through her proposal with as friendly, respectful and collegial an exchange as anyone could ask for.

At the end I said, "There's something we ought to talk about," as kindly as I could and saw her brace herself. For the next half hour we reviewed the old incident, not to attack and defend, but to learn from it and clear the air. She was mightily relieved, especially that I hadn't complained to her boss. She went on to be one of the most responsive, creative and trustworthy representatives I ever worked with.

I learned even more from the experience than she did, I'll wager.

This happened before I discovered the power of saying to myself in the midst of an imbroglio, "Consider it input." I doubt that I would have acted differently in this specific case. Things worked out well. But I would have viewed the conflict dispassionately and constructively from the outset.

And I wouldn't have been sucked into the drama of it or distracted by it.

At least I held my tongue until I had it under control.

97% Factors

Conflicts

Think of conflicts embedded in your Case History. Think of another from home.

What was each side afraid of losing?

What could or would you have done differently had you immediately viewed the attacks and counterattacks as "input?"

PRINCIPLE 1 IN PRACTICE

Being calm does not mean being passive, or weak, or silent

Many in leadership and followership roles will do anything to avoid conflict, remaining silent when the business welfare is under attack, appeasing naysayers and strong advocates instead of challenging them and getting the business back on track. Others lose their cool, making matters worse.

Instead of ducking conflict or fueling it, stay calm. That's not easy, but it pays off by taking the volatility out of the moment. Referees do this routinely in hockey games when hot tempers explode violently. They call time out and separate the combatants. Interestingly, the players know better than to attack the referee. That's partly because of the heavy penalty for doing so. But they also value his presence to prevent serious injuries to brawling players, and they rely on his emotional detachment.

In most Leadership Test conflicts, finding the underlying cause has a chance of solving the underlying problem and healing the rift. Jumping into the fray swinging only widens it. Call time out. We'll probably find that the conflict we see doesn't remotely reflect the conflict that is. And don't take sides. Taking sides compromises our ability to bring peace short of overpowering the perceived enemy. Supporting the wrong side and repairing the damage may be next to impossible.

We don't even have to react until we've taken a moment to ask ourselves whether reacting is appropriate. Sometimes the most appropriate reaction is no reaction at all. Our silence as we look from opponent to opponent communicates that we think they ought to reflect on what they are saying or doing. That's not being passive. That's silence in action.

Ask yourself who you want in command when embroiled in conflict—someone who concludes the worst and panics or someone who stays centered and calm? Then ask which "someone" would you rather be?

When someone people respect—at work or at home—
keeps a cool head during conflict and chaos,
that gives others permission to do the same.

In 97% territory, that's leadership.

We do not have to solve the problem ourselves

We may not even be able to solve it ourselves, certainly not Leadership Test problems and certainly not on the spot, even though people who want action may be facing expectantly in our direction. We typically don't and can't know enough to decide unilaterally and wisely any more than they can. In all probability the best solution will take the best thinking of you, me, the opponents, plus a cross-section of suffering stakeholders who aren't present but understand the problem intimately and want it solved too.

Avoid a knee-jerk judgment. Has anyone even paused yet to ask what each side believes to be true? Why try to solve the problem alone? Involve people in getting to the truth and the solution. That turns most situations to everyone's advantage, often avoiding conflict altogether.

I asked one CEO, who devoted almost four solid weeks to participation in No Fail Leadership problem-solving workgroups, to tell me which things that were piled on his desk before we started were still piled up unattended at the end. He pondered his desktop for a while. "Except for one medical and one legal issue," he said, "the workgroups handled everything important. And for the first time, I didn't have to solve the problems alone."

Get the fears out on the table

Think about how many times our suggestions and ideas have been rejected out of hand by people who think they know what we have in mind before we've had a chance to explain. What were they afraid of? How many times have we reflexively done that to others? What were we afraid of?

Get the fears and conflicting beliefs out in the open first and fast. They rarely have much to do with facts of the moment. They have everything to do with the deep-seated beliefs and fears each of us has brought to that point of contention, plus speculation about the direction of change. The group may find that what people fear to be true is totally unfounded. Not always, but often enough.

Expect to meet with resistance, especially from the most insecure people in the room, resistance that as leaders we must overcome. To succeed we must be the calmest, sanest person at the table. That gives others permission to stay cool and collected too. Reassure people that two ground rules are in effect—Principle 4's *Make it 100% safe to tell the truth* and Principle 5's *No blame, no excuses.*

And pass along this reassurance as well:

We do not lose our beliefs by listening to those of others.
We do not preserve them by closing our mind.

People can change: Help them believe that

Hollywood has recognized this for a long time. Think of the movies you've seen about a high-flying financial whiz who crashes or the derelict who considers himself totally worthless. Both find themselves in a new situation that calls upon talent and depth of character they never knew they had, transforming them into human beings they never thought they could be. People can change.

The naysayers and troublemakers rank among the first people I want to interview in any new assignment. Beneath the victim's armor they wear I routinely find people with insight and ideas who the company suppressed so consistently that they have decided to shut up except to criticize and complain. Listen to what they have to say. Give them a proper forum to express their often deep understanding of what's going right and wrong beneath the surface. Their contributions can prove valuable beyond all expectations. That should come as no surprise. Articulate troublemakers that attract a following demonstrate natural leadership ability. Flip their polarity from negative to positive. Not only do their disciples follow along, but the redirected leaders can become some of the staunchest, most effective, promotable advocates that management has on its team.

Learning to lead beyond the Pavement Ends sign

Principle 1: All problems stem from conflicts of belief about what's true. No Fail Leadership warns that unless believers allow in new evidence and beliefs to change, corporate adaptability is impossible. Leaders must detach believers from their past beliefs long enough to look at the truth of the present. Thus sobered, we can start solving the problems that we must solve to survive subzero winters and thrive come spring. In so doing, people find a new source of energy and joy in mastering, inspiring and leading change and a new sense of impatience with a repressive status quo.

As I have asserted earlier, we do not have to change the whole culture to invigorate the company. A coalition of leaders at multiple levels, from top executives to frontline employees, can lead the way, one success at a time. A stream of successes, whether small or dramatic, sends a very powerful message to all: The status quo is not an option. The action, attention and rewards go with the people who want to make things better. We don't pin medals on people who look for safety and status in the past.

Lead. Teach people to embrace the present and the future, not the past. That's far healthier, safer and more fun than protecting the status quo.

97% Factors

Pilot test: turning conflicting beliefs into input

Next time a difference of opinion arises and your blood pressure spikes, remind yourself that you and the other people have "conflicts of belief about what's true." View what occurs as input, then note:

Who believes what?

What does each side fear losing if its view doesn't prevail?

View what occurs as "input." Does the tension subside?

Do people detach from their beliefs long enough to get to the truth?

Corporate culture and performance

In 1992 John Kotter and James Heskett of Harvard University published the book *Corporate Culture and Performance*. In it they recounted their quest to determine what, if any, correlation existed between the two.

They hypothesized initially that a strong culture separated financial performers from also-rans. They asked the top executives in the largest 9-10 firms in 22 different industries, 207 companies in all, to rate their competitors on the degree to which a strong corporate culture influenced managerial decision-making.

To Kotter's and Heskett's surprise, they found virtually no correlation between a strong culture and strong performance. Upon reflection, that made sense. Strong cultures can be more destructive than productive—arrogant, insular, ossified and blind to the cancers within and the threats from without. Consider the pharaohs of ancient Egypt, the Caesars of the late Roman Empire and colonial governors throughout the British Empire. The closer the end of days, the more arrogant, self-serving and tradition-bound they became. As the authors put it, "Cultures can have powerful consequences, especially when they are strong. They can enable a group to take rapid and coordinated action against a competitor or for a customer. They can also lead intelligent people to walk, in concert, off a cliff."[3]

Next, Kotter and Heskett wondered if a strategically appropriate culture made the difference. They found a weak correlation. All successful companies start out strategically appropriate. But strategic appropriateness is not a forever thing. The marketplace can evolve around them while their strategy doesn't, leaving them strategically inappropriate, outmoded and resistant to change.

Next the professors hypothesized that a strategically adaptive culture separated winners from losers. Pay dirt! It did. A strong correlation. Management's compass in successful companies fixed on the subtly changing wants and needs of three constituencies—customers, employees and shareholders. And the entire company continuously synced up its course with all three. The status quo was not an option.

These winners also learned to value "leadership" at all levels over "management," which "by its very nature is somewhat conservative, methodically incremental, and short-term oriented."[4] Managers care about themselves, their immediate group, and their product more than customers, employees and shareholders. They are bureaucratic, political, and insular. They avoid risk. Even the very best of them simply cannot produce major change. They lack the boldness, vision, and energy that leaders embody and need to create large and difficult changes. The authors caution us that "in mature firms, even modestly unadaptive cultures can resist change with great intensity."[2]

97% Factors

To what extent is your organization's culture:

Strong, aligning everyone behind long-shared values, goals and methods?

Strategically appropriate, in sync with our business strategies and environment?

Strategically adaptive, helping you adapt to changes in the business environment?

---

2 John P. Kotter and James L. Heskett, *Corporate Culture and Performance* (New York: The Free Press, 1992), 143-144.

In this organization, who gets promoted: managers or leaders?

The answer to this question, per Kotter and Heskett, "says more about real values than any mission statement or credo."[6] If your company promotes managers, the authors go on, who cling to outmoded beliefs about what works instead of what's next, then you've stacked the deck against employees whose "personal values include an emphasis on integrity, trust, and caring for other human beings."

As I said in the chapter on assumptions, a business is what an enterprise tends to settle into once it begins to thrive. Enterprises like being on the move.

PRINCIPLE 2

Nothing is ever what it seems.
The truth lies elsewhere.

WE ALMOST ALWAYS FACE THE NEED to make decisions based upon imperfect, incomplete information that's not solely quantitative and easily gift wrapped with the usual metrics. Conflicts of elusive, powerful beliefs underlie the outward problems we struggle to overcome. This chapter explores elsewheres and secrets hiding in the realm of the 97% that matters. None quantify easily, and the act of illuminating them can make people uncomfortable, at least until they learn that, as Plato asserts, facing the light brings clarity that interpreting shadows on the wall cannot.

Unfortunately, we see what we expect to see, not what's really there. Lawyers, doctors and mystery writers understand this. Beneath the problem or conflict we see—the symptoms—lie deeper issues.

Yet people at all levels in business and other organizations go about their daily work and decision-making as if totally oblivious to this truism. They end up solving the wrong problem or half-solving or mis-solving the right one. People assume that the problem or conflict they see is the conflict that exists. It isn't; I have never found an exception.

An "elsewhere" that could be anywhere

My daughter Hilerie waitressed her way through summer vaca-
tions in college. This particular Saturday was the opening moment of her first day training at a large popular restaurant in the
big city. In walked a thirty-something, harried, tipsy couple with
no reservation, a ten-year-old birthday girl, her girlfriend and an
attitude. The hostess, with more than a little trepidation, ushered
them to a table. The waitress who had Hilerie in tow immediately
said, "No way! I'm not taking that crew," a sentiment seconded by
the other waitstaff stationed nearby.

"I'll take them," Hilerie volunteered.

"These would be your first customers here! Are you crazy?"

"We'll see," she said, silently resolving not to let their behavior
fluster her and pledging to be the most professional waitress these
people had ever encountered.

No sooner had Hilerie reached the table and before she could
even welcome them to the restaurant, they began yelling and
complaining. "Where is our bread? We're hungry! We're not
gonna sit here and let you treat us this way! This is the third
restaurant we've been to today and we still can't get any service!"

"OH! I am so sorry! I'm sure the kitchen just brought a fresh
basket of bread out of the oven! I will hurry up and grab that
for you while you all look at the menu. Don't you worry about
a thing! This will be a great dinner, I promise!" And so it began. The table complained about the food, and Hilerie agreed and
rushed it back to the kitchen to get redone. She offered extras at
no charge and did everything she could to make the daughter's
birthday party a party, despite the parents. She never once lost
her cheerfulness. After the dinner plates were cleared, the father
and the girls went out on the deck of the restaurant to watch the
boats pass through the harbor and for the first time a sense of
calm settled on the table. Hilerie came over to see what kind of
dessert the mother thought the birthday girl would like and that's
when the breakthrough happened.

"Thank you for today," she said. "We just found out this morning that my husband has terminal brain cancer. We didn't tell our
daughter, because we wanted her to have a nice birthday."

Before the dessert was through, the couple was fixing her up with their nephew and making plans with sixteen of their friends to come hear Hilerie sing the leading role in an opera at the Cleveland Institute of Music.

Nothing is ever what it seems. The truth lies elsewhere.

This couple didn't come to that restaurant looking for food. They came to keep a promise to their daughter. And they were lashing out against a world going blithely about its business, totally oblivious to their new, shattered reality. They were crying for help, for connectedness, expecting none....but finding it anyway.

Don't forget to follow the money. It has a weakness for "elsewheres"

Hospitals, like the human body, can be dense with elsewheres. So can organizations and enterprises of almost any kind, and diagnosing their ailments can lead to elsewheres as unexpected as the one my daughter uncovered. Here's one of them:

The hospital's CEO and medical director called me in because it took several hours longer than national standards to move seriously ill or injured patients through the emergency room and into an acute care hospital bed for extended treatment. Although these patients account for only 15% of ER visits, they end up occupying the vast majority of acute care beds elsewhere in the hospital. In terms of revenue, they matter. And they and their families were justifiably upset by prolonged stays in the ER.

It took us longer than expected to figure out what was really going on, which you may understand best by following along as the mystery unfolds. So come, Watson, the game's afoot!

We began by looking for process breakdowns. We interviewed everyone who directly or indirectly interacted with the patients, from ER arrival through handoff to the medical staff tending inpatient beds in the main hospital. We uncovered plenty of obstacles and dysfunction that, if removed, would shave minutes here and there, but not hours.

Let's follow a typical, very sick, elderly woman we'll call Grandma Jean, whom the paramedics drop off at the ER. She now lies in a room on a narrow bed on a thin, hard mattress waiting for an

ER physician to check her over. The physician's assessment, based upon her history, physical and lab tests, argues for admitting her for inpatient treatment. He calls the on-staff internal medicine physician—the "hospitalist"—for a consultation and agreement to admit her. The hospitalist says "not yet."

Why not?

First, to protect the hospital's interests. The hospitalist, per regulations, wants to make sure that Grandma Jean meets Medicare's and private insurers' tightened eligibility criteria for acute-care admission. He sends home the patients he deems ineligible, a decision that's not always clear. Inappropriate admission can mean inadequate, little or no reimbursement. No admission can mean malpractice. In Grandma Jean's sad case, as assessed by the frustrated ER doc, clarity about admission can't be clearer.

Second, even though Grandma Jean seems eligible, the hospitalist wants more tests on her before writing admission orders. That way he can fully diagnose what ails her and create a treatment plan for her stay that accelerates her recovery and discharge by 10-25%, per studies of the hospitalist model. He can also assign her to the correct hospital ward upstairs so that she won't have to be moved. At least that's the prevailing rationale.

Third, tests ordered in the ER can be done immediately and simultaneously. Tests done after admission upstairs get lower priority and take longer (a belief not usually accurate, thanks to upgrades in technology). And as insurers insist, such tests must be done sequentially to save money—i.e. he can't order Test 2 until Test 1's results justify it. That delays treatment. So, extending Grandma Jean's stay in the ER sounds logical to the hospitalist and in her best interest (even though Grandma Jean, the ER staff and the insurer incline to disagree).

The ER doctors are stressing out. Patients fill the waiting room. Unforeseen droves can arrive at any time. The ER needs Grandma Jean's bed. They counted on assessing her condition quickly and admitting her. Her family wants to get her in or out quickly too. No one likes hanging out in the ER for hours on end. That's what families complain about most, poisoning their satisfaction with everything thereafter.

Beyond that, why are the ER doctors being asked to "diagnose" at all? They haven't the time for that. Med schools train them to stabilize, "assess" and triage patients home or into the hospitalists' care. The hospitalist's specialty and job is to diagnose what's wrong and plan how best to treat it. Warehousing patients in the ER while doing diagnostic tests for hospitalists' convenience abuses and irks staff and patients alike. It also clogs the ER, putting other ER patients on hold and in jeopardy. How can that be in anyone's best interest?

What's going on? Is it a conflict of patient care philosophies? Of beliefs about who is responsible for what? Or about who's top dog?

And why here, at this hospital? The hospitalist model reportedly works seamlessly elsewhere; the hospitalists accept the ER physician's judgment, admit patients quickly, and complete the diagnostic work once the patient arrives in a bed upstairs. What's different here?

Something still didn't compute. Something had to be other than it seemed. Finally it dawned on me to ask the CEO about hospitalists' financial incentives for performance. Were they in sync or at odds with patient throughput?

Bingo! Start with hospital reimbursement. Most acute care patients are elderly and insured by Medicare or Medicaid or through HMO contracts that put a cap on payment. The hospital gets one amount for Grandma Jean's emergency care. It gets another chunk for her inpatient acute care no matter how long or short her stay or how extensive her treatment, given her diagnosis.

ER physicians' efforts affect the length of stay and profitability of the ER chunk; the hospitalists' efforts affect the inpatient chunk. The hospital shows a profit when both groups do their respective jobs well and expedite the patient's return home.

But ... it turns out that the hospitalists' annual bonuses linked to short length of stay while patients were under their care, not short length of stay from ER arrival through acute care to discharge home. The later their clock started ticking, the better they looked and the bigger their bonuses. No wonder they wanted the ER to do as many diagnostic tests as possible before accepting control.

Meanwhile, the ER doctors earned their bonuses for patient satisfaction and quick throughput—in short, for acting in Grandma Jean's best interest.

Long experience across industries says that unless Group A's success ties to facilitating Group B's, and vice versa, then one will succeed at the other's expense. And the customer's. And the enterprise's.

Follow the money. Nothing is ever what it seems. The truth lies elsewhere.

97% Factors

Follow the money

Compensation: Does the compensation system reward productive behavior and action across departments, functions, and micro-cultures?

Incentives: Does it take the incentives out of unproductive behavior?

Manipulation: Can employees work around or manipulate the system for self-serving gain?

The other side of simplicity

I would not give a fig for the simplicity this side of complexity,
but I would give my life for the simplicity on the other side
of complexity. —Oliver Wendell Holmes

Consider the U.S. Constitution. Despite the contentious, pro-tracted negotiations framing it, the founding fathers molded it into one of the most simple, vibrant, purposeful documents of all time. Consider Einstein's formula relating energy, mass and the speed of light—$E=mc^2$ —so simple, so elegant, yet so deep into the complexities of the universe.

Principle 2 directly challenges those who demand rapid im-provement in performance to look beyond the simplicity of hur-ried assessments and quick action. Some decision-makers are so lopsidedly action-oriented that problems rarely get solved well, just worked around, creating more problems later on.

Is the effort dedicated to the truth-seeking worth it? It is. We don't want to solve the wrong problem, half-solve or mis-solve the right problem, or go serenely about our business missing the problem altogether. Routinely addressing problems on the fly cre-ates a bad habit. It lowers the bar for all problem solving. People get so accustomed to superficial thinking that mediocrity be-comes the expectation—and they live up to it. Why do anything else? Ask employees to think something through thoroughly, and they don't know how. So what? Management has little patience for the extra effort. Or values it. Or knows enough to detect or credit its contribution when credit is due.

Can we measure the value of getting to simplicity on the other side of complexity? Most certainly. For openers, once we diagnose a problem as accurately as we can and map our way forward, then we can ask en route if we're on the right track to "the other side." If not, that means the problem morphed into one we didn't foresee. We can adjust, sparing us a costly continuation down the wrong road. And retrospectively we can figure out the costs and conse-quences of the trip we took versus the one we didn't.

Nonetheless, a double danger for decision-makers lurks in Oliver Wendell Holmes comment.

◆   *Never getting beyond simplicity*

We make most daily decisions in the simplicity and haste this side of complexity. Most wrong decisions too. Think of the long-term, potentially life-threatening consequences for patients regionally if the paramedics and the ER staff we met in the first chapter had decided to end their joint workgroup—before discovering and fixing the breakdown in protocols for mass casualty incidents.

◆   *Getting mired in complexity*

"We study things to death, and nothing ever happens." The closer we position our ear to the frontline, the louder the chorus of complaints we hear about the problem of "all input, no output."

Getting to the other side

No problem is ever what it seems; the truth lies elsewhere, and seek it. The time to search for the truth may temporarily delay action, but we act smarter. We do a better job of solving the right problem instead of the wrong one and solving it right the first time.

Even when we have to think and act quickly, we think smarter, one of No Fail Leadership's key objectives. We know what we need to know up-front, but don't yet know what shortcuts we're taking, what risks we're accepting, and what critical knowledge gaps we must monitor and fill quickly as the action unfolds.

Whether we're in calm or in crisis, applying Principle 2 requires a basic understanding of how our perceptions impede us from getting beyond what seems and entering the elsewhere—the 97% that matters—where truth awaits our arrival. Let's address three issues:

1. Why nothing is ever what it seems.

How and why do we inadvertently misperceive situations and what should we watch out for as we investigate and assess them?

2. Elsewhere. Where is it?

Why we are so unaware of the elsewhere in which truth lies? What consequences arise from our blindness and what does it take to open our eyes?

3. What's really going on?

What forces drive problems and conflicts, and how can we smoke them out of the less obvious recesses where they hide?

WHY NOTHING IS EVER WHAT IT SEEMS

When our children act up, deaf to our "no's," or our teen goes rogue, lost in some alien cyberspace, the reasons they give have little to do with what's wrong. And treating symptoms cures nothing. The same dynamic operates at work.

In earlier chapters, we delved into how all problems are conflicts of beliefs—pre-existing beliefs—about what's true. The power of the past, reflected in our lack of neutrality and our tendency to perceive selectively, impedes accurate on-the-spot assessments and ongoing judgments about problems we face.

Past thinking and habits feel at home in the simplicity this side of complexity. "Nothing is ever what it seems" because we rush to look for assurance that whatever the present holds, we've seen it before, and we know how to handle it. We accept evidence supporting this and ignore evidence to the contrary. We honor the past and look past the present. Why?

We solve a personal problem instead of the business problem

More than one employee, leader, company, government and even nation has been brought crashing down through paranoid, precipitous reactions to ideas and events that people prejudged or misread through personal fears projected from the past into the future.

Here's one way it works: The business problem at hand threatens us at some level and with some intensity. We conjure up images of screw-ups we have experienced before, whether we caused them or not. We fear that a repeat performance under our watch could spotlight our vulnerabilities. Thus the personal threat looms bigger and more immediate than the business threat. As a result, we act to eliminate the personal threat instead of the business threat.

That's what happened with the hospitalists. They mustered all sorts of semi-legitimate diagnostic reasons (medical business reasons) to keep Grandma Jean in the ER, but the deeper reason was personal: to protect their annual bonuses.

Unfortunately, the "business" solution we engineer to eliminate a personal threat (like warehousing ER patients to do diagnostic tests against protocol to protect bonuses) can be vastly different than a solution to eliminate the purely business threat (like "assess" in the ER; quickly admit ailing patients to the medical-surgical suites so that the hospitalists can order lab and radiology tests; and work with everyone in the testing chain to cut turnaround times in half, helping everyone long term, including patients).

Most angst resides in the unexamined simplicity this side of complexity, not on the other side. Recognize self-protective impulses and solutions for what they are. Get them out in the open before the business problem gets elbowed aside. Otherwise, our solutions will end up self-serving and off the mark, sometimes disastrously.

We often race from the past into the future, ignoring the present altogether

That leaves the present like a bewildered orphan sitting on the doorstep, unheeded, watching traffic zip by, waiting to be spotted by someone who cares. And if we're never fully in the present, blind to what really goes on around us, then how can we or anyone see the present clearly? We can't, in which case:

⊚ How enlightening is our past? Our past experiences may never have been grounded in a former present reality of any kind, ever. The "present" we remember is a photo of an old photo of a scene that never was.

⊚ How accurately can past experiences illuminate today's problems, solve them or guide our future? Our thinking springs from an altered state of reality. We superimpose it on whatever pops up today.

The opening chapter's mass casualty incident offered a stunning example of projecting the past into the future, skipping right over the present into worst-case scenarios and speculations. As you may recall, the hospital's ER scrambled an army of doctors and nurses to handle a bus full of presumed casualties, few of which showed up. When the hospital participants learned that the medics had delivered more than twice as many patients to their crosstown rival, they instantly assumed that the medics were playing favorites, as always. Embarrassed, angry and hurt, they wanted to disband the joint workgroup.

Fortunately, they didn't. The audiotapes of emergency transmissions allowed people to relive the incident as it unfolded, proving that medic preference played no role. It never had. The truth lay elsewhere. Fortunately, people looked.

In the previous chapter—Fear, conflict, consequences and Principle 1—I cited conclusions from Kotter's and Heskett's *Corporate Performance and Culture*. They talk repeatedly about how experienced, highly intelligent top executives can adhere to the corporate strategy that was responsible for the company's rise long after it became directly responsible for the company's decline. The environment changed but top executives didn't spot it or refused to respond to it. They kept coming up with brilliant solutions to yesterday's problems. Few CEOs have the stomach to calculate and flagellate themselves with the cost of mistakes like that!

Again, nothing is ever what it seems.

If you still doubt the dominance of the past in defining what we see and experience, just think how confused and vulnerable we feel when our past does not define what we see and experience. Example: our first day as a first-time executive in a company in an industry we've never worked in before.

We don't even share common definitions of what we see

During the Cold War the communist countries co-opted the word "democratic." "Democracy" once stood for freedom of speech and movement, sacredness of personal property, one-person-one-vote, equality of opportunity and other brakes on authoritarianism. But no such virtues characterized the East German Democratic Republic. It imprisoned and oppressed its people behind the Berlin Wall and redefined "democracy" as state-enforced equality of economic and other deprivation.

We assume we agree on basic definitions, but we rarely agree on the basic definitions of anything.

Look at the company's statements of mission, vision and values, or our job descriptions, or what management says it expects of us, or what our promises say to customers. Do the words mean to others what they mean to us? When someone says "soon," what does that mean? Or, "We'll evaluate that." "We're 99% in agreement." "Responsibility." "Accountability." "In the ballpark."

Ask, or you'll never know. No wonder we talk past each other. And the confusion rises exponentially when people from different cultural backgrounds sit at the same table. No one even knows what "yes" means.

What seems in our common interest may not be, at all

In Henry James' 1903 novella *The Beast in the Jungle*, his protagonist, John Marcher, lives his life obsessed that some spectacular, horrible fate—some "beast"—lies in wait for him and any woman he might marry. Hence, he keeps the only woman who ever loves him at a platonic distance, rarely seeing her, rarely even venturing out of his house into the world of people and places for fear that something bad might happen. The decades pass. She dies, old and ill. At her gravesite, his "beast" finally pounces. Marcher realizes with horror that while he has been holed up successfully avoiding some horrible fate, he has frittered away his entire life and a woman's love. He lived so afraid that something bad would happen to him that nothing ever happened to him at all.

What's true individually can also be true collectively. If you, like John Marcher, can't be sure what your best interest is, how can you be sure about mine? Or ours? And what if the others at the table aren't any clearer about their own interests than you are about yours? We end up with a collection of interests masquerading and misunderstood as the common interest, when it's nothing of the kind.

You've heard the warning, "Be careful what you wish for, because it might come true." Along with wish fulfillment comes the law of unintended consequences, which postulates that actions taken with the best of intentions can have profoundly negative repercussions. Such as defending the status quo. Or passing ill-conceived legislation, marrying on impulse, merging with another company, doubling the business overnight, or making a promise we can't keep just to make the sale. All may seem in our common interest at the time, but time often proves otherwise.

Decision-makers who acknowledge this phenomenon don't stop deciding and acting. They stop over-relying on their own intuitions, which can rush them headlong or headstrong into what "seems" right—the "right" on the wrong side of complexity—where danger awaits every footfall. Instead, they wisely work hard to uncover the critical factors operating outside their view, in the past and in the now.

But that only gets them past simplicity into complexity, into a cacophony of input. To get to the simplicity on the other side, they must hear the themes and music hidden in the noise. They need to:

⊚   Clarify their own preconceptions, biases and interests and help other stakeholders clarify and look honestly at theirs.

⊙   Detach their ego from the decision and welcome rather than squelch honest feedback. Get the wax out of their ears. Listen. Learn. Hear more clearly.

⊙   Ask everyone to stay alert for the consequences of implementation as they unfold, including the unintended consequences—the bad notes.

In the end, we and they decide differently. More wisely.

97% Factors

Nothing is ever what it seems

Personal agenda: Who seemed most interested in addressing the Case History's problem and leading the charge to solve it? Did a personal agenda play a role in the choice of solution?

The past: Did past experiences advance and enlighten the deliberations or bog them down?

Definitions: Did participants agree on basic definitions of key words or talk past each other?

Interests: Did participants agree on what was in the common interest, or did consequences, intended and unintended, prove otherwise?

ELSEWHERE. WHERE IS IT?

Even if no one else knows where "elsewhere" is, the leader had better be able to look for it and find it. The alternative is to fly blind in spite of knowing better. This section covers why we fly blind, plus what's really going on that we dare not miss.

The importance of missing information

The chapter introducing Principle 1—*All problems stem from conflicts of beliefs about what's true*—also introduced us to professors Kardes' and Sanbonmatsu's research on the importance of missing information. Their findings, recapped here, help explain what Principle 2—*Nothing is ever what it seems; the truth lies elsewhere*—seeks to achieve and why it succeeds:

- ◉ Nearly all evidence we get is limited, incomplete, or fragmentary, and a lot of it comes from "clearly partisan sources."

- ◉ People willingly make decisions based on "scraps of information," insensitive to what they omit. They form strong beliefs based on weak evidence.

⊚   Paradoxically the less we know and/or remember, the
     stronger the belief. "People are often most confident when
     they are most wrong."

Just think about the decisions we make or go along with based
upon short, persuasive presentations. Or assertions prefaced by
"everybody knows that …" Or pronouncements we accept as true
because they come from experts, leaders, and other authority figures, like trial lawyers in their "catch me if you can" mode, who
arrange the truth to out-maneuver it.

People usually don't spot omissions built in to bolster a one-
sided case. They accept half-truths and outright lies as whole
truths, especially from bedfellows. They uncritically accept research results that partisans mischaracterize by failing to disclose
troubling negatives. People assume that missing information
lacks relevance unless an objective observer makes the fact of
missing information vividly evident. *Consumer Reports* does this
with side-by-side checklists impartially comparing products and
features.

Per the professors, "It is just as important to think critically
about what we do not know as what we do know." Fortunately,
merely warning people that critical information is missing makes
people moderate their judgment calls even if they do not know
exactly what's missing. That's important. Per the authors:

*"Moderate judgments are more accurate than extreme
judgments, more readily updated as new information becomes
available, more justifiable to oneself and to others."*

"More accurate, more readily updated, more justifiable." Assert-
ing Principle 2, *Nothing is ever what it seems; the truth lies elsewhere,* early in a problem-solving session, even a private session
with ourselves, sounds a crucial warning that changes the nature
of all deliberations that follow.

Make it a mantra.

The missing information: where is it?

The total quality movement, from Deming through Six Sigma and beyond, taught us to focus first on manufacturing and other heavily transactional, production-like business processes. Documenting processes in detail helps us determine how things get done. It quantifies the errors, defects, delays and other impacts from producing and doing what we do the way we do it. We learn where problems and opportunities arise and what we need to change to better serve stakeholders and outwit competitors. Without this understanding, our diagnoses and treatment plans can suffer from flaws.

But I have seen companies spend hundreds of thousands of dollars, if not millions, defining, measuring and analyzing their processes in intimate detail. Yet when all was said and done, few problems got fixed or stayed fixed. When top managers poked their business in the belly, it giggled and then plumped back out into its old shape.

Something critical and elusive escaped serious work, namely the Leadership Test problems. They still went on. Employees blocked new ideas. Implementation plans slowed to a crawl. People failed to communicate and cooperate cross-functionally. Employees didn't understand customers' expectations or each other's. They made too many promises they didn't keep. Workarounds proliferated. Problems piled up, covered up. Employees ducked accountability and blamed others. And management wasn't clear why things went wrong or what to do about any of this.

Lost and found

Most of the input we need to solve Leadership Test problems goes unaccounted for in the tidy 3% we can measure. But it's found elsewhere, in profusion, in the disorderly 97% that matters.

The map of the Six Sigma model shows where quicksand awaits.

SIX SIGMA PROCESS IMPROVEMENT MODEL

DEFINE   MEASURE   ANALYZE   **IMPROVE**   CONTROL

Three-Percenters stride into process improvement without appreciating the danger. Their metric-minded thinking may help them traverse the Define, Measure, and Analyze boxes but not the Improve and Control boxes, even when Six Sigma and "lean" consultants and other survivors of the crossing lay planks over the hazard and post warnings. Metric-minded thinkers with eyes glued to the 3%, unconcerned about the 97% that Deming insisted matters more, can end up mired in an elsewhere they don't expect, ill-equipped to Improve and to Control, a word that doesn't mean "rule from on high" in the 97% milieu. It means "lead."

Success at Improve and Control takes joint ventures between leaders at all levels and the people they lead. And uniting people behind a common cause isn't easy.

To Improve is fundamentally a doer's endeavor, driven by the desire to get the urgent work done any way possible, whatever it takes. Overall processes, procedures and customs provide broad parameters for action, but doers will circumvent processes that get in their way and devise their own, keeping what they have jerry-rigged to themselves. Over time these self-defined, informal processes evolve through trial and error and operate largely unnoticed. They provide comfort for us as doers once they become dependable, tempting us to think like Machiavelli's self-satisfied "enemies" of change.

Unfortunately, processes that serve us well can create chaos for other individuals, departments, or the company as a whole. Eventually management steps in demanding change we resist, but reluctantly agree to explore, as long as all agree that change will not be unilateral. Or inequitably against us.

Without inspired leadership at this juncture the reluctant agreement to improve motivates "improving" far more than the thrill of it. Been-there-done-that skepticism and cynicism keep us lukewarm until trusted leaders win us over. Our best employees relish a common cause that people support, plus faith that the up-side warrants the effort. We and they especially need confidence that the individuals and groups responsible for implementing the improvements will follow through.

It boils down to this: unless employees individually and col-lectively value productivity, productivity does not improve, espe-cially in service-intensive activities. And while executives assume that employees value it, they don't really know that to be the case, a major oversight. Employees commonly fear productivity as be-ing good for management, but personally high risk. It isn't safe to be honest, proactive and accountable. Many fall into blaming, making excuses and running for cover. Even employees who have the will to raise productivity don't always have the wherewithal. As a result, process and productivity improvements undertak-en with the best intentions meet with Machiavelli's enemies of change and lukewarm defenders of it.

As leaders we need to know why these enemies, who can nest at any level, are enemies. Why are defenders lukewarm? What bar-riers—practical, interpersonal or micro-cultural—impede buy-in and implementation? And how come we walk around so blind to what's going on?

Enlightenment lies in an elsewhere we may incline to overlook. It doesn't lie primarily in activities we can easily measure. It lies first within us. It lies in our struggles to get beyond the simplicity and complexity standing between us and the simplicity on the other side. It lies in rethinking beliefs and habits from which we must detach if we ever hope to improve. And to *lead*.

Remember, the purpose of Principle 2—*Nothing is ever what it seems. The truth lies elsewhere*—is to detach us and others from the past beliefs that prevent us from perceiving clearly what's hap-pening right now.

THE BLINDNESS OF SELECTIVE PERCEPTION

We see what we're trained to see

- ⊚ *The CEO focuses* on strategic and planning issues that frontline workers rarely glimpse. Meanwhile, frontline workers see all the ways that management's best-laid plans break down during implementation. But the people don't cross-communicate.

- ⊚ *The chief financial officer looks* for quantitative evidence from the past to predict future performance, while the human resources director looks for qualitative predictors that never show up on the financial report—like talent, training, experience, attitudes, integrity and achievement. And the two don't clearly see the connections between their activities.

- ⊚ *Left on their own, the designers design* elegant websites that the programmers can't execute. Left on their own, the programmers create websites bristling with interactive features that mere mortals can't figure out.

Organizations hire us and individually assemble other technical and functional specialists to see what we don't see. That's the upside of specialization, training and division of labor. But consider two downsides: myopia and the expectation of myopia.

- ◆ *Myopia.*

Sometimes training makes us so individually myopic—so single-mindedly focused on "our job"—that our collective myopias unwittingly miss what happens to the business as a whole. Bureaucracies are notorious for this. So are departmental silos. So are businesses that require a multi-disciplinary approach but are lopsidedly driven by technologists, or accountants, or sales people, or engineers or other specialized breeds of top dog.

Myopia can also be self-imposed by individuals who don't feel confident or empowered to think outside of their box, so they seek refuge hunkered down within it. Or it can be group-imposed by peers and superiors who have swaddled themselves in the status quo. They fear ideas and imagination and enforce conformity. They ignore what goes on elsewhere and care little that their modus operandi might create chaos for others. In business, that's unacceptable.

- *The expectation of myopia.*

We tend to anticipate that employees, especially those on the frontline or in specialized disciplines, will mind their own business. When their minds wander outside their field, function or level of expertise, superiors can get dismissive with them for dabbling in something they presumably know nothing about.

I heard of one young woman who tried three times to bring a new product idea to her boss. He told her that when she'd been with the company five years, then she could talk to him. She quit, took the idea with her and made a fortune. His myopic farsightedness stemmed in part from this expectation of shortsighted myopia in others of lesser stature.

We see what we want to see and block out what we're afraid to see

Look in the mirror. How does the face you see compare with the one in last week's snapshot of the family? Younger and cooler than the dude or dudette in the photo that did you no justice?

Look back at the times you focused so single-mindedly upon a task or problem that you shut out all else as background noise, no matter how important. We're all aware that witnesses don't see things the same way. Why then are we so often surprised when people don't see them our way?

We sometimes don't even see what we trained ourselves to see, if the picture doesn't jibe with the reality we know. A minister I respected exhibited increasingly odd behavior over the course of several years. We stopped attending his church. A year later we ran into the assistant minister and inquired about her boss. "He's back with his drinking buddies," she reported. In the interlude he had been in and out of alcoholism rehabilitation. "Here I am," she rued, "a trained counselor. He paraded all the symptoms right in front of me, and I never saw them for what they were."

At home we block out lifestyle, marital, family, financial and even health problems until they swell to crisis proportions. At work we ignore dysfunctional thinking, behavior and relationships, processes and performance breakdowns, market downslides and other internal and external threats, hoping things will improve on their own with time. And when we come up with turnaround ideas and plans, we can be slow to admit that they aren't entirely working. We don't want to be seen, or see ourselves, as imperfect.

The more deeply attached we get to the ideas we come up with, the more threatened we feel by incoming ideas and evidence to the contrary. We get impatient with people who differ with us and with evidence that contradicts us. We resist change we don't initiate. We block out the truths that we fear will make us look bad.

Never forget fear. It never forgets you.

We see what advances our short-term interest, ignoring the long-term consequences for us as well as others

A colossal example of myopia-generated waste in a multi-industry value stream popped up as a case history in James Womack's and Daniel Jones' book *Lean Thinking*, the source of the earlier Porsche story. This one recounts the journey of a cola can from the bauxite mine through manufacturing, filling, then draining by a thirsty drinker. In this particular example, the journey of the cola can traverses four countries, with stopovers in seven production facilities, a retail warehouse, a retail store and a buyer's refrigerator. The trip from mine to mouth takes 319 days. Check out the itinerary.

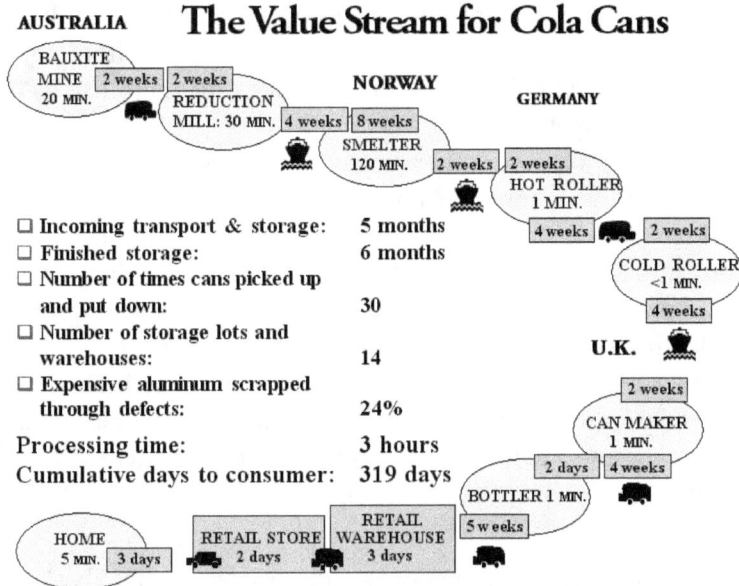

The Value Stream for Cola Cans

- ☐ Incoming transport & storage: 5 months
- ☐ Finished storage: 6 months
- ☐ Number of times cans picked up
  and put down: 30
- ☐ Number of storage lots and
  warehouses: 14
- ☐ Expensive aluminum scrapped
  through defects: 24%

Processing time: 3 hours
Cumulative days to consumer: 319 days

99% of the time is waiting. Only 1% adds value.

Three hours of processing out of 319 days! Mass production demands massive equipment operating at high speeds, with infrequent changeovers and minimal direct labor. But production efficiency at individual companies can create staggering waste between companies when we add in the indirect costs along the way for technical support, inventories, handling charges and storage costs. Each step can be a paragon of efficiency, yet the process from start to finish can be the paradigm for waste bred of self interest that is simultaneously myopic, calculated and ignorant.

We see what we are trained to see, want to see and consider important. We ignore the rest. Ask, "What could we have overlooked?"

We would rather see daily problems than deeper problems

Day-to-day problems are easy to spot. They're familiar. Known. Often easy to fix. We have experience dealing with them, so we cling to them seeking self-worth in our struggle, like an abused spouse in a codependent relationship. We occupy our day working around them or picking up the pieces when the full plate crashes on the floor. We get a kick out of troubleshooting. We become experts at it. We never run out of things to fix. We feel needed. Indispensable.

Try asking a CEO or other manager, "Suppose all the little crises went away. Do you know how to be a business without them?"

Managers that are administrators more than leaders tend to stare into the void I have just created in their mind. They haven't a clue how to be at peace with peace. If they can't even conceive of a high-functioning business, how can they evolve one?

As leaders we must look for the deeper problems, look at them, and help others to do the same. We may find people mentally retreating into a dark, cozy den. We need to shoo them out. Some symptoms of avoidance:

- All-consuming busy-ness with problems of the day.

- Complaints about the deeper problems but unwillingness to confront them.

- Denial that the problem exists at all: "We're doing just fine, for the most part."

- Vexation with people who keep sounding the alarm.

- Procrastination, in two forms:

  Plan A: Concoct ingenious workarounds to sidestep the problem for now instead of fixing it. When that fails, activate ...

  Plan B: Initiate a high-profile study of everything until the project suffocates under its own weight without answers.

At least we've made progress, yes? No? Progress procrastinating scares us less than authoring solutions and actions that press us and others to change. Probe. Blindness to fundamental problems in preference to immediate problems tacitly admits accountability for them.

No wonder people cling, not just to business-as-usual, but to problems-as-usual. There's safety there. But nothing resembling leadership.

WHAT'S REALLY GOING ON?

When people find themselves at loggerheads, the fundamental conflict often goes beyond the latest event or personalities precipitating it. It even goes beyond processes, one of the battlegrounds where conflict visibly plays out, and beyond bad processes, the usual suspects for fomenting it. But bad processes don't explain most of what's going on beneath the Leadership Test problems prevalent in the 97% that matters. A major chunk of them, I have found, falls into four categories:

1. Individual conflicts of values and mindsets.

2. Group misassumptions and misunderstandings about each other's situations and predicaments.

3. Lack of leadership.

4. The money trail.

These problems befuddle all but the most skilled, insightful leaders. We inherit some from past and present leaders. Some problems arrive fresh from new leaders, pass-alongs we haven't encountered before. Others we may have invented ourselves through our own inexperience, lack of understanding or ineptitude. Even a leadership epiphany won't instantly solve such problems, because enlightenment is only a prelude to action, not action itself. But it's a start.

97% Factors

What's really going on beneath what seems?

Several sources of problems may be in play in your Case History. As you encounter them:

- ⦿ *Check the mini-boxes* I have placed next to the subheads for flagging relevant ones, as you did on the Leadership Test.

- ⦿ *Add to the list any conflicts* not covered that played key roles in your Case History.

1. Individual conflicts of values and mindsets

Values are the lenses through which people focus power. Employees need positive, clearly understood, embraced and shared values to power productivity, along with the mindset and wherewithal to turn values into reality. When things don't move ahead or people don't communicate or interactions get tense, stay alert for individual, group and enterprise-wide mindsets and values that conflict. Such conflicts operate in an elsewhere we dare not overlook.

❑ A conflict of work ethic

Most employees take their job seriously. It's their career and their gathering place. It's their opportunity to learn, grow and use their talents for a greater good. They expect and accept conflicts of beliefs rooted in divergent talents, education, experiences, mindsets and cultural upbringing. But they do not appreciate slackers who do as little as possible, the cover-your-assers who duck accountability and the naysayers that complain rather than pitch in. All of them drive the doers nuts. They stall productivity and have inordinate power to subvert it. And hard workers fault management for allowing such behavior to go on unchecked.

❏ A conflict of mindset

People with a logical, analytical mindset tend to process and organize the world differently than people mentally predisposed to an interpersonal, imaginative perspective. Working together they can produce big ideas; working at odds, gridlock can result that leaders struggle to untangle. The conflict can go on within us, too, as the numbers tell us one thing and our gut tells us something else, until one side wins a split decision.

❏ Personal agendas and fear of loss, however ill defined

The ego's mindset comes with longstanding, deep insecurity. We find ego insecurity at all corporate levels, from CEOs to frontline personnel. It dogs achievers who feel pressured to excel by an inner drive, peers, family or contractual obligations. It haunts those who have successfully climbed their mountain only to discover they now have a mountain to defend. It disempowers underachievers demeaned into believing that their aspirations ought to extend no wider or higher than the confines of their cubicle. It can overwhelm people whose success lands them in situations they are ill prepared to handle, victims, they believe, of events, promotions or status they didn't seek.

Threatened egos, from the self-important to the self-deprecating, tend to take out their frustrations on handy individuals and groups. They are quick to identify adversaries by name, and the conflicts act out as preemptive strikes against unsuspecting targets. "Give an inch now, I lose. Take one now, I gain."

People really do have a hard time recognizing and admitting early on that their cherished idea, modus operandi or status quo doesn't work or needs rethinking. Just listen to politicians or special-interest advocates debating on a talk show, or managers and employees defending their decisions. They fear losing credibility, authority, reputation and even their career if proven wrong. They omit facts and dismiss opposing views instead of jointly perfecting outcomes for the enterprise as a whole.

And despite the eloquence of their rhetoric, the intention and passion driving it usually don't emanate from their higher, human brain. They well up from the primal 15% that's driven by deep urges and fear of loss.

Have you ever recommended action to protect your butt or advance some hidden personal agenda, such as renting an English castle for your California company's annual retreat? Or, laying a logic-heavy argument on your dad to justify borrowing the car for a double date to Friday's football game one day after getting your driver's license?

Be aware and beware of primitive instincts at work. Don't be distracted by surface logic. The truth may have been deliberately consigned to the omissions bin. Lift the lid and retrieve it. Assemble the complete picture.

❏ Bullies, victims and wiggle room

Look early on for the bullies and victims we fingered in Chapter 9. We'll find them locked codependently in one-upmanship between the "aggressive" and the "passive." That forces others to work around them just to do their job, dragging down the organization and irritating good people no end. Workflow becomes lava flow that sends conscientious employees on roundabout detours.

Victimizers and victims act equally self-indulgently. The victimizers indulge in the rush they get from exercising power and deflecting blame onto others. The victims indulge in feeling sorry for themselves, helpless, and released from responsibility for their failure to perform. Until we stop the bullies and get the victims to set aside their victim mentality, the tug of war will monopolize problem-solving sessions. And the consequences mount.

❏ The workforce in general

Employees take their cues from top management, which teaches lessons with every move it makes. Bullying abuses employees. Management that tolerates abuse for whatever reason creates a culture of distrust and fear and emboldens others to follow suit. Is that the lesson management wants to teach?

❏ Customers and other outside stakeholders

Survivalist behavior trumps customer welfare—a descent into Hades that's hard to climb out of. Is management exploiting the reservoir of customer trust to get away with underperformance when times get tough, hoping customers won't notice?

Regaining customer trust costs far more than keeping it, especially when we must rebuild it within our walls before we can rebuild it among outsiders. Stop the damage before it spreads.

❏ The victims

Once the victim mentality takes hold, victims gain an excuse to choose their own standards, underperform and disengage. Cooperation itself presents a threat, as if yielding on any point signals weakness to the other side.

❏ The bullies

Bullies are bullies by choice. Appeasing them doesn't work, because they get something out of their disruptive, abusive behavior, which will run rampant until leaders refuse to tolerate it, step in and say "no!" Saying "no" stops the flow of rewards. It also clamps down on the bullies' wiggle room by putting the responsibility for their actions where it belongs—on them, not on people, pressures, expectations, upbringing or society.

No matter how powerful, creative or indispensable bullies seem to be in other ways (positive signs that they are capable of more), they must change. Now, or else. The agony of their presence far outweighs the ecstasy. And best of all, no one will mourn their passing.

2. Group misassumptions and misunderstandings about each other's situations and predicaments

❏ Each group has logic to what it does, but the logic conflicts

Here's a life-and-death example. A paramedic team responded to a 911 call from a nursing home and found an elderly, feeble woman who had been feverish for days. The medics were angry that the staff hadn't called them earlier. In their eyes, Grandma had been mistreated, and they made their feelings known. But nothing is ever what it seems.

The nursing home staff had specific instructions from Granny and her family that her cancer should take its course without further intervention. They waited, trying to determine if Granny's fever was cancer-related and should be left alone, or if it was unrelated and should be treated.

Unsurprisingly, the medics and nursing staff found themselves exchanging words. The medics' goal was to keep Granny alive. The nursing home's goal was to help her die with dignity.

Two wrongs don't make a "right," but two "rights" can make a serious "wrong."

❏ Conflicts of culture

These can burst on the scene with an abrupt change of management or ownership. Or when two workforces consolidate. Or when operating in a foreign country with a culture and values that are vastly different from ours, even antithetical. Companies bumble into some conflicts unexpectedly with the best intentions. A Japanese consumer electronics company I worked with was one of them. In Japan, it enjoyed a workforce with a common culture and language. In the U.S., its Southern California workforce spoke 37 different languages.

❏ A conflict of loyalties

It's a side effect of training, silos, workmate alliances and other affinities that make groups clique-up and clash with each other, especially when one group feels that its success is being compromised by another.

❑ Conflicts across functions

These can reflect differences between how departments are managed and go about their work. One group may value data-driven, structured activities, while another may value aggressive entrepreneurship. One department can be a paragon of interdepartmental cooperation while another holes up in a silo. And yet another lords it over all others, a superpower among powers, such as Manufacturing over Sales in one company and the reverse in another. Leaders that play favorites make matters worse.

❑ Conflicting policies and procedures hard-wired into daily routines

Per policy, the accounting department had to approve all customer credit for purchases of their company's $500,000 machines.

Per policy, the service department—recently made into its own profit center—had to approve all credit for ongoing parts and service. It automatically put customers on C.O.D. who hadn't purchased recently.

One major new customer with sterling credit and multiple purchases finally needed some parts. The service department denied credit and shipped them C.O.D. Flabbergasted, inconvenienced and insulted, the customer blew his top. That left the sales manager and CEO to pick up the pieces, which almost didn't go back together again.

❑ Coworkers not understanding or buying into the value of what others ask them to do

On big projects some companies prepare elaborate critical path analyses that detail the dependent activities required to complete the project on time. People in charge assume that everyone knows what to do for whom by when and the consequences of missing a deadline. Don't bet on it.

We don't always take requests from coworkers seriously if their wheel isn't squeaking. Who needs another interruption and one more thing to do? So we stack it with all the messages and paperwork awaiting attention. Inaction may hold up others from completing an important task, but the priority is theirs, not ours.

How much time do you personally spend per week bugging and begging people to provide the input, collaboration or decisions you need to meet your deadlines? Five, ten, twenty hours? Multiply the hours you waste times the number of people in your organization, since everyone else suffers from the same plight. Add in the costs of delays, downtime, missed interlinked deadlines, frustrated employees and angry customers, lost momentum and lost opportunity. You get the picture.

That's waste, big time! Waste so common we accept it. We don't even think of it as waste. But it costs the business a fortune.

97% Factors

Time wasted

Do a top-of-mind estimate of the time you wasted implementing your Case History's project and the impact on speed, cost and quality.

3. A lack of leadership

❏ A lack of clear authority and chain of command

Employees at all levels frequently express confusion not so much about the published organizational chart, but about the real chain of command. Who really decides what? Where is the seat of power? Where are the seats of power? The informal chain can trump the formal chain.

When I interview employees, they often tell me that the manager who by title ought to make the key decisions doesn't make them. The CEO does. Or headquarters. Or the "sergeants." Or the favorite son. Or two people do. Or no one does.

This is a leadership problem. Command at whatever level breaks down when leadership is absent physically or mentally for long periods. The leader may be philosophically inclined to play hands off or too frightened to make decisions, intimidated by overlords or underlings. Or too new to know what's best, or too lacking in confidence. Or not respected by peers and subordinates, or not willing, competent or experienced enough to lead.

When trying to understand why performance falls short, shortfalls in command and accountability may explain a truth underlying "what seems."

❏ Inconsistent, lax standards across functions or within groups

In organizations, as in families, we cannot mind-read what others expect of us, need, and want. Each person creates his or her own standards and expectations. No wonder they vary from individual to individual. So do standards among groups, departments, branch offices and scattered facilities.

Many people—especially bullies and victims—secretly like imprecise standards. Imprecision allows wiggle room. The long-term result? Mediocrity and disunity. Ending wiggle room raises the bar on performance and accountability beyond what some employees are willing to shoot for.

Underperformance may trace importantly to standards that few understand, agree upon and uphold—or want—within groups and between them. Leaders must set the standards and enforce them. As a friend once said, "If you have no standards, you're 100% guaranteed to meet them."

❑ Ever growing piles of un-prioritized work

When management piles on work without prioritizing what to do with existing projects, the people assigned to do the work will prioritize their workload themselves. Their choices may not be close to management's or coordinated or consistent with each other's and end up cannibalizing resources on all projects.

The boss assumes—without finding out—that his project or problem takes precedence. He thinks he can shoehorn it in without disruption or consequences. Some subordinates salute and set everything else aside, including critical projects the boss had assigned earlier and were forgotten in the urgency of the moment, an oversight that could return to haunt them all. Others see their own deadlines suddenly jeopardized and protest, with some risk of being branded as obstructionists. Still others, besieged by such requests, either disengage from their job, responsibility and accountability or over-engage out of a strong work ethic, ending in burnout.

Resistance to more work may reflect frustration not at "more work," but at the dispiriting list of long-nurtured, half-finished projects that die senseless, premature deaths without accomplishing anything other than draining resources, energy and appetite. Senseless deaths build an expectation of non-completion. And the projects that die tend to be tough ones that promise to deliver high value, but require personal and corporate commitment.

❑ A history, short or long, of making promises that aren't being kept

- ⊚ Sellers make promises about products and services to attract customers.

- ⊚ Customer satisfaction and retention rest upon how well these promises are kept.

⊙ Companies that surpass others only make promises they can keep, and they keep all the promises they make. That includes promises made internally to each other and externally to customers and outside partners.

This observation may strike us as obvious and simplistic, but the damage caused by broken promises goes far deeper than customer disappointment. Like a cancer it can eat away at the company's fundamental integrity. It only takes a few, minor, promise-keeping failures before people conclude that they can't trust the whole operation and anything it does. To protect themselves, they begin policing everything that comes their way, an overhead burden they resent.

We'll get into making and keeping promises in a later chapter. For now just be aware that promise breakdowns destroy trust. What appears at first glance to be an argument over a customer invoice, an internal turf war or some other immediate, urgent issue may in fact be the latest link in a long chain of promises not kept, whether intentionally or unintentionally. Ethical employees can sometimes get so frustrated that they ally with long-standing customers against their own company to salvage the relationship.

Frontline behavior when making and keeping promises reflects the standards and example that management has set with its choices, decisions and action. Again, things may not be what they seem; the truth may lie elsewhere.

❏ 4. The money trail

Do you recall, early in this chapter, how dismayed the ER physicians felt that the hospitalists warehoused clearly sick patients in the ER for testing instead of transferring them to a hospital room and ordering the tests themselves? Had we not followed the money trail, we never would have found out why—conflicting financial incentives—and fixed the problem.

Money can motivate in subtle ways that process improvement charts don't factor in. Don't forget to find the trail and follow it. It may lead to the most unexpected, penetrating enlightenment of all.

97% Factors

Nothing is ever what it seems

Personal conflicts: What individual values and mindsets seemed most prevalent and powerful, who held what views, which ones prevailed, and with what consequences, plus and minus?

Group conflicts: Do groups truly understand each other's situations and predicaments? If not, what have been the manifestations and consequences? Do they care?

Lack of leadership: How many and which of your Case History problems trace fundamentally to problems of leadership? Which problems do not?

The money trail: Earlier you tracked the conflict between the ER and hospital doctors to conflicting compensation packages and looked for parallels in your Case History. What other ways have money or its lack contributed to the origin and persistence of the Case History problem?

Understand that we don't understand

Most managers we've encountered, especially CEOs and other leaders, admit that they know less than half of what really goes on inside their walls, especially during those countless, daily moments of truth on the front line and behind the scenes that make or break customer and internal relationships. And managers may know even less about what customers really think. Employees won't confess their weaknesses. Customers rarely volunteer opinions, unless they are very unhappy. And the typical surveys don't penetrate the subsurface dynamics churning decision-making and action.

But even when events take place right before our eyes, we still don't see them clearly. We see them fully encumbered by our past experiences, beliefs, and associations. Stay particularly alert to any conclusions reached quickly. They're probably incorrect.

Managers and employees alike pride themselves on comprehending a situation quickly, solving it on the spot and then moving on. We're impressed with people who can do this, and we reward the behavior. Paramedics at a 911 scene excel at it, and we wouldn't want it any other way. But paramedics "assess" and stabilize. They operate by design in the simplicity this side of complexity. They don't "diagnose." Physicians "diagnose." And we don't want one of them carving us up until they have diagnosed and understood the problem and planned an intelligent solution. We want the same from employees.

So, monitor the speed of your rushes to judgment for a day. Note how fast you size up each work-related or personal interchange. Merely being alert to your thought pattern may change it. You'll ask one more question, or invite a second opinion, or pause to remember that nothing is ever what it seems and ask what's really going on.

Using Principle 2: *Nothing is ever what it seems.*
The truth lies elsewhere.

You will find that people catch on to its value very quickly. It's so remarkably apropos and accurate that, before long, people apply it routinely and quote it to colleagues. To ingrain the habit all we need to do is:

- ⊚ *Assume that Principle 2 is valid.* I have never encountered an exception.

- ⊚ *Probe for the truth* until the group has uncovered what's really going on. I am not arguing that we illuminate every possible "elsewhere." We need to pick, choose and act, avoiding costly detours to nowhere.

- ⊚ *Don't ever accept the first explanation.* Position it as one that's "in the bag." You can even grant that it may ultimately be the best one. But ask for more. Appeal to the Sherlock in each of us. "Let's keep going. What else could be behind what seems to be?"

- ⊚ *At the end and along the way, remind people that* "Once again, nothing is ever what it seems. The truth lies elsewhere," because that's where you'll find it. Soon, people will do the reminding for you.

Principles 1 and 2 teach us to open our minds and dig into the eye-opening elsewheres where the truth really lies. We learn to suspend our attachments to strongly held beliefs, preconceptions, instant diagnoses, conjectures, rushes to judgment, and particularly to the presumption that coworkers value and venerate such thinking and behavior. Mental agility in the service of truth holds a critical place in problem solving and decision-making. Mental agility in the service of ego does not.

The agreement we make with ourselves and others to search for the truth and allow it into our thinking represents the first step—a giant step—along the path toward accurate problem solving, sound decisions and learning to lead by learning to succeed.

PART 4

GETTING THE TRUTH

ON THE TABLE

PRINCIPLE 3

The truth is always positive, even when it's painful.

Fear of the truth or ignorance of it costs dearly.
If leaders do not make decisions based upon truth—upon
accurate input and assessments—then what
are they making them on? Untruths?
Half-truths? Wishful thinking?

That is a recipe for disaster, in business and in life.

There is no alternative to the truth

Do you remember the workgroup meltdown that almost occurred following the Mass Casualty Incident that wasn't? Our Lady's ER staff blew up at the paramedic group for the "obvious" favoritism it showed by transporting patients to competing ERs. They wanted the paramedics to come clean and admit guilt. Fortunately, the tapes of emergency radio traffic told a different story that the hospital group had no choice but to accept. That took some courage. What took more courage was going back to their furious doctors and nurses to correct self-righteous misimpressions. The truth turned out to be positive. It graphically exposed flaws in the MCI protocols and reestablished good relations between the two groups.

Listening to the truth and accepting it aren't easy when truth contradicts our own thinking. Parents don't want to hear that the high school expelled their teenager or that the family has almost spent itself into bankruptcy. People don't appreciate their boss pointing out that their attitude interferes with job performance, or that their self-created policies create chaos for everyone else, or that a venture they championed isn't working out. Such admissions seem to admit failure.

Nothing positive comes from denial. The truth never goes away. Denial is waste. It doesn't add value. It destroys it.

There is nothing positive about denial

U.S. manufacturers made horrendous miscalculations about the threat from Pacific Rim and India. Arrogance, Complacency and Procrastination label three petards upon which a business can hoist itself. U.S. manufacturers hoisted themselves on all three. Most, believing that no nations could challenge U.S. leadership, dismissed the threat.

Today, we are paying the price. To stay in business and compete at home and globally, America's service, technology, manufacturing, financial and other industries increasingly produce or subcontract offshore, an out-migration with serious consequences for U.S. technology, knowhow, jobs and industrial capacity. The cost for us to lead pales next to the cost to catch up, but catching up late, which isn't cheap, arguably costs far less than losing yet more industries through denial and delay.

On a local scale, think of entrepreneurs you know who refuse to step aside or grow when their business outgrows them or atrophies around them, a truth they cannot accept. Or think of managers who cling to familiar paradigms for conducting business and dealing with people until the business and the people have gone elsewhere. Closer to home, think of all the truth avoidance that goes on in families about love or money or child rearing. People handle truth very gingerly, like a grenade with a half-pulled pin.

Deniers of the truth sniff a drug more toxic and common in workforces than cocaine. Cover your ass. Hide the mistakes. Finagle the numbers. Don't rat on a brother. Stretch the truth to consummate the sale. Make promises that you can't keep, getting people off your back a little longer. Tell people what they want to hear, not what they need to hear. Let someone else tell them.

When we're not avoiding the truth, denying it or burying it, we embellish it, stretch it or trim it. We've come to expect untruths, half-truths, and wishful thinking in advertising, sales presentations, business analyses, quarterly and annual reports and so on. We fear letting the truth speak for itself, especially when dealing directly with people we know. Blunt truth telling takes us aback, so we pussyfoot around the truth so routinely that qualified truth becomes the norm.

But we need the truth. Truth determines how clearly we see, how cohesively and competently we operate, how productively we perform, how competitively we pursue our mission and how agilely we lead or respond to change and opportunity.

Pussyfooting around it impacts directly on what input we report as we strive to justify the truth we tell and to defend against the truth that exists, uneasy about airing evidence that gets in our way.

Where does that leave leaders and other decision makers who are starved for input? It leaves them sifting endlessly through garbage masquerading as food for thought, hoping competitors are mired in an even deeper heap.

The truth is always positive?!

Principle 3 does not advocate turning battle plans and secrets over to an enemy bent upon our destruction. That's not positive. Or revealing trade secrets to a competitor itching to rip us off, or speaking openly with a schemer out to get inside information to use against us. If pushed, we truthfully tell them we won't tell them.

Rather, Principle 3 advocates being truthful—being accurate—with ourselves above all and with each other about what really goes on inside and outside our company's walls. We need input we can trust from people who know we want it and don't hesitate to share it.

Principle 3 also advocates being truthful externally with customers, outside providers and partners and with other stakeholders. Wary outsiders don't fully expect it and don't forget when they get it. They have to make business and personal decisions based upon what we tell them. For them, the truth is always positive.

Even when the truth is painful?!

By painful, I don't mean the sting of getting your bottom spanked for a misdeed. Or suffering the indignity of being sent to your room, ostracized temporarily from the action. Or being shunned by classmates for reporting a friend's serious offense to authorities.

Then again, maybe I do mean that. Maybe I have just described the mental image from childhood that overtakes adults reflexively when the idea of telling the truth, the whole truth and nothing but the truth seems but one end of a grayscale of options.

The red end of the grayscale

When my older son was a senior at West Point and home for Easter break, his 11-year-old sister asked him if he would visit her sixth grade class—a mixed, gifted, college-bound group—and talk about his experiences at the U.S. Military Academy.

They fixated on West Point's honor code, bringing him back to the subject three times. The code demands that he always tell the truth. They couldn't believe that "always" meant "always." Like, are you supposed to rat on your friends? Not cool. Or safe. You lose friends. There must be some exceptions! What's truth and what isn't? Not everything is black and white. How much can you know and not have to tell? What if you just know about something? Say you weren't there, but heard about it. Should you talk? Or suppose you did something, but no one knows about it. Should you rat on yourself?

After several rounds of what-ifs, my son realized that the kids were lawyering it to death. They got hung up on definitions, saw truth as "unnatural," and missed the principle. So he made it concrete by telling a true story.

West Point, he explained, trains officers who lead troops into battle. A company of soldiers on the Vietnam front line was ordered to advance to Point A. The fresh, young lieutenant, who had misread the map, found himself and his group at Point B a short distance from Point A as darkness was falling. He quickly regained his bearings, but decided to bivouac for the night, leave early, and be in position by sunrise. No harm, no foul. But when he checked in with headquarters, he didn't want to admit he'd screwed up on his first patrol, so he reported that they had made it to Point A, as ordered. I mean, like, he was almost there, right?

The black of midnight vanished in the fireworks of a hundred explosions as the company came under intense Viet Cong attack. In a panic, the lieutenant called for artillery support 200 yards west of his position.

He got it. Due west of Point A was Point B. "Friendly fire" killed or bloodied half of the lieutenant's men before he could undo his graying of the truth.

That's a hard way to learn that it's not the truth that's "unnatural." What's unnatural is not embracing it.

Truth is not unnatural because it never goes away

It lurks behind every denial, half-truth and lie, whether we initiate them or feel coerced into furthering them. Every time we lie, we experience and validate the truth behind the lie we create. We demean ourselves with our dishonesty and hypocrisy, and we know it. We've not lived up to our own expectations, and down deep that really bothers us. As one manager expressed it, "I'm so used to keeping my mouth shut or outright lying to buy time or make something bad look good that I no longer recognize myself. I didn't start out this way. Where's the 'me' I used to know? I want me back!"

To such people the truth is positive, even though they have suppressed it for personal survival or even personal gain. That basic, latent yearning for integrity energizes the courage to reconnect with the truth.

What's so striking is how positive a turn the future takes when people open their eyes, even when the turn launches them in an unexpected direction. The truth about us as individuals may seem painful for the moment or in anticipating it. So may the truth about what we think ought to work but embarrassingly doesn't. Nonetheless once the truth is out we may not experience any pain at all. The Chicken-Little fears that hold the old ways in place usually prove overblown if not groundless. The sky does not fall. It opens up.

♦   *The truth about ourselves.*

Several decades ago, I came across a list of questions human resource managers can use to get honest answers from job interviewees. At the time, I was leaving one job and looking for another. I wanted to go into each interview as prepared as possible, so I typed out brutally honest answers to each question and studied for the oral exams. I clarified what I was good at, not good at, liked and disliked in jobs and bosses, plus what I wanted in the next job and wanted to avoid. Surprisingly, only one potential employer of several asked even two of the questions. Accepting a job offer from any employer based upon the interviews would have been like marrying at the end of the blindest of all blind dates.

So, I interviewed the interviewers. For example, if they failed to ask "What kind of positions do you do best in?" I turned the questions around, asking them, "What kind of people do best in that job?" After getting their answer, I volunteered mine to the questions they didn't ask. When the fit was clearly wrong, we both knew it, but we weren't done. Some interviewers thought of a more suitable job opening for us to explore.

Over the years, I have shared the questions with friends who had been fired, felt like failures, and were pessimistic about the future. All of them came away with a more realistic view of themselves, their confidence restored, a clear idea of where to go next, and eagerness to burn rubber. Their old job, they found, was a bad fit. It accentuated their weaknesses, failed to exploit their strengths and talents, demanded that they be someone they weren't, and should have been traded in for a new job long ago.

Why had they waited so long to seek the truth? Because egos hate what they view as failure and go to enormous lengths to deny it. People make secret agreements with themselves to protect their public image, admit nothing, and damn the consequences, only dimly aware that the ego would rather kill them than cure them.

Ask yourself: As human beings, are we stronger or weaker after taking stock of ourselves? As available human resources, are we more valuable or less? Employed in a new job we are good at, do we accomplish more or less? The ancient Greeks, on the Temple at Delphi, got it right: "Know thyself."

♦   *The truth about what works and what doesn't.*

People too often won't even concede that one part of a plan is failing for fear that opponents will kill the whole thing. Think of all the win-lose conflicts between labor and management, departments, individuals, parents and schools or special interests and society where neither side is willing—nor has the courage—to concede that the other may have a valid point. Think, too, of the well-intentioned governmental programs that should have been consolidated, reformed or canceled years ago, but no one has the courage to take action. They lumber on, politically off limits to serious reappraisal, wasting money and effort that could be spent restructuring and advancing the same cause or a more practicable one with far greater payoff.

When we cannot openly acknowledge shortcomings, we lose the opportunity to learn from mistakes and correct them. That leaves us little choice but to defend the status quo in its entirety. Eventually a few rotten ideas do pollute the barrel, taking the good ideas down the sewer with them.

The serious search for truth must supplant fear of the journey

You already know people who stay ahead of the pack on truthfulness. We find them at all levels, even in difficult cultures. They make up our core of leaders, acknowledged or not. We go to them when we want a candid assessment of our thinking, performance or predicaments, knowing full well that the answer we get may not be the answer we hoped for. But at least it's honest.

No Fail Leadership validates these leaders' pursuit of truth and creates conditions that enable others to catch up, turning a core into a broader corps. It illuminates how and why Leadership Test problems take hold and resist solutions. It targets assumptions, processes and other Leadership Test practices that come into intramural conflict and into broader conflict with the marketplace at large. And it gives us good reasons and unthreatening ways to overhaul them.

We learn how heavily we have armored ourselves with misbeliefs—unnecessarily, as the whole truth reveals. We learn which practices make sense and which ones handicap us and others, a problem we may have known about or suspected but chose to disregard, practices that we never would have instituted had people been open and honest with each other all along.

We learn how positive the truth can be. Even when it's painful.

There's no truth without courage

Remember how we defined "true" in Chapter 1—in accordance with fact or reality. Truth in No Fail Leadership means accurate, correct, avoiding error, misrepresentation or falsehood. That's the truth we need.

Courage is an incredibly important precondition for such truth to prevail. Without courage, truth rarely even surfaces. Most all of us value courage, but only a minority of us can draw upon it naturally and routinely in our everyday lives. Fear of truth stands in the way. So does a lack of faith in the truth as a consistent force for good. And so does a workplace culture where embracing the truth seems riskier than equivocating it, using it selectively or looking the other way.

Without truth, we have no lodestone. We lose our bearings. We strike off in ill-advised directions, aborting far more journeys than we complete, a massive waste of most every resource we possess.

Untruths, half-truths and wishful thinking never led anyone to the Promised Land. Neither did leaders who lack courage.

Leaders at all levels must have the courage to:

Seek the whole truth.

Ask for it.

Provide it.

Receive and face it.

Share it.

Act on it.

To many, each of these entails more risk than they want to stomach except in small, sugar-coated doses. Others come well endowed with courage and high standards they expect to live up to. But they run into a wall of mediocrity that stops them in their tracks, dispiriting them no end. In fact, none of this has to be the case. No Fail Leadership endeavors to make it safer and more rewarding—not riskier—for everyone top to bottom to embrace the truth than to stonewall or skirt it.

Skeptics and cynics see this goal as unattainable and may actively sabotage progress to prove themselves right. They fear the truth and project onto others their own lack of faith in themselves to handle it.

They argue that truth leaves us (starting with themselves) naked and vulnerable, especially in business cultures where parsing the truth or keeping your mouth shut grows into the survival tactics of choice. "I need to cover my ass like everyone else." The nonchalance can't mask the anger and frustration. "When people hear the truth, half the time they don't believe it anyway, especially if they don't like it. Truth has become a tool. When it works for me, I'll use it. When it might work to my disadvantage, I'm not volunteering it."

Bottom line, they consider truth telling unnatural, as did the kids in the sixth grade class who couldn't believe that anyone in his right mind would honor an honor code.

Double-bottom line: experience, unexamined, isn't always a good teacher.

Courage to seek the whole truth

Many CEOs and other top dogs I have met with over the years, down deep, fear too much truth.

Some are too arrogant to admit that theirs isn't the hot-shot, totally checked-out organization they tout. Or that problems exist that they can't handle or worse yet haven't seen. Others get complacent with success or the status quo and believe that "while there's always room for improvement, we're doing quite well." Still others know that the business needs serious reexamination and intervention, but they procrastinate, like patients whose cardiologist has told them to quit smoking, eat right and exercise before they topple over from The Big One. Even basically honest, conscientious leaders striving for the greater good sometimes succumb to doubts that the gain outweighs the pain.

Oh, they'll all pump out numbers and reports to track financials and other impersonal performance indicators. And many will do process and productivity-based analyses of root causes. But they want no part of a deeper quest for truth among the workforce and customers at large. They want no challenge to the way they lead, hire people and conduct their business. Such feedback could force action they have avoided. It might prompt change or trigger an axing from above or a palace revolt from below.

Their resistance is unfortunate. All resistance is a cry for help. It emanates from fear-based speculation more than reality. Remember:

Nothing is ever what it seems; the truth lies elsewhere.

The problem that we think traces to our personal failure probably has many facets beyond those we see. To solve it, the facets that we don't see may need as much polishing as our own.

Our diamond may still be in the rough. We will never know without an honest, objective appraisal. Go for it. If we uncover flaws, so be it. The truth is always positive. We can't fix a problem we don't understand and fear to investigate.

Courage to ask for the truth

Some CEOs wish they knew the truth of what's going on. But they shy away from asking employees who have been quietly accepting their lot to start thinking and speak frankly. Still other executives have never allowed their people to speak frankly. To them, liberating tongues sets a risky precedent. As one CEO put it, "A little bird tells me that if you ask people what's wrong, you may have to fix it. If you ask what they want, you may have to give it to them." The bird was a chicken.

Once again, distrust coupled with fear stands in the way. The fear of asking far exceeds the actual threat from the answers, as exhibited by our cynical CEO and seconded by input from people at all levels over the years. Management expects the usual blaming, finger pointing and griping. But that's not what comes back when I interview employees in troubled companies and probe beyond complaints. I get insightful feedback into the complexity of what's working, what's not and why it's not.

Yes, some angry, stubbornly cynical employees I've encountered can't be objective, calm or positive about anything. But in others a subtle but profoundly encouraging attitude shift can take place on the spot. Instead of blurting out the scuttlebutt or their pet peeves, they think before they speak. The simplistic generalizations give way to more nuanced, accurate testimony. They assume that top execs believe them capable of it or they wouldn't have sent me to ask. Balanced thinking begins. It feels good to them. Most want more of it.

Courage to provide the truth

Think back to the story earlier in this chapter that recounted my son's experience talking about West Point's honor code with his sister's sixth grade class. The kids listed one excuse after another for not being truthful. Adults in the workplace have more excuses to add.

Asking for the truth and freeing people to speak frankly in confidence does not guarantee that they will do so. Most appreciate the chance to provide important input and are motivated to be candid. Others are reticent. They fear reprisal or the disruption of someone's coveted status quo. They lack faith that the truth ultimately helps everyone and that they can trust those who receive it to deal with it intelligently. That prejudgment says more about the trust that those who prejudge have in themselves than about the trustworthiness of those they prejudge. Their ugly truth: "If I were in your shoes, I might use what you say against you, so I must expect that you would do the same against me." Employees must overcome their distrust and fears, show some courage and seize the opportunity to contribute.

Courage is only required where there's fear. Remove the fear, and courage isn't an issue.

Courage to receive the truth and face it

Positive though the truth is, hearing it can be painful when it calls our own beliefs, blindness and performance on the carpet. Problems that we have long suspected emerge as hard realities. Problems we've never dreamed of suddenly confront us, including those caused by informal processes that we barely perceived. Misunderstandings about roles, responsibilities, standards, expectations and performance abound—open invitations to misbehavior, dysfunction and mediocrity. Receiving and accepting the truth without being defensive takes courage. Dig deep.

Besides, don't we want to promote courage throughout the company? Employees take their cues from the people at the top. When management lacks courage, so do employees. They seek refuge in the informal processes they devise to get their work done with as little personal risk as possible. That undermines the efficacy of the overarching formal processes they must work within, processes the company relies upon to fulfill its mission productively and efficiently.

Courage to share the truth

We must share the truth, deflating though it can seem, to spark change. People who think they own the truth find out that other points of view have legitimacy that competes with their own preconceptions, a step toward opening their minds. People who feel alone in their predicaments learn that others struggle with the same ones and may have already figured out good ways to deal with them. Employees whose exposure has been confined to their bailiwick, along with their perspective and conclusions, discover adjacent bailiwicks they never explored. They find smart people they never got to know doing high-value work they never understood or turned to advantage.

Truth is the across-the-board, humbling, disrupting yet enlightening breath of fresh air that revives and revitalizes whole organizations. It makes private misunderstandings and misperceptions public, where they can be addressed and straightened out for everyone's benefit. The common reaction to the revelation is, "I had no idea!"

Once again, courage is only called upon when there's fear. Set aside the fear, and courage is no longer an issue. The truth, hidden away, cannot do its vital work. Trust it. Share it. Allow it to come to our rescue.

Courage to act on the truth

In mid-1980 Procter & Gamble was informed that its Rely tampons, along with other super-absorbent brands, were implicated in menstruating women becoming sick with a new disease called

Toxic Shock Syndrome (TSS). P&G immediately began collect-
ing scientific and epidemiological data from the U.S. Center for
Disease Control, the Food & Drug Administration, state health
departments and leading universities. It turned the data over to
a scientific and medical advisory group that reviewed everything
and concluded that the connection was not yet conclusive or fully
understood. Nonetheless, TSS was on the increase, and Rely was
linked to more than its share of new cases.

P&G could have stalled by trying to deny or discredit the evidence or they could have waited until it was incontrovertible, the
tobacco industry's tactic of choice. Instead, P&G—then known
more for deliberate movement than agility and speed—scrambled
its national sales force and massive logistical resources on Sep-
tember 22, 1980. Within days it voluntarily removed every box of
Rely from retailer shelves nationwide, without external prodding
from lawyers or consumer watchdogs. It just did it, explaining
that until TSS was better understood, "suspension of Rely sales is
appropriate."

Can you imagine how costly that was, immediately and long
term, to withdraw a major consumer product from the marketplace based upon extremely limited, circumstantial evidence—
without being forced to do so? Think of the refunds and the lost
sales revenue. Time and more research proved the decision to
have been fortuitous, and the decision demonstrated P&G's high
ethical standards along with good business sense. It also demonstrated rare courage at the top. I was proud of my old employer
that day.

One more client case history: Scandinavian Airlines System,
SAS, a story about a CEO who gained control by letting go of it.

"Control freaks" are so common among people holding responsibility and authority that you almost need to be a control freak to
not be considered an exception. They nest in rigidly hierarchical
structures where "men who think" transfer their ideas smoothly
to "men who labor." The concept was the brainchild of turn-of-
the-20th-century productivity guru Frederick Winslow Taylor,
who legitimized and institutionalized it as "Scientific Management." Taylor worshipped the management pyramid as the house
of the gods. And CEOs were happy to perch on top.

As the century wore on, it became increasingly clear that as central control at any level increases, output decreases, in business and in government. People rebel. They stop caring. They disconnect. They spend more time complaining to each other and filing grievances than working. Productivity takes a dive, causing chaos and dysfunction. Control freaks wind up with a company that's paradoxically chaotic and catatonic at the same time.

One of the first CEOs of stature to grasp this truth was Scandinavian Airline's Jan Carlzon. Tom Peters told the SAS story in his best-seller *In Search of Excellence*, as did Carlzon in his book *Moments of Truth*. My firm also told it in a radio campaign when SAS was a client of ours. Here's the story, basically as told in one of the radio spots:

When Jan Carlzon became SAS's president in 1981, punctuality, service and morale had all deteriorated. SAS stood in deep financial trouble, and trade journals judged it the worst airline in the world.

One day Carlzon was sitting at his desk pondering the hemorrhaging of money and morale when one of those ego-bruising truths dawned on him:

"Thirty thousand passengers, a lot of them on business, fly SAS every day," he said, "and come face to face with our people about five times a trip. That's a hundred fifty thousand encounters a day, moments of truth that can make or break us and I don't control a single one of them."

So what did Carlzon do? He turned control over to the ticket agents, cabin attendants and others who really need it.

"If a passenger has a problem," he said, "don't worry about protocol or a few pennies. Just fix it. And I will back you 100%."

In the 1980s few CEOs had the courage or trusted their front-line people enough to give them that kind of power. Or to confess their personal lack of it. Can you imagine what happened to morale and service when Carlzon downloaded that much authority?

Incredibly, Carlzon put SAS in the black within one year, and within two, SAS was Airline of the Year.

The appetite for truth must be voracious

Don't forget:

The truth is always positive, even when it's painful.
The alternative is to base decisions on untruths, half-truths
and wishful thinking. That courts disaster.

Do not seek truth out of paranoia. People will sense your dread and question your intent. They will suspect that you mean to wheedle the truth out of them so that you can use it against them. They'll clam up.

Instead, be intensely curious about everything, like a kid with a screwdriver and a houseful of things to unscrew. Encourage that curiosity in others, for the good of all. People won't assume a downside if you are convinced that the truth is always positive and embody that conviction.

Be curious about:

- How things in the business work and don't work

- People's beliefs and fears and the conflicts they cause

- Formal and informal processes and the conflicts they cause

- How people interrelate or fail to interrelate with each other and with customers and other outsiders

From top to bottom, inside and out, be curious about what is and what only seems to be. That's never self-evident, because as

Principle 2 cautions, *Nothing is ever what it seems; the truth lies elsewhere.*

Truth seeking cannot be a sometime thing. Seek it aggressively, with perseverance and an open mind. When it needs to be told, tell it. Free others to tell it. Be open to receive it, even when it sends messages you don't want to hear, and reconstruct your reality as you digest the input. Be willing to share it with those who need it to do the best they are capable of. Seek truth so routinely and use it so wisely and unthreateningly that people expect and tolerate nothing less from you, from themselves and from each other. Succeed, and you will have established a priceless culture of curiosity.

Then, most important of all, have the courage to act on it. If you don't act, whatever trust you built by seeking and accepting the truth takes a nosedive, along with your credibility as a leader. People will stick out their neck and speak up a few times, but without follow-up they will eventually refuse. Why run the risk, they ask, if nothing is going to change anyway?

In the business of running a business, leaders can afford nothing less than the truth from everyone, because the alternative is too painful. In return, employees have a rightful stake in you acting on it. That's when the truth becomes visibly positive. That's the real moment of truth.

The Q&A exercises in No Fail Leadership aim to get to the intimate truth of your case history's unfolding. They also aim to get you to the truth of your role, for better or worse. "Worse" does not even remotely mean failure. It means input and learning. Any group or enterprise that values the truth will say the same—seeking and allowing in the truth has no downside long term, only an upside. It can put us way out front.

97% Factors

Leadership courage

List who played important leadership roles dealing with the Case History issue.

Grade them A–F on their overall courage (to seek the truth, ask for it, provide it, receive and face it, share it and act on it), noting key factors and experiences influencing your choice of grade.

Assess how their courage or lack of it impacted the events and outcomes.

Grade yourself on your own courageousness as this Case History unfolded.

PRINCIPLE 4

Make it 100% safe to tell the truth.

Why pay employees for anything less than the truth?

Suppose we bought a machine designed to measure tight tolerances and detect defects on the production line. We would want that machine to tell the truth always, and we would expect and rely on it to do so. That's why we "hired" it. We don't get mad at it for accurately reporting defects we wish didn't occur. Or whack it with a wrench. Or withhold oil. Or threaten it with dismissal. We may not like the bad news it reports, but we appreciate its unerring "honesty." We can take corrective action instead of wandering around in a state of ignorant bliss.

We pay good money for employees too. Why should we want or expect anything less than the truth? Or pay them for anything less? Or create a climate where the rewards are higher and the risks lower for telling us what we want to hear instead of what we need to hear?

PRINCIPLE 4'S GOAL AND PLEDGE

—The Goal—
Make it so safe to tell the truth that people come forward at
the first hint that something is awry.

—The Pledge—
We will actively welcome the truth and even insist
upon it. No one will levy a penalty on anyone for
bringing forward the truth.

Lisa, Arnold and The Pledge

The No Fail Leadership workgroup had met twice. Our client wanted to better balance emergency and routine service requests from business customers without under-serving customers that were kind enough not to demand instant gratification every time they needed help. A few months before, the CEO and department heads had, without much forethought, come up with and instituted a policy to solve part of the problem.

Today's workgroup had many participants beyond the management team. Lisa, a senior and respected department head, had just started going over how her people processed requests. Her team's process differed from the new one that CEO Arnold thought was in force. "Wait a minute, Lisa!" he snapped. "We've already decided how we're going to handle these requests." His impatience with her candid report was unexpected and inappropriate in front of employees, although not out of character.

Lisa shut up, and so did others. I didn't. "Lisa, I sense that you have more to say, and we all need to hear it." Turning to Arnold, I said, "This workgroup is a safe place to be honest, isn't it, Arnold?" He couldn't say no. He knew the ground rules.

Lisa described in detail how implementing the new policy created side effects so intolerably negative that she had to abandon it. The old policy wasn't ideal, but it bettered the new one temporarily until the workgroup could bring customers into the investigation. That had not been done earlier.

Arnold, who had simmered down, listened intently until Lisa finished the story. "Lisa, I had no idea what was happening behind the scenes," he said. "The new policy was bad from the get-go. Scrap it."

Why hadn't Lisa come to him before? Wasn't this the same CEO she and all the other managers had worked with for ten-plus years and knew well, the same CEO who prided himself in his open door policy inviting complete candor? Familiarity does not guarantee an open mind. Nor does an open door.

Arnold's perception of himself did not fully sync up with everyone else's. He found out what others had long known—that people did not believe it was 100% safe to tell him the truth. He saw Lisa try, saw himself shoot her down, and recognized his pattern. Had the workgroup rule not been enforced, who knows when he would have learned the truth about his policy, faced it and become an aid to solving the problem instead of protracting it? It certainly wouldn't have happened that day in that workgroup. The mind-opener was the contradiction between his self-image and his behavior. That bothered him, along with its consequences. He worked on reacting less and listening more.

The need for truth

Things *will* go wrong. But we must treat the revelation and details as input, not a screw up. It might not be one. Because, per Principle 2, *Nothing is ever what it seems; the truth lies elsewhere.*

Reexamine the Leadership Test's list of 12 problems. It presents symptoms. Beneath these lie causes symptomatic of deeper causes with deeper causes.

12 Leadership Test Problems

1. Implementation plans bog down.

2. Problems pile up without action, and some never get solved at all.

3. Problems are worked around instead of solved, creating more downstream.

4. People dimiss or block critical new ideas.

5. Management isn't clear when things go wrong or why.

6. People accept responsibility but duck accountability, blaming others and making excuses.

7. Frontline problems are often covered up; safety in silence.

8. Communication is great within groups but weak overall.

9. Departments and individuals don't respond to each other's needs and disagree on roles and responsibilities.

10. We're weak at recruiting and keeping good employees.

11. Customer expectations aren't well met, hurting satisfaction, and retention.

12. We make too many promises we can't keep and don't keep the promises we *can* keep.

Here are some of the specific, deeper problems I have uncovered repeatedly while tackling the twelve general problems:

- ◎ Misunderstandings about what's true

- ◎ Sparse, bad, missing or misinterpreted intelligence

- ◎ Wrong assumptions from the outset

- ◎ Informal processes run amok

⊚   A company, its organization, core competencies and people ill-suited for the task

⊚   Too-complicated instructions and plans

⊚   Unrealistic expectations about timing and return on investment

What are your chances of solving any of the problems in 97% Territory without learning firsthand the truth of what works, what doesn't and why? How will you get past the silence of the lambs, wishful thinking by managerial promise-makers afraid to admit that everything is not going to be okay, half-truths to cover-up mistakes, plus outright lies to push a personal or risky agenda or to deflect blame for decisions gone wrong?

Allegiance to the truth starts at the top

It starts with the one who calls the shots. If that's you, you cannot unravel such problems without honest, penetrating answers from other people, nor can you solve such problems with anything less. Faulty information spawns faulty decisions that dig deeper holes.

Do you want honest answers? Then be a leader that makes it 100% safe to tell the truth. Create a culture that honors this.

Sentinels can stand between the top and the truth

Bullies. As unmasked in "Fear, conflict, consequences and Principle 1," bullies in all forms allow only snippets of truth that advance their own personal agenda, a mindset that deeply predates their hiring. They are intimidators and chaos makers.

Alphas Dogs (which may include some readers). According to management coaches Kate Ludeman and Eddie Erlandson of Work Ethic[1], Alpha Dogs make up 70% of all senior executives. Usually male, they tend to be domineering, unemotional, impatient, distant, cryptic, and not good listeners. They have little tol-

---

1 Ludeman and Erlandson, "Coaching the Alpha"; *Harvard Business Review*, May 2004: 58–67.

erance for views and facts at odds with their own. On the upside, they can also be bright, self-confident, and successful as midlevel managers overseeing processes. They produce results. Unfortunately, as the authors explain, the strengths that accelerate their rise also accelerate their fall. To produce exceptional results as high level executives, they must coalesce subordinates behind a worthwhile cause and inspire them to succeed. Alpha skills don't generally include people skills. The subject doesn't interest them.

Bad leaders. Harvard University's Barbara Kellerman, in her provocative book *Bad Leadership*[2], identifies seven types of seriously flawed leaders at the highest levels of corporate, governmental, non-governmental and international power, arranged from bad to worst possible: incompetent, rigid, intemperate, callous, corrupt, insular, and evil. None of these titular leaders has any allegiance to the truth whatsoever, except as something to avoid, misuse or abuse for personal gain. Some may be climbing your corporate ladder now. Watch out.

The leader of last resort: the chief executive

If you or I, as the CEO, let one or more bad managers of any kind run our company or division or other group, we endorse their behavior by default, no matter how leader-like and approachable we are personally.

Employees despair about why we do nothing to stop this behavior. They wonder if we don't care, actually approve of it, are unwilling or impotent to stop it, or if we are secretly beholden to these usurpers-in-charge. Employees also learn that if they challenge a bully's will in any way or register a documented complaint, that person will take a chunk out of whoever crossed him. Or her.

Leaders on the ladder can set standards for truth in and truth out for themselves and subordinates that help protect the integrity of team members and serve as examples for others. But over the long haul, employees still need powerful allies at the top.

---

2 Barbara Kellerman, *Bad Leadership* (Boston: Harvard Business School Press, 2004).

Without the CEO, employees lack a higher court of appeal. So nothing changes, nothing improves. Things just get more intolerable and dysfunctional as employees disengage to survive.

Trust and truth from the top engender trust and truth from below.

Leaders teach through their every word and deed. The finest CEOs lead and inspire people to perform, not simply demand results "or else." Bullies and Alphas, like smokers, have a hard time breaking their bad habits, but some do kick the worst of them when clobbered with an unwelcome truth they can't duck, or direct responsibility for a personal crisis or business failure they can't offload onto others. Or a promotion—with people to lead.

SAS Airline's Jan Carlzon (whom you met in the last chapter) was an Alpha who transitioned to solid leader. As a first-time, 32-year-old airline president of an SAS subsidiary, he thought bosses were expected to do everything better than anyone else, so he made all the decisions himself. "Ego Boy," they called him. Later, at 36 and the new president of SAS Airlines, he found himself besieged by morale and service problems. As I recounted earlier, when he figured out that he didn't control a single one of the daily moments-of-truth encounters between SAS's passengers and his people, he took control away from himself and midlevel managers and turned it over to frontline employees, where control mattered most. Many in business and academia consider Carlzon's upending the management pyramid as one of the most significant leadership innovations of the last century.

The moment of truth for Carlzon's Alpha Dog ego was recognizing how powerless it was without the heroics of the frontline employees over whom Carlzon had no control. Once he recognized that good leaders can't lead without good followers, he mentored, trained and grew them. SAS gave Carlzon that second chance. Not all Alphas make the attitude shift. They plateau doing what they were Alpha-good at, which can be quite valuable. We need good followers.

Unless Alphas with ambition undergo a metamorphosis from hotshot loner to group leader, they remain trapped in their persona. Past successes fail to translate into future performance. That brings out the Alphas' worst impulses, which they unleash upon others. They become hypercritical, overbearing, and resistant to feedback. The people they need withdraw. They work around them or pay them lip service. The messengers of truth cut way back on deliveries. It only takes a few bad Alphas to transform truth telling from an asset into a liability. And the longer the truth tellers duck bullets, the harder it gets to coax them out of the bunker.

Eventually that fact dawns on some Alphas. The ray of hope is this: as much as ego drives them, so does data. By nature Alphas thrive on data-inspired intuitions, decision making, and action. They understand intellectually that decisions made upon half-truths, untruths and wishful thinking seriously jeopardize the overachievement they demand of themselves and others. Principle 4 confronts them with a business choice:

- *Protect their power by continuing their domineering ways, suppressing truth and teamwork, or ...*

- *... protect their results by making it 100% safe for people to tell the truth, upping the odds of success.*

The second choice requires a behavior change, which isn't easy, but if an Alpha does change, we have someone who knows both how to get results and how to lead to get them and potentially can rise in the leadership ranks, setting an example for other Alphas to emulate.

Allegiance to the truth percolates downward

And it can percolate fast. When I have sought input from people one-on-one, pledging anonymity of source with management's blessing, I haul away troves of hidden treasure. Employees often waive the confidentiality (which I honor anyway), because they believe that management finally wants to hear the truth through an outsider, and they are itching to tell it. Further, the openness persists through whatever problem-solving continues, especially if management participates.

In my experience, most men and women in official and unofficial leadership roles care about the job they do and want to help. They care about their subordinates and peers, their customers, and the company as a whole. But as noted, without a staunch, top-side advocate for two-way truth and oversight, power positions can become training grounds or hiding places for the incompetent, rigid, intemperate, callous, corrupt, insular and evil leaders-of-the-future that Kellerman fingers. And because driven people seem to get things done and move up the ladder, wannabees may believe they have license to mimic that behavior and inflict it on the employees they manage.

Unfortunately, top leaders may face a self-created complication: namely, their standards for truth and truthfulness, let alone for work ethic or excellence, may be no clearer than their employees'. As stated earlier, "no standard" is a standard. It's a standard everyone is 100% guaranteed to meet. Employees selfishly take advantage of the ambiguity by doing things their own way, even while criticizing those who do the same. The real danger comes when Alphas step into the void and fill it with standards they self-define to suit *their* purposes—namely, getting results the Alpha way. That leaves subordinates marching to an imperious Alpha drumbeat instead of the pulse and purpose of the enterprise, a plight they didn't bargain for.

Top management must commit emotionally and intellectually to the proposition that reciprocal truth is always positive and make it 100% safe to tell it, especially when solving Leadership Test problems and evaluating the decisions put into action.

I can affirm that getting the truth does not contradict getting results. They interdepend. Alpha Dogs, managers and supervisors who wake up and start asking for honest feedback from their subordinates can morph, with a little practice, into leaders. The shift of thinking, like Carlzon's, can transform an organization dramatically in ways that people cheer.

HOW TO MAKE IT SAFE

Within every organization we find people who will speak up and people who won't. Those who will speak up are not necessarily daredevils. Many simply perceive no risk. They seem to feel secure in the situation, in their position, or in themselves as individuals. We rely on them. They are the vertebrae that give backbone to the organization.

Those who hold back feel at risk, for themselves, for others, for the project, etc. Above, below or next to them may stand people with status—bought, earned, bestowed, usurped, or claimed opportunistically—who intentionally or unintentionally intimidate them.

I have asked competent top-level executives how open they can be with their CEO. Most say that they have to be very careful what they say, when, where, why and how.

I have also asked members of management teams how free they feel to speak up among peers, per the organization chart. All peers are not equal, they say. The pecking order depends upon credentials and credibility, plus who is and isn't part of the inner circle.

These people are not wallflowers. They are hands-on managers. Impediments to truth telling must be removed. That's not quick or easy. We face significant hurdles inviting the truth and getting it, not all of our own making. Here is what works:

Commit

Teach by example.

- ⊚ Insist upon the truth from ourselves and others. Make it a two-way street. We ask for the whole truth because we want it, all of it—not only its tastiest morsels. We embrace the input, feedback and learning that come with well-crafted experimentation into what works and what doesn't. We will listen to it even when it's personally distasteful, rewarding those who tell it.

- Don't allow a penalty to be levied on anyone by anyone for coming forward with the truth about what works and what doesn't, the quicker the better. Penalize *not* telling the truth, holding back, covering up, and allowing things to deteriorate.

- Never use today's "whole truth" to cut off further input, because "nothing is ever as it seems." Tomorrow's input can unravel today's whole truth overnight.

- Trust others enough to share with them candidly the truth about what's working and what isn't. We want them to factor that into their thinking and learn from our, and their, miscalculations and mistakes.

Such teachings humanize the leader. Trust and truthfulness bond employees to their leader *without* compromising the focus on results. Indeed, allegiance to the truth *sharpens* focus by filtering out the opinionating and speculating that cloud issues.

Midlevel managers who value truthfulness need high-level moral support and empowerment to press for honesty and openness in others. As fear and distrust subside, communication warms up within and between groups. Esprit de corps slowly awakens. I have even seen powerful, internal, joint ventures emerge spontaneously to deal with longstanding problems, long avoided.

Meanwhile, midlevel Alphas lose their ability to operate without challenge or accountability. They and everyone else see the CEO connecting with people through a common allegiance to the truth and achieving better results than the Alphas achieve Alpha style. That sends a message: Unless Alphas start connecting instead of disconnecting with people on their own team, they will always be managers, never leaders.

Use truth as a tool to set people free

Remember our working definition of "true" and "truth" from the chapter on Principle 1:

"Truth" and "true"

In accordance with fact or reality: accurate, correct, avoiding error, misrepresentation, or falsehood

This is the common-sense definition that science uses to pin down truth. Practitioners of production-bred Lean Six Sigma and its offshoots use it in manufacturing and service-intensive activities as they too conduct experiments, plus measure and track errors, defects, delays, successes and failures of all kinds in the 3% they can measure.

No Fail Leadership applies this definition of truth in 97% Territory as well. Here truth may be harder and sometimes impossible to quantify, such as with major problems that happen once or rarely. Further, we are dealing with human interactions with processes, outsiders and each other, where reports from the workforce tend to be heavily anecdotal or withheld out of fear of speaking up. But we are still after the facts—what's accurate, correct, avoiding error, misrepresentation, or falsehood.

Here's your opportunity to teach what kind of issues and what kind of truth ultimately matter.

Issues: The Leadership Test provides examples of 97% Factors that No Fail Leadership tackles. Your enterprise undoubtedly suffers from 97% issues not covered. So will individual departments, functions and managers. All those fit on the table.

The goal is to "make it so safe to tell the truth that people come forward at the first hint that something is awry." Thus, at a minimum, any input reflecting what works, what doesn't and why falls into the 100% safe zone. Bitching, blaming and complaining do not. Make sure people know this.

Truth: the best lesson of all is Principle 2—*Nothing is ever what it seems; the truth lies elsewhere.* When someone comes to you with a problem, ask what evidence—what facts—he or she has accumulated so far that validates the problem as stated. Ask what else the problem could be. Figure out how to get preliminary answers to the question and prioritize the alternatives. Set a date to reconvene.

People will learn to probe first and more deeply next time, what to look for, and the kinds of places to find the truth behind what's going on. The fear of the pursuit should dissipate as pursuers become seasoned truth seekers, observers, analysts, reporters, and users. Not everyone in the workforce has to be equally adept at this, but all should know top management considers the truth of what works and doesn't vital to the success of the enterprise and values everyone's contribution.

Some executives will say, "Don't come to me with a problem unless you have a solution," an order worth taking one step further. The "what else could it be" question will prompt people who are impatient for a single culprit and a simple solution to think one solution deeper than they might have, even veterans. The question can work particularly well on blame throwers who discover that they almost scorched the wrong target. You do not want to encourage and accept superficial solutions to superficially understood problems. You want less of both, not more.

Be patient

When asking employees to open up, be patient. The bullies have secrets to keep; the victims fear retribution. And the greater the resistance from either, the shakier their position feels to them and the more they wish that they weren't stuck there. They want help and a way out.

Keep in mind that conflicting ways of operating arise from conflicting beliefs and fears (Principle 1). As leaders, we must understand the preconceptions and misperceptions clearly enough to induce adherents to loosen their grip on their current thinking. Only then can we assess current processes and workarounds dispassionately, cultivate good ideas and weed out the bad ones people cling to.

When something goes wrong, assume it's no one thing. Don't leap to conclusions. Be patient. Make it safe to tell the truth. Encourage people that test the telling of it. We need their input. They need our permission to give it.

♦ *Expect perception, not reality.*

We each live in our own bubble, often tiny. Be patient with people who haven't popped theirs yet.

It's okay to accept their anecdotes—within limits—of what goes on inside it as preliminary input into their daily predicaments and the underlying dynamics. Ultimately the details of their combined perceptions raise so many new questions that they pop bubbles for everyone, illuminating a larger reality fraught with problems we never knew existed.

♦ *Expect skepticism.*

Just because the boss suddenly puts out the welcome mat for truth and declares a safe haven for those who tell it, don't expect employees to break down the door. People have been burned, sometimes badly, by broken promises and violated trust dating back to childhood, school, previous employers, loves and losses. Survivalists who grew up in dog-eat-dog cultures may rarely, if ever, have taken words like "honesty," "integrity," "trust," "openness," "caring," "cooperation," "work ethic," "responsibility," and "accountability" seriously and can't even connect with them, especially when mouthed by bosses whose past acts belie their affirmations.

Most people, fortunately, are wary but not terminally jaded. They will play along with a leader who wants to try out the "make it safe" ground rules. If the leader's truth tolerance proves to be low, participants, like advisors surrounding a dictator, will reveal only what's pried out of them or what they think the boss wants to hear. If truth tolerance is medium, they will tell some of the good and some of the bad but will omit troubling observations that might boomerang on the messenger.

Truth tolerance must be high for people to risk telling it. Give people permission to be honest. Be patient while they experiment with the idea and get used to it. Pile the rewards on the side of candor. Word will spread.

Honesty without fear is such a unique experience for many that it can transform their lives in profound ways, at home and at work. When you as leader become a catalyst for this transformation even in one human being, which can come quite suddenly, you may think you've witnessed a near miracle. Maybe two of them, theirs and yours. Honesty without fear can also change you just as profoundly as the person whose conversion you've inspired.

Keep your ego out of the way

As Barbara Kellerman points out, "Leaders acting alone are not responsible for bad leadership."[3] I might add that they are not solely responsible for good leadership, either. "Leaders cannot lead unless followers follow, passively or actively," she continues. And "the leader, the follower, and the context (are) hard to separate one from the other."

So don't get all puffed up when things go well or self-protective when things go wrong. Followers take their cues from leaders, good and bad, throughout the hierarchy, who cast long shadows.

If we lead, we bear responsibility for the workarounds and dysfunction that have evolved in our shadow. Don't protract problems because our ego won't accept our contribution to them. Employees won't level with an ego. Keep ours out of the way. Ask for input with curiosity and an open mind. Appraise input objectively, defending no one's stash until we grasp the ramifications of what we have decided and done.

This quest does not signal weakness or indecision. It seeks honest tracking of productivity and performance at the level of informal processes, workarounds and human interactions that we should have been tracking all along. Only the ego, which fears the truth, stands in our way. Make truth-telling safe. The feedback may seem painful in the moment, but as with childbirth, the pain is soon forgotten.

---

3 Ibid.

Don't fall for the myth of the open door

Some CEOs and managers, especially in smaller companies, pride themselves on their open-door policy and cite this as evidence that they want the truth and get it. Let's not fool ourselves. We may get to dispense Solomonic advice about personal problems, demonstrate a caring attitude, and, in a display of enlightened despotism, even intervene on behalf of the petitioner. But wary managers or employees may not readily disclose problems that they can't or aren't handling. They are even leerier when speaking frankly about problems concerning management's decisions, plans, implementations, and leadership—even though such issues cry for attention.

Deep down, employees don't believe it's safe to tell the truth about serious matters. And deep down, many managers don't want to hear it, or at least employees think they don't. Don't assume that an open door means your office stays fully stocked with the up-to-the-minute lowdown.

Don't penalize truth-tellers

If you ask for honesty and get it, use it wisely.

I remember a meeting in the CEO's office of a small company. One of the workers—a single mom—desperately needed someone to cover her shift on one Saturday a few weeks away. Her daughter and horse had risen through the local and regional riding competitions to the state final. Her mom was going to get her daughter there no matter what. So she started early asking co-workers to help, but none could or would. Then she went to the scheduling manager, and the two of them exhausted all other options. The mom finally told the manager flat out that she wasn't coming to work the date in question. She would come in Sunday and work a double shift, or on Monday on her day off, but not Saturday, regardless of the consequences.

The scheduler talked to the chief of operations, who voiced a threat to fire the lady. Word of that got to the CEO, who called a meeting of the chief of operations, the mom's immediate field supervisor, and me.

The COO argued that the company had been having a horrible time filling summer slots because of people calling in "ill" for themselves or their child on the day of their shift. Since employees worked in teams of two, one missing partner disabled a whole team with no easy way of pairing up singles. The Saturday in question loomed as one of the season's busiest.

Besides, he said, approving this medic's day off at such a crucial time would set a bad precedent. Granting her request would trigger others, and the company could be accused of favoritism if later requests were denied. In his opinion, it was time for the company to put its foot down.

Her immediate supervisor considered her to be one of the more conscientious workers, even though she had a confrontational streak in her. He wanted to approve her request and ask her to keep quiet about it.

The CEO asked my opinion. At the time we were in the midst of No Fail workgroups, insisting that Principle 4—*Make it 100% safe to tell the truth*—be observed unswervingly. While she may have been contrary in the past, behavior I had never witnessed, her attitude in the workgroup had been entirely positive. And her contributions ranked her among the more valuable participants. Further, her extensive, sincere efforts to find someone to cover her shift demonstrated her commitment to her job and the organization's welfare. Finally, she had a fallback position that, out of honesty, she elected not to invoke: call in "sick."

Why, I asked, would the company want to penalize honesty, which we'd been preaching, when she could simply have lied, something the company would have had to go far out of its way to prove? Worse yet, why encourage dishonesty by making lying more advantageous than honesty? To me she was a "keeper," and whatever the company did to help her out would be repaid many times over.

The CEO saw it as a simple tradeoff: She'd be absent. That could be with the company's blessing or without it. Either way, a spot would go unfilled. Some employees abused their sick-day privileges routinely. He'd deny their request, and if they quit, no great loss. If he denied her request, he could lose her in attitude if not in body. Then he'd really have a hole to fill. Bad choice. What about the "bad precedent?" He said, "It may never become an issue. If it does, deal with it then. Tell her we'll make do one way or another, and wish her luck."

Her daughter placed third in the state. Mom continued to volunteer for problem-solving assignments and leadership roles, an asset to management and frontline employees alike.

Even a mildly acrophobic homeowner, in a fit of do-it-yourself frugality, can forget his fear of heights if he has to scamper up and down his 16-foot ladder thirty-five times a day to refill his paint tray. The same goes for truth telling. The more often we tell it, the easier that becomes. And the process of telling it can be made routine. Here's a case in point.

A healthy dose of the truth about failing

The field supervisors at one paramedic-service client were supposed to mentor, train and evaluate new employees by riding with them and a senior medic on a specified number of 12-hour shifts. Supervisors couldn't always do the job because of the 24/7 nature of the business. The company offered extra pay for seasoned medics who would agree to partner with and train trainees when the supervisor couldn't. But most medics didn't want a green trainee as their only backup in a major emergency.

The few medics who were willing weren't always those you'd hand pick. All were experienced, but they spent most of their time in the field, learning by doing. Many hadn't kept their knowledge and skills current. A program with a manual for training recruits had been developed a couple years before but never implemented for lack of priority and a management champion. What the trainers taught usually fell within established protocols, but not always. The methods each had evolved for handling patients differed and so did what each one taught the trainees who rotated among them.

To make matters worse, the operation as a whole was short-staffed, and recruits were scarce because of a tight job market at the time. Management wanted supervisors to get trainees into full-time assignments as soon as possible. It evaluated trainers partly on the percentage and number of trainees who graduated—without giving supervisors the authority to enforce trainer and trainee consistency and quality. That undercut supervisor credibility.

The supervisors acted in what seemed the organization's immediate interest and their own personal interest. They scheduled the number of shifts the trainees needed in order to fulfill their requirement expeditiously. But the shifts weren't necessarily the high call-volume ones needed for maximum training value. They cut the trainers a lot of slack on the content and rigor of what they taught so that they wouldn't refuse teaching assignments. And both supervisors and trainers cut the trainees slack so that they wouldn't drop out of the program. Instead of evaluating trainees candidly and quickly, supervisors postponed giving the Ds and Fs that the marginal ones deserved, hoping that they would come through at the end, which also tended to get postponed.

Really confused, questionable trainees made it through the probation phase and into full-time positions, where dismissal for ineptitude became much more difficult. The medics as a whole were frustrated. They resented the hit-or-miss quality of the graduates who were their new, full-time partners, and they resented the burden they had to assume for finishing the job the supervisors and trainers hadn't finished themselves.

The trainer medics, meanwhile, felt imposed upon and under attack for what they had been teaching, which others later retaught to sync with their own ways of doing things, which might not sync up with anyone else's.

And the trainees felt ill prepared for normal situations, let alone high-stress ones. They wanted consistent, comprehensive instruction and candid feedback, and they felt they weren't getting it.

Supervisors felt thwarted too. They lacked the authority, incentive and management backing to flunk trainees who shouldn't pass or to blow the whistle on lukewarm medics who had become detached, behind in their skills and sloppy in their work.

As expected, performance excellence overall was hard to maintain. Truth had been sidelined, the company's reputation stood at risk, field staff morale was slipping, and people felt powerless to do much about it. No one wanted to rain on anyone's parade, and it was anything but safe to tell the truth.

Here's what happened. Upfront investigation uncovered the basic dynamics at work here, and the subsequent workgroup fleshed out the details. Fortunately, all stakeholders were represented—the CEO, the VP of human resources, the headquarters training coordinator, two regional managers, plus supervisors, senior field staff, junior field staff that had recently completed probation, and trainees.

Their assessment

The whole training effort suffered from conflicting objectives. Management wanted more medics, the field staff wanted better medics, and the supervisors wanted to keep everyone happy.

No one ran the show. Neither the supervisors closest to the action nor anyone else had operational responsibility and authority.

Bad habits leading to bad senior medics started with bad training from day one. Problems only got worse and harder to correct with time.

Trainee training must not be taken casually any longer. It deserved high priority, high standards for graduation, and high-quality trainers and resources.

Infrequent evaluations got in the way of truth-telling. Each evaluation assumed such critical importance that evaluators hesitated to be totally honest.

Open, honest communication must become the welcomed norm. Trainers, who know where trainees stand and their chances of success, must evaluate trainees candidly and routinely. And trainers, medics, supervisors and everyone who evaluates must expect equally candid evaluations of themselves.

Their plan

They put the management-level training coordinator in charge of each intern's training from orientation to end.

They turned interns who passed the in-house orientation program over to a field supervisor and three senior field personnel for in-service training. Ultimately, all had to agree on the candidate's worthiness before he or she gained membership to the regular team.

They replaced their old objective-by-default—a high gradua-tion rate—with a new one: Identify the winners, quickly weed out the losers, and get the survivors up to speed as fast as possible. Su-pervisors not only had the authority to recommend terminating an inept intern, they also had the responsibility to do so as soon as success seemed in doubt.

They updated a list of all the things the trainee needed to know to pass probation. Field trainers attended a refresher course to in-sure the currency of their knowledge and consistency of content, a major problem in the past.

They made evaluation routine. Field trainers filled out a daily performance review, with a copy to the lead supervisors and one to place in the intern's handbook. Trainers discussed the reviews with the intern each day, pointing out areas of competence and areas needing work. They discussed reviews weekly with the field-training group, including the management training coordinator. Besides completing the fieldwork, the intern took didactic and practical tests along the way, plus a final exam. Graduation re-quired passing the tests, plus securing the recommendations of the entire training team and the company's operations manager.

The impact

The caliber of new, full-time employees rose immediately as the company let losers go early, freeing more time for trainers to spend with winners. Along with the authority trainers needed to turn out quality trainees, they also got the responsibility to insure quality and the kudos for achieving it. That meant relearning the basics they were expected to teach with across-the-board consis-tency. Their own knowledge and skills rose markedly.

Senior employees who were not trainers found themselves pres-sured to upgrade their skills to keep from looking ignorant to the graduates moving into the regular frontline workforce. Manage-ment dismissed senior medics who refused to get back up to speed, and no one was sorry. Everyone knew these medics were dragging down quality, performance and morale. Consistency of service improved company-wide.

Supervisors no longer found themselves in limbo between management and frontline employees but firmly planted as true managers. Field trainers saw their stature rise along with their paychecks for extra duty.

Management gained new respect for having sided with the employees who cared about their profession instead of siding with the malcontents who, although once energetic and committed employees, had sunk to caring mainly about themselves.

97% Factors

How safe is the truth in your organization?

Is it 100% safe to tell the truth?

Who wants and accepts the truth?

Who doesn't, even though some of them may assert otherwise?

The goal and the pledge:

How likely is it that your leaders, managers and employees would fully sign on to and honor the goal and pledge? Why? Why not?

If they had signed it, what would be different today regarding:

    Your Case History problem?

    The Leadership Test problems?

Input:

Discuss Principle 3's and 4's statements plus the goal and pledge informally with trusted peers.

What is their reaction, pros and cons?

What differences would they foresee if the principles were honored?

What stands in the way?

PRINCIPLE 5

No blame, no excuses.

Blaming makes accountability impossible.

WHAT HAPPENS WHEN SOMEONE BLAMES YOU of something, whether the accusation is true or false? Everyone I have asked answers that they either attack in their own defense or they withdraw, depending upon the situation, knowing that the blamer wants to divert attention and accountability from himself and isn't interested in any explanation other than his own. Communication ends. So does any hope of getting to the truth or finding a solution. The blamer only knows what he thinks he knows. As we will see, this can be far off the mark, misremembered, or even fabricated. How can narrow, self-serving thinking and behavior possibly serve the interests of accountability?

Don't forget that *All problems basically are conflicts of beliefs about what's true*, and *No problem is ever what it seems. The truth lies elsewhere."* Suppose you are the blamer, acting on skewed or partial information. Your blaming just makes matters worse. You drive people with knowledge and insight about the problem underground for self-protection. You may kill off a few vulnerable dissenters, but that doesn't solve the underlying

Leadership Test or other problems that blame and excuses can never solve.

"Without blaming you can't have accountability"—it's a myth that plays into the hands of blamers bent on ducking account-ability.

What's blaming?

*Blamers seek a single culprit and simple solution
to a complex problem.*

So do those who make excuses. Blaming and making excuses may seem like separate acts since the blamer attacks and the accused defends with excuses—but in truth, the faces of blamers and ex-cuse makers occupy two sides of the same penny. They are made of the same alloy and share the same motto: "Don't blame me!"

Blaming is excuse making. And excuse makers, just as much as blamers, seize upon an external cause to blame for their own per-ceived underperformance or predicament. Culprits can include an individual, a group, a decision, situation and an idea. And so-lutions tend to be quick, superficial, and personally safe despite the sometimes profoundly negative, unanticipated consequences.

Remember what Oliver Wendell Holmes said—"I would not give a fig for the simplicity this side of complexity, but I would give my life for the simplicity on the other side of complexity." Blaming entrenches firmly on this side. Accountability occupies the other.

Then what's accountability?

*Accountability means being answerable for acts,
decisions and outcomes.*

What does it take to be answerable? Study the Seven Prerequisites for Accountability on the next two pages before proceeding.

THE SEVEN PREREQUISITES
FOR ACCOUNTABILITY

1. The talent and will to handle the assignment

We cannot throw someone with limited or inappropriate talents into the fray and expect stellar performance or accountability. Nor can we expect it from someone forced to take on a responsibility he fears he can't or won't be empowered to handle.

2. The knowledge and skills to succeed

Some assignments demand specific knowledge, such as computer programming. Others require broader knowledge, such as running a start-up company. If the person lacks the needed knowledge and skills, the chances of success remain slim until we fill the gaps one way or another.

3. The resources

Whatever it takes to succeed. The right resources at the right time in the right amount, neither too many nor too few.

4. The responsibility for the outcome

"When everyone's responsible, no one is responsible." We've all heard the cliché. Yet instances of unassigned, diffused or divided responsibility abound. Someone must accept responsibility up front. Guaranteed, if things go wrong, a scapegoat will be held responsible later.

5. The authority to make happen what needs to happen

Time after time people with heavy responsibility for specific performance lack the authority over employees in other departments critical to success—and get no help from above or colleagues.

6. Incentives that reward cross-functional cooperation as well as individual performance

We've said it before: Follow the money. If Group A's performance depends upon Group B's cooperation, and Group B's incentives don't depend in part on how well it serves Group A, then under pressure Group B will serve only itself.

7. Top management commitment

Management must commit to supporting the effort with requisite manpower, money, equipment, facilities, outside expertise, CEO horsepower, and so on. Lukewarm support from the top can fatally undermine the authority of the assignment's leader, causing the effort to die a potentially expensive death.

If any prerequisites go unmet, so goes accountability

I once asked a new, mid-level department manager to pull some baseline data so that we could track the progress of a performance improvement test that was underway. I explained exactly what we needed for the presentation to top management, but the data kept not showing up, despite renewed promises with each unmet deadline. Finally she returned with guesses backed more by anecdotes than facts. I asked her whether she had ever worked on baselines before. She answered no.

How could she possibly succeed? Or be held accountable? She lacked the talent and will to handle the assignment (Prerequisite 1) as well as the knowledge and skills (Prerequisite 2).

I asked her superior to teach her. He couldn't. Most others, I found, were equally unschooled, including some senior managers. They insisted upon end-result "metrics" but didn't understand tracking, value it or have interest in trying. Problem solving and accountability were all talk, no walk. No crawl. Just rocking in place with little concept of going somewhere.

The more complex the business is, the more probable that prerequisites remain unsatisfied, sometimes even the most obvious ones basic to accountability, like talent and will, knowledge and skill. Yet if a project bogs down, management will still look for a scapegoat instead of into its own oversights, motives, methods, and decisions.

97% Factors

Accountability as a subordinate

When your superior delegates important projects to you with responsibility for the outcome:

Does he/she arm you with all seven prerequisites?

Which prerequisites are lacking?

Do you feel that their absence relieves you of responsibility for the outcome?

Do you feel that you have been set up for failure, inadvertently or intentionally?

What were the consequences on speed, cost and quality of outcome?

Accountability as a superior

When you delegate an assignment to subordinates:
Do you arm them with all seven prerequisites?

If not, can you honestly hold them 100% accountable for the results you seek?

Do you unknowingly put them in a no-win situation? Are you fooling yourself to think otherwise?

Breakdown in authority

Consider what happened to Joan, an aggrieved mid-level manager. She called a meeting of her colleagues, with her boss's blessing. She described a cross-functional problem impacting severely in her area that could not be solved alone. Everyone agreed that something needed to be done and that all had a role in the solution. Joan made a project list. The participants divvied it up by function and established deadlines. The meeting adjourned, and then reconvened two weeks later, as scheduled. Some work had been completed; some hadn't. Joan granted more time. More meetings and more extensions followed until the project got elbowed aside by projects with newer and higher priorities in the departments Joan asked to help her, which, it turned out, viewed assisting Joan as low priority from the outset.

Why? Because Joan's problem wasn't theirs. Joan possessed the talent, skills and knowledge to facilitate a solution and, as the prime stakeholder, she had shouldered the responsibility for fixing it. But no one, including her boss, held overall, cross-functional responsibility and authority personally or by management proxy to sustain the priority, commitment and momentum. Her colleagues had no incentive to do their part. They may have had incentives not to. She gave up.

Joan wasn't alone. Other managers went through the same routine with the same result. Eventually no one trusted anyone to follow through on anything, a prophesy that self-fulfilled because no one with power insisted on persevering to completion. Deep-seated, longstanding problems never got solved.

Does this mean you can't expect anyone to be accountable for anything? No.

Accountability is possible

Some people accept accountability without a second thought. Suppose you are an auto mechanic. You fix transmissions in high performance sports cars. Customers trust your competence. One drops off his Lamborghini. You sign him in, dismantle the transmission, diagnose the problem, give him an estimate he approves, fix the transmission, test drive the car and talk shop with the customer when he picks it up and pays. You have absolutely no hesitation about accepting the responsibility and accountability. You trust your expertise. You have full command of the job. And you stand behind your work without blaming or excuses if you don't get it right the first time.

Accountability is possible, as you can see, with one person doing one skilled job. Corporate armies rely heavily on specially trained soldiers motivated to do the best they can against all odds. Multitasked managers and supervisors admittedly have more complicated jobs. They must interact with several levels of management and employees, departments, customers, suppliers and other stakeholders. Responsibility and accountability pile high on such people. And the best of them take personal responsibility and accountability as seriously as that mechanic.

Why then do two-thirds of the Leadership Test-takers say that their coworkers "accept responsibility but duck accountability, blaming others and making excuses," a percentage that holds across industries? What's going on? Are people behaving one way when alone and another way when together?

Doesn't accountability scale up from one to many?

As commonly practiced? No. Not cleanly or particularly effectively. Prerequisites go unmet, undermining accountability. And the higher up the ladder we climb the likelier this is. We fool ourselves and abuse others by thinking otherwise.

Like it or not, we cannot achieve accountability simply by demanding it. Leaders and managers routinely hold individuals who report to them accountable for things outside their control, then "kick ass" or otherwise censure them when they don't perform. Survival in such situations and cultures degenerates into blaming others and making excuses. Trust, connection and communication end. So does cooperation for the common good. Everyone is too busy kicking ass or protecting their own.

I am not arguing against the critical value of accountability in organizations. Not at all. I am arguing that we can only achieve it by making it a core competency for accomplishment through collaborating rather than a tool to coerce individual performance.

Our first, big step is to accept that individual accountability has limits that vary by situation and must be viewed realistically.

> *By identifying and acknowledging the limitations in each circumstance, we can set aside the blaming, excuses and scapegoating and adjust our expectations, strategies and tactics for achieving the overall objectives.*

Does that mean that some projects go ahead with no one accountable at all? Yes. Already, no one is truly accountable because prerequisites for accountability aren't in place.

> *By being realistic we can stop the blame game and succeed jointly where individual accountability is impossible.*

Does anyone succeed in spite of everything? Yes, some do. They must be amply endowed with the first prerequisite—the native talent and the will. Given these, plus ingenuity and an ability to learn quickly, they may accumulate the missing knowledge and skills. They may even take on personal responsibility for a pet project and present it fully finished at the end. But a personal project may demand no outside assignment of responsibility and authority over anyone other than its advocate. A cross-functional or interdepartmental project involves people over whom the person accountable has no routine control. A person may be assigned or take on larger responsibility, but without authority the odds of success go down.

Absence of top management commitment

One exec from the manufacturing sector went to work as VP of Process Improvement at a service-intensive company that wanted to introduce some principles from lean manufacturing into its operation. He interviewed well-regarded middle managers and others, asking what superior performance might look like, what stood in the way of it, and what interviewees wanted to work on first. He presented the short list to the CEO and other VPs, who approved it.

The workgroups he assembled dove in and developed some solid ideas into plans to "pluck the low-hanging fruit." Soon the VPs—who had been encouraged to participate but declined—began putting obstacles in his way, cloaked as, "I can't detach my people." The VPs felt threatened, in part by the improvements but apparently even more by the revelations of widespread dysfunction and the commitment needed to end it. The "not in my backyard" mentality took over, which surprised the new VP. He had never encountered a management group so insecure. That revelation alone said volumes about pervasive dysfunction.

Did the CEO insist upon full management support? No. He stayed conspicuously silent. Was he afraid to challenge his execs to cooperate? Was he as unnerved as the rest by what the disclosures might reveal about top leadership? Was he unnerved by lean manufacturing? By quicker action than the old guard could accept? By a threat to the status quo? No one knew. The projects had validity and value, and the workgroup participants certainly were committed. The critical person who wasn't was the CEO. The effort soon died. And this was just the tip of an icy fear-berg.

The bigger question is this: Why should we have to struggle within our own house to get something accomplished? Why do top executives allow the bullies and victims, blamers and excuse makers to sandbag action and drag whatever gets done down to survivalist mediocrity?

Either our leaders don't understand blaming and how to deal with it, or they understand its dark side too well.

If anything scales up, it's The Blame Game

We learn the blame game in childhood. And we use it—from occasionally to always, reflexively to deliberately—until death does us part. We blame family, playmates, classmates, workmates, employers, employees, communities, groups, institutions, societies, governments, nations, cultures and the world at large. Did I leave out human nature? And God? Blaming scales up without limits. But most consistently, we use it against ourselves.

We experience its sting early in life when parents discipline us for misdeeds, not lovingly to instruct and correct, but punitively to lay on the guilt, to teach us to fear loss of approval for missteps, and to expect punishment. In response, by observing and interacting with older siblings, parents and playmates, we accumulate strategies and tactics for denying responsibility for infractions and deflecting blame onto others. And parents and other adults unwittingly help us perfect our methods.

Parents ensnare easily. They get suckered into he-said-she-said sibling confrontations that they, as authority figures, think they can sort out and settle—not only "can," but also ought to and are expected to. Which sibling wins? The odds favor, in order:

- *A parent's favorite*

- *The first to accuse*

The accuser has time to prepare the accusation and present it to the parent, often without the accused being present. The pre-sold authority figure, with accuser in tow, confronts the accused. The accused must improvise a defense under pressure, knowing that Mom will render judgment on the spot.

- *The most persuasive*

Seniority usually confers credibility advantages. The older child has dealt with blaming situations more often, speaks more articulately, and makes excuses more convincingly. Besides, adults presume more mature conduct from the older child, unless history shows otherwise.

- *The least subject to guilt*

Lay enough guilt trips on a child for minor infractions, and parents can condition some children to accept total blame if the accusation contains even a speck of truth. Other kids reflexively

deny responsibility for anything, no matter how dirty their dia-
per. Over the short and medium term, odds of winning the blame
game favor the deniers as they gain prowess.

We parents can inadvertently implant the blame game and scale
it up through our own counterproductive assumptions, starting
with these:

> *"We understand the game. We were kids once too.*
> *They're not going to pull one over on us! We see right through*
> *their shenanigans and won't allow them."*

Just because we recognize the game, that doesn't mean we know
how to cope. How well did your parents handle it? We teach what
we have been taught, even lessons in dysfunction. If our parents
had no idea how to stop our blaming and excuse making, what do
we know about stopping someone else?

Sometimes the methods used on us hurt us too much to inflict
on others. We vow to teach the direct opposite, trusting that un-
bridled permissiveness achieves what strict discipline does not, or
vice versa. But what do we know about the opposite? We haven't
lived it. A fed-up city slicker can't simply buy a Montana spread, a
horse, dog, chair, move, and expect to feel good.

Blaming and excuse making flourish at both extremes, oppressive and permissive.

> *"Our kids won't behave unless we intimidate them into*
> *compliance with strict controls and fear of punishment.*
> *Left alone or given a choice, they will do as little work*
> *as possible. Fear got more and better work out of us faster*
> *than otherwise, and we came out all right. It ought*
> *to work on them too."*

What kind of children do we want? Intimidated, compliant,
fearful kids who eventually live up to our dismal expectations of
them? Or do we want self-reliant, venturesome youngsters who,

with our encouragement, test boundaries and expand them to encompass rich new territory?

Fear of punishment does not equal discipline. Discipline that lasts a lifetime comes from within. Discipline from without dies with the discipliner, if not earlier. Kids get tired of hearing "no." They are much more unconstrained, observant, opportunistic and fast-learning than we give them credit for. Too many "no's" and too much punishment and they will master blaming, excuse-making and truth-bending to avoid punishment. Before long we won't really trust them and they won't trust us. Sadly, our own beliefs produce the wedge. We drive it in. We split the log.

> *"We need to decide and act on the spot. Failing to decide, choose sides and act shows weakness. We parents must be strong. Decisive. Act. Show them who's boss."*

How are we going to do that? We've scared our youngsters away from openly telling the truth. When the blaming, excuses and he-said-she-said confrontations start, we hear even less of it. We profit from what has value. Only the truth has value. Where's the profit in hearing less of it?

How can we intelligently resolve anything? As parents we typically don't fully agree on standards of conduct or on disciplinary measures to begin with. Our thou-shalls and thou-shall-nots seem more theoretical than practical, age-appropriate and enforceable. Many arise situationally as ultimatums based on improvised standards-of-the-moment. And we don't apply them equally to all members of the family.

In truth, no one really knows what to do and what not to do. Even to us, our own standards, snap judgments and penalties seem arbitrary. Thus as authority figures we threaten but hesitate to follow through. When we do act, our decisiveness risks serious injustice and our discipline smacks of vengeance.

So our kids stay out of our way, do what they want and hope no one will notice. Notice triggers excuses or blaming. And why not? We punish instead of guide. Honesty invites punishment and the crimes and consequences don't sync up. Let someone else take the hit.

What have we as parents taught and we as children learned? To judge without evidence or standards, to punish "sins" instead of correct errors, to blame, make excuses, manipulate the truth, avoid responsibility and fear accountability. In short, we have taught—and our pupils have learned—how to divide a house against itself.

Is this any way to run a business!?

No. But I repeatedly find reenactments of childhood scripts in business settings at all levels—top, bottom and middle. Haven't you? We try to parent our organizations and people based upon lessons learned as our parents parented us, whether we pass them on verbatim or teach the exact opposite. As authority figures like our parents:

We assume that we know what's going on.

But most of what we know comes from the selective perceptions that peers or those who directly report to us choose to reveal in staff meetings or in private. What's really happening slips under our radar.

We agree to simplistic, wrong solutions that preserve the status quo and stifle change.

We prejudge and misjudge. Our limited past experiences, plus our fears, beliefs and intuitions lead us astray.

We cave in under pressure. Strong personalities and special interests lobby us to adopt their biased views and self-serving solutions. Pacifying them does not solve the problem and may make it worse.

We enable distrust and fear to become the status quo. We stifle new ideas that threaten it and tolerate the safe harbor that short-sighted defenders think it provides. Problems stay unresolved, opportunities unexploited.

We assume that employees won't perform unless intimidated into performance by strict controls and fear of punishment.

We have been taught to assume that employees, like children, are too self-serving to be motivated by anything else.

We treat mistakes as sins to be punished, not errors to be corrected. And we have no idea how to correct anything without threats, public and private displeasure, censure or worse. We never learned an alternative.

We pick and play favorites.

We support whoever has seniority and a long relationship with us. We value and protect the equity we have in each other. We consider colleagues to be credible unless overwhelmed by facts to the contrary.

We defer to Alpha Dogs. We fail to recognize the inequality of managers of equivalent rank on the organization chart. Some will be subordinated to entrenched heavyweights—the buddies and bullies that will serve their own interests without regard to others. They have huge advantages in the blame game that seriously hamstring the ability of others to perform accountably.

We favor whoever speaks first and persuasively, whether that's the blamer or the excuse maker executing a preemptive maneuver. When we choose sides and buy into one without honoring the views of the other, we inadvertently become a co-conspirator.

We defend the accuser against the accused. We jump to the conclusion that the charge "must be at least partly true." The burden of proof falls upon the accused.

We apply discipline and penalties inconsistently and unequally.

We find ourselves taking no serious action against the people we like for screw ups that would get anyone else fired or put on probation. Instead, we cover up.

We promote infighting and power struggles.

We find ourselves engaged in un-civil civil wars that polarize the people we rely upon to cooperate, innovate, solve problems, make decisions and implement them without great ado.

We blame and scapegoat impulsively to appear decisive without getting or honoring all the facts.

When swamped, we look for single culprits and simple solutions to complex problems. To save time we defer to the assessments of others. "He hasn't fixed it. Fire him." We succumb, hiring and then axing one executive or manager after another, solving nothing, capturing no history of the attempts and learning nothing from them. The problem isn't the scapegoat. It's the scapegoaters.

We endure endless bitch-and-blame sessions figuring out what went wrong.

Then we write off the waste in time and money as if putting back together pieces that don't fit is worth it.

The consequences are far more than theoretical

When we run our business like bad parents we seriously undermine productivity, performance and accountability—not only in our own bailiwick, but throughout our enterprise and out into the world we claim to serve. The signs are everywhere:

- ◉ *Problem-solving and plan implementation*
  We work around problems instead of solving them. Implementations bog down, making matters worse.

- ◉ *Accountability and culture*
  People dismiss or block new ideas. They may accept responsibility but they duck accountability, cover up, make excuses, blame others, and seek safety in silence.

- ◉ *Workforce interactions*
  Departments, levels and individuals don't communicate actively, respond to each other's needs or agree on roles and responsibilities. We have trouble recruiting and keeping good employees.

- ◉ *Customer-perceived value*
  We don't really understand customer expectations. We make too many promises we can't or don't keep.

Recognize the list? It recaps breakdowns singled out in the Leadership Test. The common denominator is fear, distrust and disengagement—a destructive trio that underlies dysfunction and anchors it in place. The trio empowers victimizers and promotes infighting and power struggles. It wastes untold time and money. It demotivates human beings and can even destroy them. The kind of accountability that remains is the kind of blame-riddled, excuse-riddled accountability we all can do without.

OVERHAULING BREAKDOWNS IN RESPONSIBILITY, ACCOUNTABILITY AND LEADERSHIP

Glaring examples of diffused responsibility often involve work handed off between departments that operate autonomously without consideration for each other's needs. The consequence?

Consider the case of an insurance company mismanaging one of its most critical business functions. Watch for breakdowns in all 12 Leadership Test areas and on all 7 Prerequisites for Accountability. You'll also find a story of heroism under fire by employees who cared.

Like companies everywhere it consisted of multiple departments, each with siloed people, functions, and responsibility—with no one clearly accountable overall. Farthest upstream chugged the sales department, the revenue engine, pressured by sales goals, customer urgencies and competitive threats to sell and process employer-group applications quickly, many with customized, nonstandard benefit packages. To make matters worse, the Sales department often forwarded applications to the enrollment department with incomplete or guesstimated information "to get things moving." The enrollment manager vividly described the hardship this inflicted:

"You are sitting alongside a stream watching it flow through your town when, once again, you see a baby float by. So you wade in and pull it out. You spot another one and rush back in. Soon you find yourself surrounded by babies. You grab them and toss them on shore as fast as you can, shouting for help. The village responds. People stand knee deep in babies, tossing them into waiting arms. Finally, it's over. You and the others fall exhausted on the shore, thankful that you rescued them and feeling like heroes. Meanwhile, the people around the next bend, who saw none of your heroics, spot two babies that slipped through. And they give you hell.

"But no one has time or energy to find out why the babies wound up in the stream in the first place. You don't even feel free to ask. Your people gripe about Sales' bad attitude and all the extra work they create, but isn't 'support' what support departments are for? Just accept the crap and deal with it?"

The enrollment department sat on the hot seat, criticized by Sales for being a bottleneck and by the group downstream for the occasional but costly errors that slipped through. We assembled people in sales, enrollment and downstream departments to address the situation. They were astonished to discover:

- ⊚ How little they understood about each other's jobs and predicaments.

- ⊚ The myriad opportunities for upstream errors and omissions from Sales.

- ⊚ The number of mistakes that Sales and sales support groups did not correct and how incidental they seemed to the people who made them.

- ⊚ How hard they were for Enrollment to detect, yet how often, when something smelled wrong, they sniffed out the problem, fixed it and saved Sales' butt.

- ⊚ All the rework and re-handling, customer dissatisfaction, added costs and compromised service that people had to deal with all the way downstream.

What explained the indifference of the sales people? Follow the money. Top management tied all kudos and performance bonuses to incremental sales volume. Preparing paperwork thoroughly just stood in the way of making more sales calls. And the most aggressive sales people could not be relied upon to gather the complete package of client information, which they considered the sales coordinator's job. Unfortunately, this wasn't Judy's job or expertise, and the better the "Judys" became, the more overwhelmed they were. Plus, sales people insisted that the coordinators forward the documentation to Enrollment, even if incomplete or inaccurate, to cement the sale. "We'll fill holes and make changes as fast as we can." (How comforting!)

Meanwhile, Enrollment's evaluation hinged on fast turnaround and error-free handoffs to the next group downstream. Auditors audited the documents for completeness and transcription accuracy but not for quality of content, which had never been defined. They also missed the heroics performed by Enrollment to maintain a high score. Bad input from Sales meant vast extra work and bad output from Enrollment unless someone smelled a rat and trapped it.

The lesson: Each department can do its job as ordered, even heroically, while the system as a whole ends up dysfunctional. Everyone was expected to cooperate, but no one was responsible for oversight. Responsibility remained diffused and divided among managers who worried about their own objectives first, the company's later. They left others to clean up after them and no one set them straight.

Blaming the enrollment group for Sales dereliction could not survive truth. Cross-functional understanding set everyone straight and stimulated cross-functional teamwork.

Round and down the blame drain

Blame and intimidation feed off one another. Accountability, misconceived and misapplied, quickly becomes polluted with the blaming and self-excusing that send thinking, behavior and action spiraling right down the drain. You've heard of cultures of blame? They are real. They thrive in the septic tank at the end of the blame drain.

Blaming makes most people who witness it squirm. It's heavy with emotion, superficiality, injustice and vengeance against the past situations, events and people that deprived and threatened the blamers and against a future we fear might be even worse.

A LESSON IN THE HIGH COST OF BLAME
AND INTIMIDATION

The extreme example coming up is not singular.

The young professional worked for a sizeable company's two-person department that provided ultra-sophisticated design and development support to over a hundred computer programmers. His boss, who was only five to ten years older than he, spent most of her time on the road schmoozing clients and leaving him with the heavy-duty work. He found himself dealing directly with clients in her absence, managing projects, meeting every deadline and earning the respect of everyone except his boss. She found fault with everything and acknowledged nothing positive. She blamed him for making bad decisions if they weren't totally in sync with what hers would have been if she had been there to make them. None of the mistakes were serious, all were correctable, and almost all involved a difference of opinion about the right thing to do. He never lost his cool and kept a positive attitude, at first as a lesson in how to keep cool and positive, then as a lesson in handling difficult people, and later, when he learned that she was suffering from a long-term, fatal degenerative disease, as an act of compassion. But the unrelenting criticism eventually started making him doubt his own competence.

The more positive his attitude and performance, the more abusive her behavior became. He finally told her and her superiors that unless the abuse stopped, he would leave. It didn't. He did. And went to work for a company that needed even higher-level thinking with no less work but a much more empowering and supportive environment.

Within three months he was functioning as an untitled project manager and getting superior evaluations from everyone, including clients, with whom he soloed. He also got far more work done. His comment: "I'm twice as productive in the same amount of time. That's because I no longer have to spend half it covering my ass."

Think back: How many otherwise productive hours at work and at home, creative energy, personal and corporate resources and valuable relationships have you thrown away covering your ass? And that's the initial cost.

Why would we want our number one asset—our people—awash in adrenaline attacking others and defending themselves? Most employees resent a company culture or a manager that provokes them to call upon their worst impulses to survive. Eventually many neither recognize nor like themselves. Self-respect and self-confidence plunge. So does communication, cohesion and performance, especially if other departments are not similarly afflicted. The contrast is stark. Are the employees fundamentally different? Probably not. Just the managerial mindset. The messages. The cues. The failure of leadership.

PLUGGING THE BLAME DRAIN

We must wean ourselves off of blame and excuses. They serve no purpose. They separate and divide us one from another.

Let's lead. Let's set a standard for others. Give them permission through our own example to reject blame and excuses, welcome input and facts from all quarters, and make decisions based upon them. The sink with the blame drain needs a plug. Let's plug it.

Make telling the truth safer than not telling it

The goal is to evolve a culture where people feel safe coming forward with a problem they may fear they created, trusting that there is more to it than meets the eye, and that they and others will get to the root cause, fix it quickly before it happens again, and move on.

That cannot happen in a culture of widespread blaming to avoid accountability and a culture of accountability so intimidating that people become blamers to survive. We must put an end to both blaming to duck accountability and intimidation to enforce it. They separate us from each other and from the truth that we need in order to decide, unite, act, adapt intelligently and embrace accountability.

Stop the blaming and excuses before they start

Blaming, excuses and intimidation atrophy into irrelevance when the first four principles of No Fail Leadership take hold. Let's look:

- **Principle 1**: *All problems stem from conflicts of belief about what's true.*

We believe one thing to be true. Others believe something else. We wind up in conflict that may seem personal at first but simply reflects divergent beliefs. Divergent beliefs are natural and inevitable. We cannot intimidate anyone into believing our beliefs. So we ask stakeholders not to give theirs up but to put them on hold, suspending judgment and attack and comparing notes honestly and expeditiously until we can encapsulate who believes what as prelude to focused problem solving.

- **Principle 2**: *Nothing is ever what it seems. The truth lies elsewhere.*

To blame we must believe that the problem we see is the problem that is. It isn't. Retrospection leaves no doubt. Far more goes on than we know, a fact that once admitted makes blaming inappropriate even to blamers. Repeated demonstrations of "nothing is ever what it seems" can even cause intimidators to think twice.

- **Principle 3:** *The truth is always positive, even when it's painful.*

Basing decisions upon untruths, half-truths and wishful thinking severely handicaps performance and courts disaster. Only truth has value. We can only find and access it when we get the blaming, excuses and intimidation out of the way. Once we learn this, the refreshing clarity of understanding and quality of our decisions and actions far outweigh any momentary pain. Truth takes the wind out of blamers' sails.

- **Principle 4:** *Make it 100% safe to tell the truth.*

We will never hear truth any other way. Levy no penalty on anyone for bringing forward the facts. On the contrary, we must actively welcome the truth—even insist upon it. Once we listen to it courageously, people will find the courage to tell it. Ending the intimidation ends the fear. Ending the fear ends the blaming.

Allow no blame, no excuses and no intimidation

People get thoroughly fed up with all the finger-pointing and excuses. When presented with a safe environment that tolerates no such nonsense, they jump at the chance to experiment with putting all such impulses on hold. And they actually have fun at it. They self-correct. I hear a lot of, "I'm not blaming anyone, but …" And then they struggle with recasting their thoughts from accusation into inquiry about what's really going on.

I'll never forget the first workgroup where I introduced the no-blame concept, admittedly with some trepidation. I wasn't sure whether the participants would think me batty. But even though a few people crossed their arms to hold their harrumph in check, they played along with the no-blame game.

Rachael, a young woman whose participation was important, happened to be on vacation and missed the first three sessions.

Meanwhile, the group settled quite comfortably into the no-blame mode and made considerable progress by the time she joined in. She listened awhile to get the gist of the deliberations, then spoke up to add her insights into the problem, blaming it first on one person then another. The others listened in clearly uncomfortable silence until she finished, pondering the stark contrast between where they too had begun and where, almost overnight, they now were. One finally said, "Rachael, we're not doing blaming any longer." I sat back without a word as the group explained No Blame to her.

Be realistic about the accountability we assign

Look for prerequisites that we haven't covered adequately. Either fill the gaps, even if that means reassigning people and accountability, or assess the risk of not filling them and adjust our goals and tactics to sync up with reality. And, allow no blaming, excuses or scapegoating when some of the results we hoped for leak out of the gaps and onto the floor. We took a risk with eyes open. Track what worked and what didn't. Learn. Do better next time.

97% Factors

Reality check: Case History accountability

The 7 Prerequisites for Accountability:
Did each key player have all seven prerequisites to be fully accountable for responsibilities assigned?

Which of the seven were not in place? Any pattern? Commonality?

What were the consequences for performance and outcomes?

Blaming, excuses and intimidation: What role did they play?

Leadership: What could leaders have done better?

No-Blame pilot test

Be alert for a predicament ripe for blaming and excuses. Set aside all impulse to react.

Quietly assess the accountability situation of key players overall relative to the task.

Assume that if you or someone else screwed up, then some factor outside your or their view or control may have been the root cause.

Proceed with that assumption, participate in the search for answers, and note what transpires.

PART 5

FROM INPUT
TO UNDERSTANDING

Principle 6

Work from facts first, opinions later.

FLASH BACK TO THE STORY that opened this book: the clash between Our Lady Hospital's ER staff and the EMS Ambulance paramedics.

Each believed the other's performance was unprofessional, and they had been working together to iron out the wrinkles when an SUV hit a bus of high school athletes almost head-on in the middle of nowhere. Our Lady's ER scrambled medical teams to stand by for a Mass Casualty Incident, but the "mass casualties" never showed up. EMS transported five victims to Our Lady, none seriously injured, and twenty-three to rival Downtown Medical Center.

Our Lady's staff, furious, charged "medic bias-as-usual" against Our Lady, and would have ended their workgroup had they not cooled off and listened to the 911 radio tapes between hospitals, medics, fire and police. The tapes erased all accusations of medic bias and uncovered alarming protocol violations by everyone involved. Our Lady and EMS acted quickly and jointly hosted a conference of emergency services region-wide to update and reassert protocols that had been forgotten for years.

From the outset they got "facts first, opinions later" so backwards, so frontloaded with heated opinions, that "facts" almost didn't make it to the table. Unusual? Not at all. Per Principle 1, *All problems stem from conflicts of belief about what's true.* Conflicts routinely flare up as "opinions first, facts later …or maybe never." Call time out. Look for 911 tapes.

This case also bared the need to get beyond the 3% we can measure into the 97% that matters. No metric tools were in place to track protocol violations. People hadn't taken the protocols seriously because they had created their own. That's what happens in 97% Territory. And nothing on the 911 tapes was quantifiable even though the tapes told the whole story. 97% Territory was where the facts of what happened all lay.

Principle 6 trains us to look for and incorporate evidence from the 97% deliberately and systematically into the input mix, especially when facing the kinds of people-intensive problems the opening case study and the Leadership Test point out. Sometimes 97% Factors in the form of opinions and other ambiguous signals are almost the only factors we have to work with at first. The facts underlying these factors, though hidden and hard to quantify, often constitute the only evidence that brings the picture of what's going on into focus. And sometimes it's the best evidence.

Let's talk about the 3%

Experienced, conscientious leaders rely heavily upon quantitative input and feedback for making decisions and evaluating what transpires, measuring everything that's measurable and worth measuring as a way to rein in opinion-based decision making. The whole "quality" movement, past and present, strives to replace opinions with facts. Lean Six Sigma practitioners go through intense training to be certified as "black belts" in the martial art of business combat. They emerge as warriors in the war on waste armed with all the Define-Measure-Analyze-Improve-Control weapons, plus more, in the Six Sigma arsenal. They believe that all problems fundamentally trace to quantifiable process breakdowns, and they attack them with missionary zeal. They believe so wholeheartedly in the rightness of their cause and methodology that they can get impatient with managers and employees who sense that something critical is being overlooked or devalued.

Indeed, no one can question the movement's contribution to the exceptional quality of goods and services that we now enjoy from many industries. The technology revolution would hardly have been possible without the defect reduction methodologies W. Edwards Deming pioneered. In almost every organization I have worked with, however, I encounter people with power who overindulge. They so fixate on the 3% they can measure that they summarily dismiss everything unquantifiably human as too fuzzy-wuzzy to be relevant, like beliefs and behavior, relationships and influence, individual agendas and management styles. I've even witnessed some metric militants get angry when a peer or subordinate tries to inject the idea that human factors count too.

I confront them with this red flag waved by Dr. Deming, father of the entire fact-driven, metrics-driven movement they espouse as gospel:

> *The 3% you can measure misses*
> *the 97% that matters.*
> *— W. Edwards Deming*

Deming's blunt assertion seems so heretical—so off his statistical avenue to quality control—that his disciples must wonder if he whipped a U-turn when they weren't looking. So, with hardly a tap on the brakes, they drive on, refocusing their attention on the 3% they can measure because "numbers don't lie" and steer clear of the other 97%, writing off the immeasurable inefficiency as an irritating but normal cost of doing business.

Fortunately, some disciples and leaders discovered that Deming knew what he was talking about, especially for service-intensive activities and enterprises where the Leadership Test problems are most evident.

The "facts" may not add up to the truth

*A fact is something that existed or happened
that can be verified.*

As we know from courtroom dramas, news reports, and political speeches, the so-called facts may not be accurate, complete, verifiable or the whole truth. Indeed, truth is what's left after we have stripped away the misinformation, manipulation, opinions, anecdotes and wishful thinking. What's left may not be much.

But don't equate fact solely with quantifiable data and quantifiable data with truth. That's what numbers-driven people try to do when they insist that we only allow quantitative input on the table. In search of certainty and safety they risk over relying on Define-Measure-Analyze-Improve-Control-type tools that can mire them down in complexity.

A case in point. One healthcare institution hired an outside firm to do a massive process analysis of urgent care and emergency patients from arrival through discharge to compare the number of stops made along the way, hospital people seen, and the average patient times spent per segment versus national norms. When the study was completed the charts covered the walls of the conference room and indeed, showed slower patient progress than the norms. One executive asked why the variances. No answer. Many process lines showed homegrown processes with no national norms. "What are we supposed to do with all this?" No answer. The consultants had quantified the processes and throughput, but management was still in the dark about rationales for processes, causes of delays, and what to fix first. The answers lay with the people the consultants timed for efficiency but never really got to know.

Facts encompass far more than data. Facts include things people have said, done, observed, reported and written, plus events and other happenings and evidence that don't quantify neatly. The answer to "what next?" ultimately came from asking departmental employees to cite specifics underlying bottlenecks, and then getting leaders and stakeholders from targeted segments to put the clues together, diagnose the problems and agree on a solution.

Surprisingly few of the participants were schooled in management problem solving. Their schooling ventured little beyond their healthcare specialty and managing on the job. As expected, opinions sprinkled with facts opened most personal interviews, but by interview end, participants were often digging deep for facts—or where to find them—about important, new, unanswered questions, intrigued by the quest for answers.

Knowing what people don't know may ultimately count far more than what they do know, especially when they discover their own knowledge gaps. None of us would want to fly west in a Cessna based upon yesterday's weather report. Why would we sanction ignorance over input and act upon unexamined opinions when piloting our company?

Humans don't do most things by the numbers

We grow up and live in families, groups and societies that condition us to form strong opinions based upon limited evidence. We act on the spot based upon opinions, a contemporary echo of our distant, survivalist life on the savanna and in the forests. That imprinting carries over into our workplace. Particularly when pressured for results, we tend to overly trust past experience, intuition and good intentions. We resist getting slowed down by metric-driven methodologies or sidetracked by too much data and logic that challenge our intent. We bet incautiously on our reflexive beliefs about what's true, when the truth lies elsewhere.

This conditioned, survivalist mentality spawns the more troublesome opinions and actions I have witnessed. As intangible and elusive as our underlying beliefs and fears are, they are too powerful and active to discount.

Whether today's leaders hover at 15,000 feet or 500 feet above the front lines, the forest canopy still hides the action going on at ground level. The standard metrics and research usually tell more about the site and size of the problem than about why it's a problem in the first place. Even standard "root cause" analysis often doesn't root out the cause. We still won't know why communication, teamwork, implementation, and all the other Leadership

Test breakdowns wreak havoc in the 97% or how to make them disappear. Employees at ground level usually don't document their informal processes and workarounds or base them on thorough data gathering, analysis and sober, meticulous planning. A different dynamic is at work.

Opinions are facts of business life…and much more

Opinions matter. Opinions can buoy an enterprise or sink it. They manifest the individual beliefs, anecdotal experiences and scuttlebutt that feed them. And we seriously underappreciate them. Whether misguided or clairvoyant, opinions influence activities on and behind the front lines irrespective of what management wants. They can sway management at all levels to take action that's out of sync with the real predicaments and corporate mission. Strong opinions advanced early in a meeting by a person with leverage can intimidate people into silence, shutting down the search for truth in an instant. So can strong opinions rooted in an ossified status quo. Even solid data that gets in the way of intent can end up brushed aside.

Opinions inhabit the 97% we can't easily quantify. We must find out what the people we depend upon think. Opinions about the company's purpose that are out of sync with management's provide early signals that employees—or leaders—have lost their way. Informal processes—employees' unofficial opinions of how to get something done better—alert us to potentially serious dysfunction. Opinions can be weathervanes for entrenched fears and misbeliefs that, once out in the open, we can deal with without threatening the belief holders. Best case, opinions have some top insights and ideas underlying them that we want to hear.

Opinions—whether secretly harbored or openly advocated at the top or on the battle lines—are facts of life.

And we badly mismanage both opinions and opinion holders

- ⊚ We brush off less gifted, educated or experienced opinion holders as unworthy of holding a valid opinion outside their box.

- ⊚ We disregard opinions of others altogether or downplay them.

- ⊚ We suppress opinions by cutting people off whose opinions conflict with ours.

- ⊚ We let opinions run wild when we don't know how to manage them.

- ⊚ We cave in to them when they back us into a wall.

We cannot tell people not to have opinions or try to make opinions go away by not listening to them. Suppression just fuels the underground resistance that creates Leadership Test problems. Nor can we let talkers monopolize conversation, cutting total input and dishonoring others with something to say. Leader pacifism in the face of high-pressure opinion holders doesn't make strong opinions go away.

Mismanage opinions and opinion holders, and performance and productivity will never reach full potential. We dare not adopt and enact someone's agenda or viewpoint without examining its intent, validity, implications and consequences. That isn't leadership. That's follower-ship.

Principle 6 turns the quest for truth into a joint enterprise. It sensitizes and trains people at all levels to put input from the 97% on equal footing with the 3% so that we understand both the strengths and limitations of opinions and facts and moderate our judgments until critical evidence is in. It also shows ways to get past the distrust and fears of loss that keep employees from talking about things they know aren't working.

THE GOAL OF PRINCIPLE 6

Go beyond what we measure into the 97% that matters so that we can solve the right problem right the first time.

The immediate problem we see rarely is the real problem or the problem we need to solve. Top management sees different sets of problems than midlevel and frontline people, and it views common problems differently than they do. Individuals within departments see different manifestations than their colleagues. And customer viewpoints can differ markedly from any of our views from inside. If we try to solve a problem as any one observer or group perceives it, we will not solve the right problem. We risk making matters worse. And with each fumbled attempt we resist trying again.

The truth lies in a composite "elsewhere" we need to fully understand and respect. An astounding accumulation of fact and fiction, beliefs and misbeliefs, actions and inactions, breakthroughs and breakdowns hides in this elsewhere. So do the distrust and fears of loss that anchor the problems in place.

Obviously we cannot know a complex, evolving "elsewhere" quickly or in total. Knowledge accumulates as we focus on pieces of it that demand attention. We get smarter. When crisis demands a rapid response with limited input, we will respond with acute awareness of the risks our ignorance creates. Instead of plunging headlong into action on faith or intuition, or doing nothing pending macro solutions, we can start small, conducting action experiments designed to scale up quickly as feedback fills crucial gaps in knowledge. Such trials by fire value instant, honest reports from the front so that we can adapt. The trials engage opinion holders and often convert them from enemies or lukewarm supporters of change into valued and essential contributors.

The problem with opinions

They're ours.

Like our children, we nurture them and have high hopes that they will do us proud. We take offense when dissenters question their value and potential, and we defend them beyond good sense. Opinions, whether long held, conceived under the gun, or blurted out in eagerness to contribute, all tend to suffer from common maladies:

◆ *Opinions arrive pre-packaged in our old beliefs.*

Beliefs are conclusions we accept or adopt as true with or without verifiable evidence. They are often formulated by others and indoctrinated.

Dogmas, doctrines, biases, bigotry, righteous causes, family and other values fall into this category. Beliefs predate opinions. Beliefs can be so ingrained and obscure in their origins that we never pause to examine them seriously. Yet we defend and act upon them as if they were indisputable facts.

We place a far lower bar for evidence that confirms our bias than for evidence that runs counter to it. Nonetheless, we confidently believe that we make informed, pro/con judgments when deep-seated beliefs actually govern our choices, nudged one way or the other by our even deeper instincts to fight or flee.

Opinions are conclusions about what's true, valid or probable that we come to based upon what we think is "evidence." Unlike beliefs, opinions more readily come and go. Some change and evolve. They lie between impressions and positive knowledge.

This "evidence" typically consists of a headful of past experiences, anecdotes, opinions of others, intuitions and hearsay, plus a few "facts" that we have gathered incidentally along the way. Often, the facts have gone out-of-date, or we remember them inaccurately, or they may have been inaccurate or incomplete right from the beginning.

We recognize that people routinely examine the same evidence we do, interpret it differently, weigh pros and cons and arrive at conclusions we don't. Subjectivity leaves our opinions open to legitimate dispute. Robust challenges make them harder to maintain intact. Still, as vulnerable as they are, opinions stiffened by beliefs strongly govern how we define the present and compose the what-if scenarios we project into the future.

Opinions overly attach to the past

Clichés begin life vibrant with color, wit and resonance. Eventually, the color fades and the wit dies from overexposure. But people drag the corpses around for years as if they still communicate something "right-on."

"Been there, done that, won't work" has just enough life and relevance left in it to be dangerous. It's a powerful de-motivator. It evokes a perceived history of botched attempts. Who'd dare to brave another attempt, especially when people claiming firsthand knowledge forewarn us that its reception is doomed from the start?

I've watched top executives, especially those running service-intensive organizations, back off at the first signs of internal resistance, particularly when considering another round of process and performance improvement. They start out ambivalent in their own mind based upon limited knowledge. They happily defer to the opinions of disenchanted veterans who give the impression that they know what they're talking about. Listeners who have merely heard complaints can quickly nod in agreement.

But the blanket assertion "won't work" cannot go unexamined. Accept it, and the business-as-usual mentality wins.

The question to ask is this: "Where have you 'been,' what have you 'done,' and why didn't it 'work?'" Maybe the objector *has* been there and done that and it didn't work. The input may help us avoid repeating someone else's mistakes.

On the other hand, our naysayer could have been to a *there* quite different from our *here*, and what he did differs markedly from what we contemplate doing, superimposing his old experiences and fears on new problems and ideas where they don't apply. Or he may have leapt to conclusions or have a stake in preserving the status quo or have personal reasons to deflect the truth or merely parrots the "been there done that" cliché in a display of faux wisdom.

The more forcefully someone advances the "been there, done that, won't work" opinion, the deeper we should probe. Remember the paradox of strong beliefs: the less that's known and/or the less that's remembered the stronger the belief. The stronger the belief, the stronger the opinion. And as the researchers discovered, "People are often most confident when they are most wrong."[1]

It takes a determined, coolheaded leader to swim up the "been there, done that" stream.

♦ *Opinions leapfrog over facts to solutions that make things worse.*

State Senator George McManus, now retired, was a member of Michigan's healthcare committee. One day a fellow senator arrived at the committee meeting fuming about what had happened to his mother at her nursing home and proposing legislation to end such "abuse" once and for all.

Apparently his mother had managed to lower the guardrail on her bed when none of the staff was present. She tried to get out on her own, which she knew she wasn't supposed to do. The bed was high enough that when she sat on the edge her feet dangled without quite reaching the floor. The drop caused her to lose her balance, and she fell, hurting herself.

So her son, the senator, wanted to legislate lower heights for hospital-high beds. (Costly, adjustable beds were not common in nursing homes at the time.) Fortunately, one of the senators knew why the hospital-style beds stood the height they did. Nursing home staff performs a lot of physical work on patients, turning them, cleaning them, lifting them, and more. Lower beds meant more bending and less leverage. That caused more staff injuries,

---

1 Frank R. Kardes and David M. Sanbonmatsu, "Omission Neglect. The Importance of Missing Information," *Skeptical Inquirer,* March/April, 2003: 42-46.

more time off work in an industry strapped for employees, and more workers' compensation claims.

The legislation died in committee. But what if it hadn't? What if no one at the meeting knew the history? McManus said that it was scary how many laws were enacted based upon one person's experience, an emotionally charged opinion, good intentions and few facts. Even scarier was the number of such laws that made it to the floor for a vote and passed, creating chaos in whatever industry they affected.

I wonder what we would find if we identified and costed out the wastes of manpower, money, resources and common sense caused by all the Chicken-Little legislation that governments pass to save us from lightning strikes on clear days.

◆   *Instant opinions solve the immediate problem, which is probably the wrong problem to solve first.*

It's easy to point fingers and attach blame to people, processes and things that appear to stand in our way, and then assume that the problem we see supersedes all others. But the problem could merely show symptoms of deeper problems and not even rise as the most important one. Here's a case in point:

The exasperated parts department supervisor in a heavy-equipment manufacturing company slapped a stack of order forms on the workgroup's table. "Wrong part numbers, just from yesterday! That's what this group needs to work on. The service techs are driving me crazy!"

Saner heads wanted to know what else was screwed up. So, the parts department kept tabs for a week and returned with the following chart of the frequency of errors.

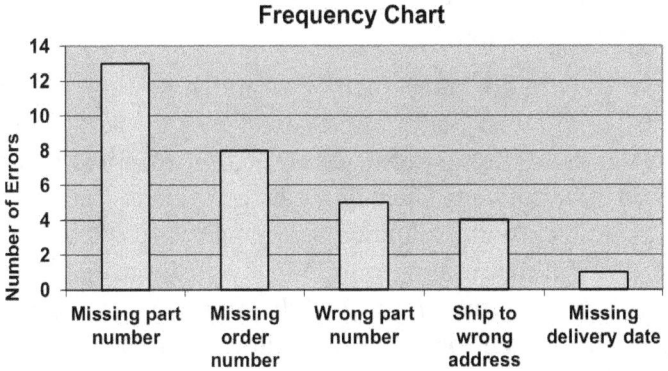

It turned out that missing part and order numbers occurred more often than wrong part numbers. The group then identified the cost of the direct and indirect waste in each category and the investment of time and assets needed to eliminate each problem. Opportunities to ship to the wrong address or miss a delivery date—the two least frequent problems—were harder to spot up-front and cost the most to correct. And when not caught, they cost customers dearly in extended downtime that could trigger penalties and jeopardize contracts. Further, the problems inter-linked. Eliminating wrong part numbers wouldn't solve the whole problem and might even have exacerbated it. The department fixed the shipping and delivery problems first.

Problems that get headlines don't necessarily belong at the head of the list either, despite the passion of those who consider them-selves victims or saviors. The obvious example is special interest groups that badger their targets to advance their cause ahead of and, if necessary, at the sacrifice of all others. They argue, "If we could just start this or stop that or increase the budget to fix this, then the problem would be solved." Don't believe it.

Go back to Principle 2: *Nothing is ever what it seems. The truth lies elsewhere.* Solving the immediate problem first probably solves the wrong problem. And the immediate solution is probably the wrong solution. Facts first, opinions later.

Use opinions as portals to what's in play
in the 97% elsewhere

People usually do know their jobs and how they accomplish them. They know what promotes excellence in their cubicle and what stands in the way of it. About half of frontline people say that no one, not even their immediate superior, has ever asked about problems and solutions before or hasn't asked for a long time. Once initial training ends, employees figure out how to get their job done on their own. And the more service and relationship intensive their job, the more latitude they generally have for personal ingenuity.

What they see and experience from then on is their reality. They tend to generalize from it. The generalizations can be accurate or way off base. We are privy anecdotally to what happens in our immediate back yard. But we have only a vague idea of the facts of what's happening more broadly and how our actions influence the whole. Managers and coworkers alike find themselves taken aback by the breadth, depth and longevity of misconceptions about each other's work and by the certitude and fervor with which people hold on to misunderstandings.

But important information and insights may lie within people's reality and opinions about the obstacles they face, how they get around them, and the assumptions and logic behind their workarounds. Time and again a perceptive employee close to the action sees an opportunity or threat in patterns no one has discerned before. We usually will not see their picture unless we ask for it.

Incorporate the best of what the 3% and 97% can
contribute without being undone by the worst

Opening the door to opinions early on may seem to violate "Facts first, opinions later," but, as noted earlier, opinions are facts of business life. They animate activity in the 97% that matters. What counts up front aren't the opinions themselves but the latent knowledge, facts and insights supporting them, adding new dimension to "facts and truth." Principle 6 plops us down on Oliver Wendell Holmes' path from simplicity into complexity and ushers us well along the way to the simplicity on the other side.

- ◎ Upfront we define the Leadership Test problems that go on in the 97% we don't measure.

- ◎ We dig into simplicity—the legitimate facts and promising opinions found in the limited 3% we can measure plus in the 97% as we begin to explore it as well.

- ◎ We disassemble opinions and other hard-to-measure factors in search of the underlying facts—fodder for analysis.

- ◎ We combine the findings into a holistic, upfront picture of what really seems to be going on, how and why.

- ◎ We track clues in the resultant complexity until paths to simplicity begin to emerge through the mist.

But we're not there yet. The mist, although nowhere near as dense as the fog of complexity, arises from what we still don't know that blocks our way.

Opinions based upon fact, once everyone has the same facts, have value

Upfront we accept that critical information gaps exist in our personal and combined perspective and strive to fill them. We shelve instant opinions instead of challenging or defending them until "elsewhere" has been explored. And we help others within and outside of the enterprise to do the same.

We listen to each other, drawing out input and insights that would never emerge in impatient, ironhanded meetings. We want the truth and make it safe to express it untrammeled by blaming or excuse making. We learn to separate fact from everything else and extract useful content quickly and efficiently. We learn that logic underlies what others do, even though the logic may conflict with our own, and not usually with hostile intent. We will be too savvy for superficial or self-serving opinions to prevail. Remaining opinions will be informed, enlightened and contributory to the composite view that leaders need in order to lead.

Once evidence from the 3% and 97% is in, we will know what really goes on in "complexity." We can then agree on the likeliest routes to "simplicity," mark them out, and work together to pave them. And whatever problems we still must overcome, we will have upped the odds of solving the right ones right the first time.

97% Factors

Facts vs. opinions

Role: Which played the stronger role in diagnosis, prescription, implementation, and evaluation of outcomes—facts or opinions?

Availability: Were facts available for both the 3% you can measure and 97% that matters more?

Leadership: How well were opinions and opinion-holders managed? What could be done differently next time?

PRINCIPLE 7

Get input from frontline people *before* making decisions they must implement, not after.

THE BEST IDEAS OFTEN COME FROM THE FRONT LINE, where business processes take place. The worst "good ideas" often come from the top. As Peter Drucker asserts in *Managing for the Future*, "In knowledge and service work, partnership with the responsible worker is the only way; nothing else will work at all." [1]

Principle 7 insists that leaders get major frontline input and engagement up front. Doing this connects the top and bottom. It helps cultivate partnerships based upon mutual respect and trust that outlast the project at hand.

Building partnerships Principle 7's way

No Fail Leadership, most boldly through Principle 7, attempts to engage management in doing what management has often failed to do—get the input that really makes a difference in advance and along the way, cultivate the workforce to engage and unite behind a common cause, and secure buy-in to the solutions before implementing them.

---

1 Peter F. Drucker, *Managing for the Future* (New York: Truman Talley/Dutton, 1992), 107.

Executives and down-line managers I work with often claim that they feel closely in touch with the people under them, thanks to team meetings, daily business encounters, open doors and friendly conversations over lunch. That's nowhere near enough. It's useful but too one-sidedly incomplete, because nothing is ever what it seems; the truth lies elsewhere. Leaders need input—unfiltered and unspun. If we're not making decisions based upon truth, then what are we making them on? Wishful thinking? Half-truths? Outright lies?

When a client asks us to help solve a problem, we pick the brains of employees cross functionally until we capture the point of view of every stakeholder group in detail. That takes time, immersion and investigative work. Many frontline employees say that they have never been asked for their input before. They feel honored to contribute and want to do more.

As leaders we may not have time to dig deeply into every problem that comes our way. To increase our visibility we could create a splash in as many troubled ponds as possible, moving quickly from one to another. Or we could focus intently on one or two at a time, immerse ourselves in the problem, and work shoulder to shoulder with problem solvers.

Give serious consideration to the second option. It's Principle 7 in action: *Get input from frontline people before making decisions they must implement, not after.* Immersion builds respect and successes. Respect based on successes builds leaders. As leaders we might not work with as many employees initially by focusing on a few problems at a time, but we will establish close working relationships with people we do work with, and we will succeed at what we do. Through us, employees will learn our vision and goals, both for them and the enterprise. They'll learn how to settle on solutions that are strategically on target and how to implement them successfully, including fast-track implementations under pressure (more on all of this later). People will also learn about us as leaders—what we are like to work with, our standards and expectations, and how we see employees' role and importance in overall success.

Importantly, pick problems that involve different areas and people each time. Our network of cross-functional relationships will expand quickly. And so will word of the successes we have led, spreading far beyond the employees we worked with directly. Once again, it's Principle 7 in action.

Isn't there an easier way?

If you knew of one that beats close involvement, you would already have taken it, wouldn't you? Early on we're rousing employees to think about the business in a new way. Giving them boxes to check on an employee survey, even with blanks for comments, won't smoke out thinking and details as effectively as good, old-fashioned detective work.

Even executives of huge consumer service companies I've talked with say that, despite generous research budgets, they still lack answers. And despite massive investments to computerize, centralize and standardize every process and product they can, they still consider their company "only 85% there," as one put it.

If they are "85% there," why should they care? Isn't 85% good enough? No, not in highly competitive industries. Competitors are 85% there too. The last 15% makes all the difference. It's the toughest to deliver and management doesn't know what goes on in it.

Why are they stuck at 85%? Because to get un-stuck, they need to dig into the informal processes, action, inaction and dynamics at work near and on the front line. That means talking with the people in the trenches as well as up the chain of command.

Skeptics question whether spending as much time with individuals as Principle 7 advocates warrants the investment. They especially question our emphasis on frontline and frontline support people.

"The one-on-one conversations take too much time. They open Pandora's box. They slow things down when we need to act now!"

Well, "act now" expediency all too often comes from fear in the face of urgency. We can't solve problems we don't understand. We'll never understand them if we don't seek answers. And we will never solve them if we work around them. The intangibles are substantial, pervasive, long-standing and deeply rooted. They stand squarely in the way of process and performance improvement.

If leaders want to turn that last 15% to its advantage, then they must go where the intangibles constitute the main obstacles to tangible progress. Do less, and service breakdowns will remain too common, silos too problematic, plan implementations too bogged down, and feedback too tardy and short on candor.

The hidden danger of failing to get input

I have asked veterans of No Fail Leadership workgroups how they feel about past problem-solving sessions where they were not interviewed in advance by someone who could get their views on the table anonymously on their behalf. To a man and woman, they said that, by comparison, past sessions were "a waste of time." Please think of pounding the mental streets as essential investigative work. A case in point:

The client was a service company bent upon streamlining its customer intake process. One of four workgroups did not make as much progress as the other three. The three most successful ones had been populated mainly by people interviewed in advance and cultivated to volunteer. The fourth consisted of half that had been interviewed (the Customer Intake Group) and half that had not (the Customer Destination Group). Those interviewed knew why they were there, were prepped, united in a common cause, and ready to let everything hang out for all to see and ponder. Not the Destination group.

Why not? Because the senior VP who engaged us questioned the Destination Group's relevance to the intake problem and nixed its interviews. Besides, no such interviews had been conducted in the past. He was afraid of mission creep. "Stick to Intake," he ordered.

That was ill-advised. The Intake Group's problems were linked to interactions with the Destination Group. The latter was invited to the workgroup only after that reality became clear. By then it was too late to interview Destination Group managers and supervisors, and we could not interview any frontline people at all.

The Intake Group proposed a cross-functional pilot test to improve customer handoffs. The Destination supervisor agreed. But back in her department, her people felt threatened by the test's procedural changes to their MO. They refused to even entertain the proposal. They felt left out because their group hadn't been interviewed while the other group had been. Their viewpoint had never been sought nor their predicaments expressed and honored. To them, they were outsiders up against a workgroup of energized insiders with a big head start and intent to scapegoat them.

That perception wasn't accurate at all. The Intake Group had already gotten past finger-pointing and blaming thanks to the interviews and workgroup sessions. To them the truth was emancipating. Their only interest was to invite the Destination Group to help solve a mutual problem as co-stakeholders in the outcome. The issue escalated into a management-employee confrontation that expanded interdepartmentally. Eventually a less ambitious pilot test materialized that took a baby step, but progress badly trailed opportunity.

Meanwhile, a separate management-frontline workgroup was considering a way to solve a different problem. At my urging, they put planning on hold a couple days while frontline participants asked four question of colleagues who hadn't been interviewed:

- ◎ "Is this a problem?"

- ◎ "Is it worth solving, and why?"

- ◎ "How would life be different if it were fixed?"

- ◎ "Will you help?"

The answers, unanimously, were yes, yes, much better and absolutely. They finished the plan and implemented it with solid buy-in and stunning success.

The contrast between the two workgroups could not have been more dramatic. One was engaged and eager. The other wasn't, illustrating two dangers:

- ⊚ Assembling people to solve a problem without first having found out what they privately know and think breeds skepticism and lukewarm engagement.

- ⊚ Charging ahead with a plan without getting frontline input about its underlying assumptions, wisdom, and implementation details before making decisions that workers must live with unleashes enemies of change.

These omissions, per my travels, appear to be the norm. People attend as conscripts, not volunteers. They may have been briefed and asked to bring data and reports to first sessions, but their personal input—what they really see and think—stays behind. The key people we need at the table aren't there either. We don't even know who they all are. Major stakeholders are missing. So are frontline employees who really understand what goes on in the briar patch. The few who do attend may not feel free to speak candidly. And where are top managers who can liberate people to speak candidly, guide problem solving, and approve recommendations on the spot? The net consequence is disengagement and dysfunction. Resentment. Sluggishness. Progress trailing opportunity.

The immediate danger of leaders disconnecting from the front line

We dare not disconnect from the people who do the work, especially employees on the front line and in close support roles.

If we disconnect before we make decisions by failing to get input from responsible workers on the front line, then we compound management misunderstandings and miscalculations about the nature of the problems and the right ones to solve.

If we disconnect during decision making by failing to incorporate stakeholders at all levels as partners in problem solving, then we won't develop successful solutions or get buy-in to the plans we implement.

If we disconnect after making the decisions, even joint decisions, then the implementations will lose momentum and bog down.

If we disconnect habitually, then no one will volunteer much of anything. When we ask people for input we may get back a guarded fraction of what they would tell us if they felt safe to speak candidly.

The long-term dangers of disconnecting

Decapitation. A corporate body without a head. The leader's job is to:

◎   Articulate the forces and principles responsible for the prosperity of the enterprise.

◎   Champion them down into the depths of the workforce.

◎   Make sure that employees understand their vital, personal role in furthering the welfare and integrity of the mission.

Admittedly, the job gets harder as growth stretches the connection between the leaders and the workforce. But the importance of connecting grows too. And the consequences of disconnecting aren't trivial:

♦   *Diffusion of purpose.*

Individuals at lower levels may know little to nothing about how they and their job fit into the overall scheme. Employees that trickled in over time may have had no meaningful contact with the key leaders ever, even after years on the job.

Managers promoted from the ranks of the untutored don't suddenly infill with missing knowledge and wisdom about what made this business succeed. Neither do managers hired from outside. Instead of following the principles that top leaders evolved and embodied with success, they improvise or import their own methods and institute them, a prime source of disunity and dysfunction.

Each new layer of managers and supervisors distances top leaders further—and sometimes firewalls them—from teaching and guiding the workers responsible for the work.

As leaders we cannot operate while only hazily aware of workers' ignorance of the purpose of what they do, of mid-management's self-created MOs, and of leadership's weakening connections with the front line. Disengagement poses a major threat to effective leadership.

◆   *Diffusion of practice*

The leader is also responsible for keeping track of how the internal mindset morphs over time:

- Spotting any deterioration in the integrity and viability of the business principles in practice

- Reasserting principles that have been sidelined

- Adapting those that need updating

As leaders, we cannot accomplish any of this without input from responsible workers, not just from top and mid-level managers but, especially from frontline employees immersed in the action.

◆   *Leadership complacency and miscalculation*

Long-reigning, highly respected leaders may think that everyone still knows them and syncs up with their vision and methods of achieving it. Not likely. The members of the close-knit band that engineered and drove the growth know each other perhaps better than they know their spouses. But as the organizational chart expands, so does the distance between the boxes, which connect fraternally only at the highest levels. Leaders, even legends in their own time, end up connecting with employees mainly by the shadow they cast.

Other "leaders," some of the worst, disconnect by disposition or preference. They communicate from afar without really connecting and see nothing wrong with that.

Well, something is "wrong with that." Whether the leaders detach through complacency or intent, they do the enterprise and everyone in it a costly disservice. Here are just two of many ways:

⊚ No one knows what their leaders like, dislike or intend. That seeds clouds of uncertainty and fear that drizzle coldly on employees year round, distracting them from their primary assignments and subverting their ability to understand and grapple successfully with the problems at hand.

⊚ The leaders lose track of work in progress. Ignorant of the workload, they pelt employees with their top-down inspirations and urgencies of the moment that can cripple existing high-value projects mid stride, without giving savvy implementers a chance to object or remedy the unintended consequences.

Learn to lead by solving the right problems, right, the first time

We must learn to succeed. And "practice makes perfect."

We all know what it's like to do something without succeeding, and most of us know that we can't "succeed" without "doing." As someone said, "God can't move a parked car."

Competent leaders usually have hit lists of strategically important problems to solve and high-value opportunities to exploit. They may even have a list of subprojects to complete, some of which may be underway. Such projects offer us leaders and emerging leaders a credible, unthreatening reason to familiarize ourselves with the inner workings of the business. Once there, we can inspire open, honest exchange and build close working relationships. And selfishly, we can also gently bias efforts toward "learn to succeed" solutions that help solve other problems on our strategic hit list.

Principle 7's call to invite frontline people to supply input for decisions that affect them offers a way in. Once there, our mutual objective, for our future and theirs, is to carefully pick the right problems to solve and solve them right the first time. Here's what to look for:

The right problems satisfy two upfront criteria

•   *They can be solved with a high probability of success.*

Choose problems that, if solved, will make a difference in performance, productivity and customer satisfaction.

Choose short-term problems that promise a quick, high return on the effort with low financial investment.

Choose "first domino" problems. Glue the first domino upright, and it stops toppling dominos down line, leveraging the effort.

•   *They require cross-functional, multilevel effort.*

Cross-functional, multilevel problems cannot be solved without major increases in communication, honesty, mutual understanding, teamwork and ultimately trust. Finding solutions and implementing them connects people more intimately than ever before.

The right solutions

•   *Solve problems holistically.*

Holistic solutions recognize the interdependence of the parts and the whole. We learn to think cross-functionally, bridging hierarchies and including all directly affected stakeholders in the deliberations. Most of all, we create win-win solutions for everyone involved.

- *Stretch us without setting us up for failure.*

Overly ambitious attempts face far more intertwined variables and obstacles than we can foresee and contend with. They risk achieving little if anything and can do unforeseen, costly and even unalterable damage, however unintended. People learn to succeed in bite-sized chunks. Success scales up about as fast as failure.

- *Scale up.*

Holistic solutions to first-domino problems that also look downrange can scale up fast to encompass broader problems. They often solve so much of the broader problem that surprisingly little remains to be done—and at little cost. Small, solid, forward-looking successes teach us to solve complex problems faster and better than sink-or-swim immersions in big seas.

- *Promote engagement instead of resistance.*

Solutions that seek and honor frontline input engage people from first contact through implementation and beyond. Engaged, committed employees inspire engagement and commitment in others, generating broad-scale buy-in of the highest order.

Principal 7: *Get input from frontline people before making decisions they must implement, not after*

Without ongoing participation from frontline and support groups, decisions can drift far enough off the mark that they have to be scrapped or revised later at high cost, bloated by the extra cost of fixing collateral damage. None of this builds confidence in the decision makers.

Furthermore, what better place to find early warnings of Leadership Test breakdowns than on the front line where the principles are tested every day? And what better way to establish an early warning network than by using upcoming projects to build relationships with frontline employees?

Principle 7 provides the entrée and sets up success. It tells us what we must do to up the odds of succeeding.

Input: Ask for it and listen rather than avoid and ignore it. Value what employees say instead of brushing it off. And don't stop with arms-length input. Jump into the melee. Witness the predicaments and needs of frontline and support people first-hand.

Decisions: Armed with that input, jointly prioritize which problems people want solved that actually need to be solved first, not only from their perspective but from management's. Involving employees in the choice assures buy-in to what happens next and intercepts "big solutions" that cannot succeed.

Initial input is never enough. We need to turn the problems inside out in order to build viable solutions that work cross functionally—a new experience and good training for many employees.

Implementation: Think through implementation plans from every point of view, in detail—yet another new experience. And teach participating employees to track, in detail, what works and what doesn't, why and why not, so that plans can be adapted expeditiously to exploit opportunities or deal with obstacles.

I end this chapter with its beginning

The best ideas often come from the front line, where business processes take place. The worst "good ideas" often come from the top. As Peter Drucker asserts in Managing for the Future, *"In knowledge and service work, partnership with the responsible worker is the only way; nothing else will work at all."*

What's next

Principle 8: *Only make promises we can keep, and keep all the promises we make.* It's about choices, and its link to Principle 7's admonition to get input from frontline people before making decisions they must implement is strong:

⊚ Who makes the promises that drive the enterprise? Its leaders, managers and others with authority.

⊚ Who's responsible for keeping them regardless of who makes them? The people on the front lines of frontline departments.

⊚ Who pays the price when promises aren't kept? Everyone, from leaders to employees at every level, plus every outside stakeholder that depends upon the enterprise. Ultimately, the enterprise itself.

Principle 8 ventures into decision-making territory involving promise choices that can prove treacherous for the unwary.

97% Factors

Frontline input

Source: Was frontline input served up by managers, supervisors and other proxies that claim to know what's going on at the front?

Or was it discovered by talking directly with frontline employees embroiled in the action? And with customers and other
stakeholders?

Quality/quantity: What consequences flowed from getting or
not getting frontline input?

Value: Ask peers and others you trust how they felt about past
problem-solving sessions where they were not asked to give
their input and put their views on the table up front.

Where they contributed in advance.

PART 6

FROM SOLUTIONS

TO IMPLEMENTATIONS

PRINCIPLE 8:

Only make promises we can keep, and keep all the promises we make.

EXECUTIVES, MANAGERS AND EMPLOYEES in every company I've worked with know deep down that they make too many promises to customers and each other that they don't have the manpower or resources to keep. Yet they make them anyway and sacrifice employees to keep them. Working relationships get overstretched. So does customer goodwill. The fabric of the organization begins to unravel. So does quality, performance, productivity, customer satisfaction, camaraderie, and morale—potentially beyond repair.

When leaders give real thought to today's most serious problems, they quickly realize that overpromising and under-delivering explain or exacerbate almost all of them. And perpetuate them. And cost the company a bundle, unnecessarily, I would contend, both strategically and in the daily conduct of business.

I have encountered many organizations that commit to keeping promises and expend huge resources to do so. I have rarely found an enterprise deliberately organized with optimizing promise making and keeping as the guiding light. Most organize around optimizing processes, quality and profits. Well-conceived, well-oiled processes can help reduce errors, defects, delays, costs and price, upping quality and value. That helps back up product promises. But the most perfect processes cannot guarantee that promises will be kept or that the outcomes will satisfy anyone other than the process police.

Keeping promises or not keeping them impacts profoundly on a company's relationship with its employees, suppliers, middlemen, and most importantly, with its customers. Are we restraining our temptations to promise more than we can deliver? Are we keeping all the promises we make? Over-promising can stretch us beyond the breaking point, creating untold waste internally and jeopardizing vital relationships. And when we make more promises than we keep, we disappoint those on the short end.

Principle 8 (*Only make promises we can keep, and keep all the promises we make*) raises issues of purpose, attitudes, activities, honesty and integrity individually and corporately, not just at the top but deep within the organization. Issues like what we can do and what we cannot. Plus issues of what we could deliberately gear up to do if we believed in the upside. Instilling and honoring Principle 8 starts at the top. Leveraging the power of promise keeping depends upon leaders committed to championing and enforcing it.

A promise

A promise can mean one of two very different things to its maker. It means only one thing to its receiver.

To the maker it can mean a commitment to perform—a contract, tangible or implied. "I will." Or it can mean a statement of *expectation* to perform—an intention, genuine or professed. "I might."

To the receiver, it always means, "You will."

From promise to commitment to delivery

The delivery phase then triggers new rounds of promises and commitments to customer personnel, outside vendors, and each other internally as we process, fill, ship, bill, and follow up on the order. Then comes after-sale support that can range from almost none for supermarket goodies to endless for medical treatment or new aircraft or software or manufacturing equipment, where staying functional and keeping up never end. And so do the risks and rewards of customer retention.

We make more promises in more ways than we realize

An individual can promise and deliver on his or her own. But in multifunction organizations entirely separate individuals, groups, and "media" can be key players at each stage, with upstream people making promises that they expect others downstream to keep:

- ⊚ *Company to customer.* We presell customers and raise their expectations via our reputation, image, marketing communications, pricing, contracts and myriad other arms-length encounters, from initial awareness through the end of the relationship.

- ⊚ *Product and service to customer.* Customers and product reviewers test our promise-keeping ability first hand. They evaluate product and service fit and quality, product and people performance, reliability, aesthetics, warranties and presale and after-sale support. The user experience as a whole counts by raising expectations or lowering them. And customers and reviewers aren't quiet about disappointments.

- ⊚ *Employee to customer.* Through face-to-face, phone and other direct contacts, our people interact with customers throughout the life of the relationship, promising satisfaction in one area after another.

- ⊚ *Employee to employee.* Employees make oral and written "I will" promises to each other top down, bottom up and across functions and departments every day.

⊚   *Company and employee to value stream shipmates.*
    Promises flow both ways as we interact with suppliers,
    sales and after-sale intermediaries, plus other
    stakeholders upstream and downstream that we rely on to
    conduct business.

Each one of these promise-making encounters with customers
and each other constitutes a "moment of truth," a concept fathered
in the early 1980s by Jan Carlzon, CEO of Scandinavian Airlines
System, as discussed earlier in "The truth is always positive."

Moments of truth

Carlzon defined "moments of truth" as those countless encounters between customers and employees that motivate customers
to come back or take their business elsewhere. These "moments"
overwhelmingly take place outside of management's purview and
control. Primary control rests with frontline and support employees who deal with customers every day.

Now let's factor in Harvard professor Ted Levitt's insight (in
"Assumptions") that all "products" are basically intangible, because neither "tangibles" like cars nor "intangibles" like taxi rides
can be tested *reliably* in advance. Hence, people really don't buy
tangibles. They buy *intangibles—promises of satisfaction.* Services
ooze intangibility. Employees manufacture and remanufacture
services, not in factories but on the spot as they interact with
customers and make judgment calls. That complicates achieving consistent quality and managing the making and keeping of
promises during those moments-of-truth encounters.

The long-term trends tracked by the Claus Fornell International
Group (CFI), an organization of University of Michigan econo-
metric statisticians, bear this out. Over the years its annual American Consumer Satisfaction Index (ACSI) findings show that the
more service intensive the company or "product," the lower the
average customer satisfaction ratings.

No Fail Leadership vastly expands the contact arena beyond
personal customer encounters to encompass all the ways we make
promises listed above. Each encounter, per Jan Carlzon, challeng-

es us with a moment of truth that can make or break us. They occur not only within functions but across them, often simultaneously. Promises made in one arena frequently must be kept by players in another or several other arenas. And the promise makers should consider the ability of the promise keepers to keep the promises before making them. There's the rub. They often don't.

Attracting customers with the right promises is important but not enough. Keeping customers means keeping promises. Breaking a promise breaks the trust upon which customer relationships build and last. And that goes double for promises made to each other within an organization, where people must depend upon and trust each other day in and day out.

As I said: A promise can mean one of two very different things to its maker. It can mean an "I will" commitment or an "I might" intent.

To the receiver, it always means: "You will."

Promise Gaps

The gaps between promises made and promises kept—Promise Gaps—jeopardize credibility and trust externally and internally. They waste more money, time, talent, opportunity and goodwill than almost any other performance factor within company control, including lousy processes and process breakdowns.

Broadly speaking, promises made by our company, our products and services and our employees target two categories of stakeholders:

- *External:* Customers and other outside suppliers, middlemen, partners, watchdogs, and the like.

- *Internal:* Employees in the corporate family, sometimes geographically dispersed.

The promises employees make to each other may constitute a category as critical as promises to customers. If promises to colleagues in other departments, functions and nearby cubicles break down, so do promises to customers. And we often don't take internal promises seriously enough. In fact, we may not even think of them as promises, as commitments, or as moral obligations, just tasks with deadlines it would be nice to meet: "I might" versus "I will."

Think back to the Leadership Test and some of the breakdowns it cited: bogged-down implementations, problems that pile up without action, blaming and excuse making, weak communication, individual and group unresponsiveness and conflict, dissatisfied customers and, "We make too many promises we can't keep and don't keep all the promises we make."

The last one sums it up. Unkept promises permeate every problem. We may not even understand what customers internally or externally expect because we don't know what promises they have heard. We work around the inevitable problems and uncertainties the best we can on our own, but we feel left in the lurch. Even processes meant to minimize errors and defects can be too outdated, ill-conceived, inept and rigid to succeed. Hence, we duck accountability, communication and contact with each other to avoid "I will" commitments or the blame for not having kept them.

"I might" thinking destabilizes the first domino

The waste of time, manpower, money and resources that "I might" thinking precipitates mounts fast. Let me show you how.

NASA developed "critical path" scheduling in the 1960s to organize the hugely complex endeavor of putting a man on the moon in the least amount of time—an extraordinary promise and undertaking. We still use this tool today.

In brief, a critical path lists all the tasks required to finish a project. Some tasks can be worked on simultaneously. Others—the "critical" tasks—cannot proceed until requisite tasks have been completed. We cannot design, build and launch a spacecraft without the quality, on-budget, on-time contributions of thousands of employees, contractors and subcontractors, plus fast-track decision making by all the government agencies, armed services, political and other national and state stakeholders involved.

Our daily projects don't normally require critical path project management. But every task we undertake, even if important but not urgent, has a critical path that completes it in the shortest possible time.

When someone makes a promise to complete something critical for us and fails, the first domino falls. Then others. Our whole project runs late by the length of the time it takes to prop the fallen dominoes back up.

97% Factors

The high cost of commitments not kept

Guesstimate the hours you actually expended to complete some task. What's the total?

Total the best-case, critical-path hours for you to complete the task if everyone meets deadlines.

Subtract the best-case from the estimated actual total, factoring in time for extra prodding, rescheduling, meetings, client service, mistakes, redesign, etc. Is the difference double, triple, ten times the hours you ought to have spent?

Estimate your labor cost per hour and multiply. What's the total?

Every penny constitutes waste. And we've only talked about your piece of the larger project and your hours. We haven't calculated the other costs that accumulate waiting for the larger project to finish, which could be holding up others.

What about all the other projects and tasks on our list?

Our project and task list documents promises of accomplishment by a certain date, even though we may not think of the list that way.

How many projects are on it? Do they suffer the same critical-path fates as the single task? Then so do everyone else's. Our delays set our colleagues back, compounding the hours, days and months lost. Further, we may have to put our other projects on hold while we turn our organization upside down trying to get the first project back on track. More delays. More collateral damage. And scrambling to catch up instantly raises the chances of human lapses and errors occurring despite established processes.

The result: do it once, then do it over. To the rework, add the waste in manpower, lost opportunities, profits and competitiveness from projects finished late or not at all, plus the toll that the frustration takes on us and our colleagues.

How did we get into this mess!

We make some of these promises to customers to get their business. We make some to people internally so that they can complete their assignment. Some promises others make to us so that we can complete our assignments.

We make some promises voluntarily, as part of our job or in a show of collegiality. Some promises our superiors or their superiors make for us and assign us to fulfill them, like it or not.

We find ourselves scrambling to meet expectations—theirs, customers' and our own. Out of frustration and desperation, we come to treat interdepartmental projects we don't initiate as someone else's problem, a distant second to our own. Some promises we can't keep or never should have made at all. Worst case, we deny we made them, but they stack up anyway.

No wonder implementations bog down and problems pile up without solution. No wonder major projects languish and die and we disappoint customers and each other, pointing fingers to escape blame.

Beware of pawning these off as process problems

The overpromising and under-delivering go on despite well-engineered processes, sabotaging our best laid plans. Do poor processes get in the way of promise keeping? Absolutely. They spawn many of the workarounds that toe no line and the failures that occur when workarounds don't work.

Do well-oiled processes safeguard us from our failures to perform? To a point. But we can't end overpromising and under-delivering through standard process improvement. We make promises by choice. Bad promises reflect bad choices even when good choices abound, for reasons ranging from naiveté to business pressures to personal ambition. The consequences reflect promise breakdowns to be fixed, not through process improvement but through promise improvement. Promise improvement starts with this recognition and admission.

Are we blind?

No. We have chosen not to see. We expect others to keep promises, but we don't want to eyeball ourselves in a mirror. So we tacitly agree with coworkers to chalk up miscarriages to human nature, too much work or other forces beyond our control. Or to someone's ineptitude. We zealously perfect our processes and then beat each other up with the "accountability" brickbat for not meeting deadlines or expectations. It doesn't occur to us that the larger problem of making and keeping promises goes beyond processes and accountability. Processes cannot solve promise problems, or they already would have. The usual models don't incorporate the concept.

We need promise improvement, not just process improvement

I have found that "promise improvement" motivates people far more powerfully than "process improvement." Processes are impersonal. They emphasize and reward conformance over individual talents and strengths, initiative, ingenuity and adaptability. Making promises and keeping them are deeply personal endeavors that activate most people's innate desire to live up to their own expectations as well as the expectations of others. In service activities this impulse makes the difference between mediocre and outstanding performance.

We need to think carefully about the promises we intend to make before we make them and be prepared to commit to fulfill them. Then we need to organize and align ourselves to be better at making and keeping promises than any competitor.

BUILDING A PROMISE-CENTERED ORGANIZATION

STEP 1: Find a promise that breaks new ground.

What do customers need, want and value?

We think we know. But do we? Maybe we did once upon a time, but losing touch proceeds as relentlessly as aging. Customer perceptions about us and our promises do not have to be current or accurate. If customers consider our products and services second-rate, they're second-rate, no matter how good we think they are.

Value as customers perceive it counts far more than value as sellers perceive it. Sellers don't call all the shots. Customers have minds of their own.

What customers really value and what we want them to value can be miles apart, resulting in bad choices of promises to make and where to focus promise-keeping resources. Market and customer research alone cannot give us the answers. We need to figure out what perceptions and misperceptions shape the decisions we make.

What do competitors offer, promise, deliver and fail to deliver?

Sales, technical support and customer service employees that field questions every day can accumulate a patchwork of general knowledge of how we and competitors stack up on features, benefits and product and service performance. For most, assessing prowess on promise performance ventures into new territory.

Consider doing a "promise" analysis of companies, brands and their products and services that you regard as relevant competitors. Examine everything each one promises to potential and existing customers in advertising, web-based communications, collateral, and public relations efforts, news and independent watchdog assessments, plus verbal promises and promise failures reported by customers, field sales people and others.

Single out what promises each competitor makes, which promises are unique and which ones aren't, which they live up to and which they don't. Out of this marketplace of ideas will emerge an illuminating and often surprising picture. You will learn:

- What the marketplace and individual competitors think that customers value, which as we know could be way off the mark

- Each competitor's vulnerabilities that we can exploit when helping customers weigh relative costs and benefits

Each competitor presents what it believes—and wants us to believe—that it excels at and its competitors do not. Most make the expected overall superiority claims, but their supporting evidence differs. It ranges from demonstrable uniqueness to me-too reassurances of parity performance to absence of comment altogether.

Omissions can signal things they're not good at, believe irrelevant or haven't thought of. What a competitor fails to talk about can raise a red flag, like a new wonder-drug with hush-hushed side effects.

We will find that some companies have a clear concept of where their competitive advantage lies and stay on message. Others try to be all things to all people, shot-gunning us with every sales pellet they can stuff into a shell, hoping one will hit the mark. For us, gaps and vulnerabilities offer opportunities.

How good is our business category's promise of performance versus kindred categories?

We need to know the state-of-the-art of our industry's prowess—not just the best competitor's prowess—in understanding and fulfilling customer needs and wants, making promises and keeping them. We may be better than any direct competitor, but our industry can pale compared with others. Remember the once-shining airline industry? It now scores near the bottom on customer satisfaction. All those frequent flyers that covet their various Apples, stay in major hotels and eat at full service restaurants know when they are well served and when they're not.

What do we *currently* offer, promise, deliver and fail to deliver?

Now let's add our enterprise to the promise analysis, assessing ourselves as we assessed others.

What *could* we offer and deliver of unique value in the marketplace of promises?

Despite protestations to the contrary, even the most service intensive companies I have studied spend far more time thinking about themselves than about their market, customers and mission in life. Just making it from one day to the next jousting with the windmills of internal dysfunction diverts attention and energy from asking "where next," from clearing the path and then reaching the destinations that matter most.

Our businesses aren't philanthropies, but thinking beyond our parochial interest to survive can birth new ways to enrich our customers, employees, stakeholders and communities. Stand in customers' shoes. Think of the predicaments they find themselves in every day as people trying to make emotional and survival ends meet. Is there hidden value in our enterprise, products or services that makes us even more valuable than we know?

Consider ServiceMaster's "higher purpose."

When management guru Peter Drucker asked ServiceMaster's company directors what business they were in, they answered: "housecleaning," "insect extermination," "lawn care." Drucker said, "Wrong. Your business is to train the least-skilled people and make them functional."

So that's what ServiceMaster did. "Least functional" doesn't necessarily mean "least intelligent or industrious." It can mean "bright, ambitious, but unschooled." Cleaning and tending homes became a magic carpet to success, an occupation with honor and dignity, neither demeaning nor petty. Business grew to $3.5 billion, thanks to Drucker's insight.

I can almost guarantee that there is some higher purpose in your business too, and chances are that no competitor will have spotted it in their own. Find it. It's a rich source of breakthrough ideas and promises worth gold.

Answering these questions will take you a long way

◆ *What's missing, what's overlooked?*

What do serious customers need, want and value that neither we nor competitors have recognized or sought to provide? Almost invariably, something critical we have overlooked fuels a breakthrough, big or little, but significant nonetheless. We miss it because everyone is busy playing to each other, blind to what over time has come to count.

- ◆ *What unique, meaningful value could we offer, promise, and deliver?*

What could set us apart from our most direct competitors and potentially pioneer entirely new markets? That's what Apple achieved in mobile phones and computers and Microsoft in business and personal software propelling them into higher orbits that left competitors in their stardust. And think of the extraordinary standards Disney's parks set in serving and entertaining families.

What I'm talking about goes way beyond advertising and selling. These are wars of promise making more than promise keeping. Promise keepers may feel no particular attachment to whatever the promises promise makers in marketing put on parade. The unique, breakthrough promises we're after invite workers enterprise wide to join in a mission-driven, competitive adventure that they believe in and leadership supports.

Step 2: Gear up for bolder promises, better kept.

What bolder, interim promises could we make right now while gearing up to make and keep the game-changer we've got in our sights?

Bolder promises

We must be selective and realistic. We need to identify and articulate the promises we currently make, can legitimately make and legitimately cannot (at least not yet)—overpromising leads us down a dark path that promise makers too often ignore. Each interim promise should chisel a step up our Mt. Everest, not up lesser mountains we may have been climbing thus far. And each foothold should be firm enough that we can keep promises we make while chiseling out the next step higher up, building trust among today's buyers and users for the bolder promises we'll be making tomorrow.

Better kept

A myriad of promises emanating from our company's people, products, and services circulate among employees, customers, business associates and the public, usually with inconsistent, disconnected coordination and oversight. How can we align promise making and promise keeping so that they don't operate at cross purposes, short term and long term? Three ways: situational, methodological and holistic. Promise improvement takes effort on all three fronts.

Aligning interim promise making with promise keeping

◆   *Situational alignment as problems arise*

We exploit promise breakdowns as opportunities to experiment with better ways to keep the promises we already make, both to customers and each other:

- ◉   We take stock of our day-to-day, cross-functional predicaments and misunderstandings.

- ◉   We jointly segment these into what's possible, problematic and impossible to accomplish.

- ◉   From that list we agree on what we can and cannot promise.

- ◉   Working together, we stretch ourselves to keep the critical promises by eliminating obvious disconnects that undermine promise performance.

This tactical, operational approach may not be comprehensive, but it generates quick results. Employees usually want the bottlenecks removed and pitch in to find solutions. If the leader also understands the methodological and holistic approaches, then workarounds and other interim solutions can be upgraded into pilot tests of forward-looking solutions with potential to scale up.

Be careful. We must not make even legitimate promises or conduct promise-delivery experiments without alerting and readying the promise keepers. Employees need to know what they are up against, where they as individuals and groups fit into the promise-keeping picture and what's expected of them. Current ways of operating may be overtaxed or inadequate to deliver as promised. Informal processes may have to supersede old ways, at least temporarily, particularly under pressure. Employees with experience and ingenuity can fill cracks, but only if armed with knowledge of the larger context and purpose of the endeavor.

When I work with frontline and support employees, I find that they know too little about the basis for the work that upstream departments send their way. They know even less about the marching orders and predicaments the senders operate under and what they expect the receivers to accomplish beyond the obvious. People farther downstream seem just as ignorant as everyone else about the larger "why" behind the "what" they do. That creates the costly disconnects and promise failures that informed employees could have finessed completely—"If only I had known!"

◆   *Methodological alignment—through process, technological, and other improvements that serve promise performance ends*

When we stop thinking of what we do as "getting work out" and start thinking of it as "making and keeping promises," then everything changes.

We will view processes devised to ensure defect-free throughput as means to a promise-keeping end, not as ends in themselves. We will see handoffs between departments and functions as make-or-break baton passes in a team relay, not casual exchanges.

We don't scrap Lean Six Sigma and other production-bred processes. We redirect, refine or redesign them. Build upon them. Implement them cross-functionally. They establish one aspect of a companywide methodology for keeping routine promises that are repetitive by design, such as filling and shipping orders on time.

But the purpose of such processes is generic. And despite their utility, generic processes can seem more inflexible, impersonal and oppressive than empowering and helpful. Like IQ tests, they deal best with problems where a right answer already exists, such as what constitutes "no errors," "no defects" or "no delays" in specific situations.

Ambiguity, not by-the-book responses, permeates moment-of-truth encounters that challenge us with the unexpected. We need to create solutions, experiment and sometimes adapt on the fly. The underground world of informal processes flourishes to contend with this reality.

Step 3: Align strategically and holistically behind a common cause.

What would our enterprise look like if we realigned it to keep the strategic promise we intend to make? How do we band together in this common cause?

The third way

The strategic, holistic way surpasses others long term. It takes paradigm shifts in thinking about what's really possible. Promises are far more than disposable expediencies for selfish advancement. Promises by their very nature carry moral and ethical power. Gutsy promises emanating from the mission benefit from that fact. The resolve to keep the promises bridges cross-functional gaps by not tolerating gaps. And employees have no doubt about what counts and what doesn't. That turbocharges performance and eliminates carloads of waste. I find few companies endowed with this clarity.

In organizations, the clarity springs from the "mission," the much maligned, misunderstood mission that all too often enshrines clichés instead of a cause. Not all missions are like that. Let's start with a powerful, chillingly clear exception:

The United States Army:
The management of violence

It's a mission we must not fail to achieve. What's its promise? To win any war by managing the violence. Like it or not, war is violence. Which side would you rather have managing the violence, the enemy's or ours? That'll get the adrenaline pumping. And recruit a volunteer army. Beyond that, this mission gives the reason why the Army has had no interest in patrolling our borders to stop illegal aliens—that's not mission relevant. As mission examples go, this one ranks among the best. It's short, clear, motivating and narrowly focused on what counts.

The Army's current mission adds the objectives of post-combat governance and rebuilding to consolidate victory. Military planners once left that mainly to civilians. Managing the violence to oust Saddam Hussein went like clockwork. Managing governance and rebuilding of a nation demanded a whole new skill set the Army has had to accumulate through experimentation, "market" feedback, adaptation, innovation and evolution, not unlike in business. At least we now know what not to do—attack and win handily amidst "the fog of war" without a plan to manage the aftermath and adapt agilely to "the fog of governance."

**The mission: A promise that matters plus
a promise to deliver**

- *A good mission defines the long-term purpose of the business, one that's worthwhile for the company and for society.*

The word "mission" means *outreach* (L. *missus,* to send) and so does "promise" (L. *promissum,* to send forth). But most companies reach no farther than "quality products and service, happy employees, and profits"—in short, self-preservation.

+   *It creates a promissory relationship between customers and the company, its employees and its other stakeholders.*

Above all a mission statement is a promise of performance to the people we claim we serve. If we don't first honor the promise to them, then we will disappoint the employees, partners, investors and other stakeholders that expect to see long-term returns on their commitments of career and money.

+   *It provides clear direction on where to focus energy, thought, activity and resources most productively, adding value.*

When Scandinavian Airline's CEO Jan Carlzon handed off the handling of moments-of-truth promise keeping with customers to frontline employees, he also empowered them with the authority and resources to handle the encounters on the spot. Employees loved the new freedom. And they used it wisely. Other CEOs that tried to transplant the SAS model into their own organizations met with mixed success. Liberated employees ran off unchaperoned on misguided empowerment sprees.

Carlzon's mission for SAS provided the focus. First, he knew that SAS did not have the size or resources to survive in competition with major airlines for both business and tourist travelers. He picked business travelers and penned a superlative mission statement with a promise no competitor had ever made:

SAS: To be The Business Airline

Relevant, focused, simple, clear, and unique, a flag around which Carlzon's troops wanted to rally.

+   *A good mission clearly identifies what not to do, eliminating waste.*

Next Carlzon went over the annual budget line by line. Remember that SAS was $50 million in the red at the time and considered the worst airline in the world. The test was this: If a budget item advanced the mission, SAS would spend more on it. If it didn't, he eliminated it. If it looked more yes than no, he left it alone. This was mission-driven budgeting, no waste exempted. But no person axed. He couldn't. The workforce was unionized. So he reassigned people.

Have you ever gone over your own budget Carlzon's way, red-, yellow- and green-lining each item based on mission relevance? Try it. If nothing changes, check your mission for relevance, focus, simplicity and clarity.

SAS's discipline didn't end with "The Business Airline" mission and the budget review. The mission disciplined decision making, behavior and action as well.

Example: SAS's Tokyo office proposed that its burgeoning number of Japanese tourist groups stop over free at SAS's Anchorage hotel instead of flying direct over Siberia.[1] They could arrive rested in Scandinavia late morning, sightsee and save one night's hotel expenses. The idea was good for tourists, but bad for business travelers, who would rather get there fast, pay for a destination hotel, rise early and do business all day. Per the mission, Carlzon vetoed the stopover idea.

◆   *It inspires, mobilizes and empowers mission driven,*
     united, heroic effort on the front line and
     cross-functionally behind it.

SAS heavily trained its employees on and near the front line to follow Carlzon's lead. If the act of the moment advanced the mission, employees went ahead with it. If it didn't, they didn't.

Examples: If a businesswoman snagged her hose on a loose screw, flight attendants could dip into petty cash so the passenger could buy new ones before leaving the airport. No forms. No checks in the mail.

Employees could even marshal expensive resources to aid a business class traveler in a legitimate fix. One supervisor arranged for a limo to meet an SAS plane arriving late in New York from

1 Jan Carlzon, *Moments of Truth* (New York: Ballinger Publishing Co., 1987), 56.

Copenhagen. He offloaded the businessman on the tarmac, expedited customs, and rushed him to a helicopter that flew him to a gathering of businesspeople worldwide to sign a contract with a 5 p.m. drop-deadline. The passenger arrived with four minutes to spare. Business class travelers received this largess directly. Tourists benefited through service improvements that benefited everyone.

- *It draws to itself energetic, like-minded talent.*

How about the National Aeronautics and Space Administration's mission at the beginning of the space race?

NASA
*Put a man on the moon
and return him safely to earth*

NASA had no trouble attracting the most brilliant talent in the U.S. Neither have Microsoft nor Apple nor other pioneering enterprises whose products and services provided value to humanity far beyond any the founders could have envisioned.

- *It wins wars.*

The United States Army's "The Management of Violence," SAS's "to be The Business Airline," and NASA's race to the moon succeeded on all criteria for superb missions—a rare feat—and won their wars.

We cannot build a promise-centered organization without a promise that's so powerful and meaningful that keeping it deserves our total commitment to the people we seek to serve in a competitive marketplace and also to us as promise makers. Without that powerful "why," the promise-keeping efforts of the most dedicated workforce ever assembled will be a tragic waste. That "why" comes directly from the enterprise's mission. And its foundation rests upon mother lodes that others have not discovered.

As leaders we need a mission as concise, unambiguous and inspiring as the U.S. Army's and SAS's.

Don't do battle without one.

Missions that lead nowhere

When I find a business that stretches its dollars, people and resources too thinly and without sharp focus, I usually also find a business with one of three problems:

* *An obsolete or wrong mission*

The company squanders its time, money, talent and energy committing slow suicide treading yesteryear's paths into what has become a desert.

* *A mission that's more cliché than cause*

The mission sounds lofty, but unlike SAS's, it provides no clear direction for what to do and critically what not to do.

I once asked the president of a hospital, whose mission was to improve the health of the community through superior care, "How would you know if you were succeeding?"

"I don't know," he replied after a pause. "I suppose we'd have less business. Fewer people would need us."

"Well," I responded, "how're ya doin'?"

"We're growing."

A mission with its embedded values gives leaders the direction and authority to focus and unite people behind a high-power, high-value goal. What about your company's mission? Does it mobilize people passionately behind a common cause? Win wars? Or is it just so many platitudes and clichés?

Without a compelling mission, all activity is just vibration. Top management, pressed by deadlines and bottom lines, becomes distanced from people on the front line. That leaves employees without a leader or a cause. We get distracted by opportunities and problems of the moment that divide and disperse us on wild goose chases. We may perform our duties conscientiously and process-perfectly, but we toil without esprit de corps, conviction or the old missionary zeal. Promises suffer, and so do service and quality.

+ *No mission at all*

Businesses that spring up to exploit an invention or hot market opportunity tend to "exploit" first and think about their long-term purpose later. The company points everywhere and nowhere, a rudderless ship that's content with producing, selling and staying afloat. Eventually it drifts so far off course that employees forget why it sailed.

Go, team, go!

Stephen Covey's book *The 8th Habit: From Effectiveness to Greatness* reported the results of a disturbing Harris Interactive poll of 23,000 employees from various industries:

- Only 37% said they had a clear understanding of what their organization was trying to achieve and why.

- Only 1 in 5 was enthusiastic about their team's and organization's goals.

- Only 1 in 5 workers said they had a clear "line of sight" between their tasks and their team's and organization's goals.

- Only 15 percent felt that their organization fully enabled them to execute key goals.

- Only 13 percent had high-trust, highly cooperative working relationships with other groups or departments.

He then breathed life into the stats. He applied them to a sports team: "If, say, a soccer team had these same scores, only 4 of the 11 players on the field would know which goal is theirs. Only 2 of the 11 would care. Only 2 of the 11 would know what positions they play and know exactly what they are supposed to do. And all but 2 players would, in some way, be competing against their own team members rather than the opponent."[2]

The statistics and message from this huge survey certainly paralleled the gist of the findings coming out of No Fail Leadership's 12-question test despite its far smaller sample size. Employees report feeling disconnected and disengaged from their employer, the mission, their leaders, coworkers and customers. They question the work they do and the value of doing it.

And we can quantify the financial consequences.

Employee and customer satisfaction predict financial performance

When customer satisfaction improves, sales improve. The same holds for employee satisfaction. When satisfaction improves, sales increase. When satisfaction declines, sales fall.

This makes sense. You and I return to sellers we learn to trust, in part because we haven't the time or inclination to research all options on all purchases. We appreciate quality products and service and expert advice. We may even get to know and like the staff. It reciprocates by going out of its way to exceed expectations. That raises our loyalty and price tolerance and lowers our susceptibility to the lures of competitors.

But as sellers of products and services, we had better not take anything for granted. Our product quality does not guarantee our service quality and vice versa. We can be great at one and terrible at the other. And service quality today does not guarantee customer satisfaction tomorrow. Today's promises, even when we keep them 100%, can look paltry compared to a trend-setting competitor that ups benefits, halves delivery times, lowers costs, and captures the imagination.

Customers benchmark our promise making and keeping against all industries, not just our own. The bar inches up with every improvement, challenging us to jump even higher and potentially emerge as our industry's premier bar-raiser.

---

2 Stephen Covey, *The 8th Habit: From Effectiveness to Greatness* (New York: Free Press, 2004) 2.

A good mission is hard to find and promises are hard to fulfill, but the payoff is worth the effort

A good mission makes a powerful, competitive promise of satisfaction that we stand ready, willing and able to make and keep.

But even the most powerful mission can't leap off its monument and implement itself. It needs a champion, generals and an army. Bringing the mission to life changes the way we conceive and produce our products and services. A compelling mission changes the promises we make, how we make them, and how well we keep them during those critical moments of truth. It also changes the way customers perceive us and their level of satisfaction. Deliver as promised, and up goes the company's reputation. And so do its fortunes.

Over time I have become increasingly convinced that breakdowns in making promises and keeping them do more damage to performance and productivity and create more waste than almost any factor under management control, including process breakdowns.

Whether the promises of performance are made situationally as employees interact with customers and each other, methodologically through quality processes, products and services, or strategically by the mission and corporate communications, the promises must be the right ones or they cannot and will not be kept.

The right promises ...

Are ones we can legitimately make ... and can keep.
Stretch the company ... but not the truth.
Offer exceptional, meaningful value ... as customers see it.
Leave competitors in the dust and ...

... are kept.

97% Factors

Promise making in your enterprise

What promises were made or implied?

Which were kept and not kept?

Looking back, were the overall performance breakdowns process or promise breakdowns?

What is needed most: promise improvement or process improvement?

The promise-centered enterprise

What promises are stated or embedded in your mission?

Does your company deliver what it promises? More? Less?

Does it out-compete or lag behind others on promise performance?

Is your company's mission even relevant to what the company does, or is it more cliché than cause?

PRINCIPLE 9

Etch all decisions in jell.

Everything we do in life is a pilot test.
Even doing nothing is a pilot test of doing nothing.

WHETHER WE RECOGNIZE IT OR NOT, everything we do is an experiment. Picking a college. Parenthood. Home ownership. Switching employers. Taking risks or playing it safe. Making it big or going broke. Or both.

How much did you really know about the college you chose on your first day in your first class? Or about your employer your first day on the job? Like settlers heading west in a covered wagon, we have plans, hopes and maybe even expectations. But we have no certainties. Just pilot tests.

Doing nothing is as much of a pilot test as doing something. Dawdling while reality strides by, barely noticed, has ramifications, like obsolescence and irrelevance. We wake up in a future we don't recognize, scrambling to catch up.

Decisions are educated guesses

Decisions are no better than the best that we can make at the time. View feedback, decision readjustment—even reversal—as continuous improvement, not a negative reflection on our ability to decide. The most important decision we may ever make is the decision to embrace the truth, change and grow. That's called, "learning."

Principle 9, *Etch all decisions in jell*, presents a strategy for adapting with agility, managing risk under fire and out-distancing competition. Following it has its upsides:

- ⊙ We make increasingly sound decisions the first time, under normal circumstances, under pressure, and when in crisis. We learn what to look for at thirty thousand, three thousand and three feet. We also learn how life, problems and solutions intertwine.

- ⊙ We devise better, more holistic solutions and implementation strategies for problems we can solve that readily scale up to solve larger problems. We ask the right questions, detect and diagnose the right problems, and preempt solutions with unintended consequences.

- ⊙ We spot implementation problems quickly, intervene early and fix them before they metastasize, upping the chances of immediate and long-term success.

- ⊙ We document, absorb and apply lessons learned to each new venture, upping the odds of ultimate success.

"All decisions can't be etched in jell!" What happened to staying the course?

Certainly anything that took a major investment in time, money and manpower to create—or a long time to settle into—can be hard to change, like production lines, company software, and comfy status quos. That doesn't exempt them from readjustment.

In reality, no conflict exists between staying the strategic course and etching plans and implementations in jell. Most tactical and short-term decisions achieve strategic long-term results more consistently and fully when etched in jell than in stone. So do ambitious, long-term undertakings. If strategically relevant endeavors fail despite superb execution, then we have reason to rethink the corporate strategy. Clumsily executed endeavors on the other hand tell us nothing about the validity of the overall strategy, only about the clumsiness of attempts to advance it.

Naysayers love clumsiness. Decisions etched in stone provide stationary targets they can chip into rubble, advancing nothing. Decisions etched in jell absorb blows, adapt, and come out stronger than ever. Success gets closer, not farther away.

We know less than we think we do

If we really knew as much as we like to presume, then how come we don't really know:

⊚　Why implementations, performance and productivity bog down.

⊚　Why we work around problems, run for cover, blame others and let problems pile up instead of solving them.

⊚　Why internal groups complain about and avoid each other instead of communicating and cooperating in solving mutual problems.

⊚　Why we fail to understand or meet customer expectations, make promises we can't keep, and don't keep the promises we can keep.

If we knew more we'd have these Leadership Test problems behind us or under control. And we wouldn't be so mystified and frustrated why they're not, despite our best attempts. The greater the general frustration, the greater the pressure management feels to appear in control, act decisively, project certainty about the outcome, and perform as pledged in every detail—even in the most ambiguous, fluid, precarious situations.

Mindsets: Pre-etched to flourish or fail

Fear of personal loss is a common denominator in dysfunctional organizations. It underlies the misguided decisions carved in stone that litter the business landscape.

But something even deeper goes on here that starts with individual mindsets preprogrammed to etch decisions in stone instead of in jell. I have been puzzling over this phenomenon in leadership circles for years without finding a good answer.

Stanford professor Dr. Carol S. Dweck has one.

Why do some people, she asked in the late 1960s, achieve their potential even in the most dire, chaotic circumstances? Why do others succumb to them or end up as the paragons of the ineptitude and bully-hood documented separately by Harvard professor Barbara Kellerman in *Bad Leadership* and Stanford Professor Robert I. Sutton in *The No Asshole Rule?*

Carol Dweck's *Mindset: The New Psychology of Success* bares the roots. Her early research asked, "What makes a really capable child give up in the face of failure, where other children may be motivated by the failure?" She found that children who interpreted repeat failures solving problems as lack of ability gave up prematurely, even in areas of known competency. They self-fulfilled their prophesy through "learned helplessness." The researchers trained other children to try harder. These kids worked until they succeeded, expecting no less.

Dweck tells the story of youngsters who were instructed to think out loud as they solved increasingly difficult puzzles on the blackboard. One boy finally ran up against a problem he couldn't solve. He "pulled up his chair, rubbed his hands together, smacked his lips and announced, 'I love a challenge.'" [1] Failure wasn't an option. It wasn't even failure. It was a key to unlock a door leading to other doors with more difficult locks and more interesting rooms that quitters never learn to enter.

Quitters would rather look smart than learn. They duck challenges where success isn't certain. They look for easy wins that prove how smart they are. And, per Dr. Dweck, the level of ability did not differentiate the showoffs from the learners—not the

1 Carol S. Dweck, Ph.D., *Mindset: The New Psychology of Success* (New York; Ballantine, 2006), 3.

I.Q. or natural athletic, artistic or other talent. "Every situation is evaluated: Will I succeed or fail? Will I look smart or dumb? Will I be accepted or rejected? Will I feel like a winner or a loser?"[2]

Dweck next wondered why some students fixate on showing off their ability while others focus on learning. Ability, she realized, had two meanings: "fixed ability that needs to be proven, and a changeable ability that can be developed through learning."[3] The two meanings birthed Dweck's two mindsets—"fixed" and "growth." Dweck's table, which I have augmented with other critical points she makes, compares the two.

FIXED MINDSET	⇨ ISSUE ⇨	GROWTH MINDSET
Intelligence static, innate. "I am what I am."	INTELLIGENCE	Can be developed.
Look smart, performance is everything.	INNER DRIVE	Stretch, learn, develop; fulfill potential.
"I'm a failure." (my identity) Setback, loss, rejection threaten the ego. Proves lack of ability—a secret to protect.	FAILURE MEANS	"I failed." (an action) A natural, necessary stepping-stone for learning and improvement. Not failing = not growing.
Repeat easy wins. Avoid challenges that risk performance failures.	CHALLENGES	Thrive on challenges, innovative solutions. Explore where curiosity leads.
Give up easily.	OBSTACLES	Persist in the face of setback.
Effort fruitless; can't learn "I'm no good at that." Or worse: "Superstars don't need to train." Effort bespeaks imperfection.	EFFORT	The path to mastery. If you fall short, then try again and harder. Effort *makes* you smarter, more talented.
Ignore useful, negative feedback or squelch it.	CRITICISM	Learn from criticism.
Feel threatened by the success of others.	SUCCESS OF OTHERS	Find lessons and inspiration in the success of others.
Plateau early, achieve less than potential.	RESULT	Reach ever-higher levels of achievement.
Deterministic world.	WORLD VIEW	Sense of free will.

---

2 Ibid., 6
3 Ibid., 15

Recognize anyone?

Think about your family, friends, boss and coworkers. Or about people in positions of power or in the public eye. Or, most of all, yourself.

How many are so driven to look smart that they avoid challenges, give up easily, see effort as an admission of imperfection, lash out at critics, ignore useful feedback, and feel threatened by the success of others? These are Dweck's fixed mindset youngsters all grown up. Some don the trappings of royalty, others of victimhood. Either way, they come with inflated self-esteem, fragile egos, and an entitlement mentality. They crave status and power and use both to control and demean others. They carve decisions in stone to look all-knowing and intimidate critics. Then they deny responsibility and blame others when things go wrong.

Dweck fingers Lee Iacocca, CEO of Chrysler during its rise and fall, and tennis champion John McEnroe, the CEO of his own rise and fall. Per Dweck, Iacocca met the invasion of Japanese Hondas and Toyotas with angry demands for government tariffs and quotas instead of building better cars[4]. He fired critics, plus underlings who came up with good ideas he hadn't thought of. And he spent time fiddling with his public "hero" image while Chrysler burned. McEnroe rarely lost a battle because an opponent outplayed him. The fault lay with a backache or fever or tabloid reports, or being too fat or thin, undertraining or over-training, a day too hot or cold, or because of noise from a courtside cameraman.[5] Above all, because of stupid line judges.

Conversely, how many people do you know in business who love to learn, relish challenges, persist in the face of setbacks, view criticism as vital input, succeed and find lessons and inspiration in the success of others? Dweck features Jack Welch of GE, Lou Gerstner of IBM and Anne Mulcahy of Xerox, who breathed life into their exalted-but-sick companies following near-death experiences.[4]

Dweck's telling observation was this: "In not one autobiography of a fixed-mindset CEO did I read much about mentoring or employee development programs. In every growth-mindset auto-

4 Ibid., 125-133

biography, there was deep concern with personnel development and extensive discussion of it."[5]

Which CEOs do you think will seek you out and value what you and other employees think when the going gets rough? Which CEOs will insist upon honest feedback? And which won't hesitate to admit mistakes, learn from them under pressure, adjust quickly, and not worry about credit or blame? Which will prevail? Not Dweck's fixed-mindset people. Not the incompetent, rigid, intemperate, callous, corrupt, insular, and evil leaders Professor Kellerman skewers. Not Professor Sutton's "assholes."

Fixed-mindset people will select options that best avoid personal risk, even if this puts the company in jeopardy. Iacocca refused to entertain good ideas about better cars because he didn't author them. And if they didn't work, he'd look bad. McEnroe shunned mixed doubles for fear of embarrassing himself again after losing in three embarrassing sets at Wimbledon.

Welch, Gerstner, and Mulcahy deliberately ferreted out fixed-mindset people in their organizations and got rid of them. They kept the people who were intent on learning and growing.

And that's who we want with us in the foxhole under fire. They're looking out for everyone, not just Number One.

Reprogramming fixed minds

In business, the more intense the pressure stakeholders put on management for short-term performance, the more pressure managers feel to promise quick, certain results. Stakeholders that demand ironclad commitments in uncertain times deify fixed-mindset thinkers, excommunicate growth mindset thinkers, and then intimidate everyone to clear-cut whatever looks green to meet short-term financial goals.

Remember that fixed-mindset people don't trust themselves to perform to expectations. They believe that others have the same flaw and will slack off unless spurred into an all-consuming race to a finish line on a short track. They have no patience with etched-in-jell thinking. It scares them.

---

5 Ibid., 112-113

Encouragingly, people who have followed the first eight Principles generally accept "etch all decisions in jell" as a logical extension of the Principles that led up to it and have already traveled far toward unfixing their fixed mindset.

HOW NO FAIL LEADERSHIP'S PRINCIPLES BUILD GROWTH MINDSETS

1. All problems stem from conflicts of belief about what's true.

We put beliefs and conflicts on hold, etching them in jell while examining what's really going on. Once aired, instant solutions based on simplistic beliefs look lightweight even to the fixed-mindset showoffs that float them.

2. Nothing is ever what it seems. The truth lies elsewhere.

We actively look for truth, etching judgments in jell. Even thoroughly conceived plans cannot uncover everything relevant up front and foresee all consequences. Each surprise awakens us to "elsewheres" filled with truths and mind opening lessons. Looking together reveals enough surprises to give fixed mindsets reason to pause.

3. The truth is always positive, even when it's painful.

If we're not deciding based upon truth, then what's our foundation? Wishful thinking, half-truths, outright lies? Why carve simplistic decisions in stone? Truth will just jackhammer them into rubble. Decisions made under pressure but etched in jell bounce back, remolded.

4. Make it 100% safe to tell the truth.

Agility necessitates quick, accurate news from the front, good and bad. Fixed mindsets only want news that validates their prejudgments. But once they experience safety and value in truthful feedback, some wake up in growth country that's far less threatening than imagined.

5. No blame, no excuses.

When we don't lay blame, we don't have to make excuses or listen to them. Etching decisions in jell makes honest feedback natural and normal. Get the hang of it, and the growth mindset takes hold unnoticed.

6. Work from facts first, opinions later.

The weaker the evidence is, the stronger the opinions people hold and the likelier that their decisions will be wrong. When as a team we etch a decision in jell, we replace opinion with fact gradually and gracefully. Fixed mindsets discover the relief of not making snap judgments that snap back when evidence piles up. We all learn together. Decisions get better fast, with buy-in.

7. Get input from frontline people before making decisions they must implement, not after.

People embroiled in the daily battle will ask questions and tell us things we never thought of. Above all, we will know what we don't know, especially about unintended consequences. The details can threaten the superstar image of fixed mindsets: they already know all they need to know. Pausing for frontline input they consider dubious jeopardizes adoption of their ideas and agenda. Input shared makes matters worse for them. Too many people know too much. If results fall short people know the perpetrators, think them inept, and hold them culpable.

On the flip side, the Principle 7 "pause" to *get input from front-line people before making decisions they must implement* can help fixed mindsets and everyone else avoid rash, bad decisions they'd later have to explain or blame away. Frontline input introduces legitimate uncertainty into top-down decision making. Decisions get etched in jell, because stone isn't a palatable option. That's growth thinking.

8. Only make promises we can keep, and keep all the promises we make.

Promise making and promise keeping evolve as the makers and keepers strive to keep up with each other's demands. As cautioned earlier, each promise makes a hard commitment that we dare not etch in jell. To its maker it can mean "I will" or "I might." To its receiver it always means, "You will." Promises must not outstrip our ability to keep them, but we must keep perfecting our techniques and raising our bar. So, promise on the safe side of realistic. Stretch further as ligaments limber up. The better time to etch promises in jell is before we make them.

9. Etch all decisions in jell.

No room exists for fixed mindset thinking in these Principles. They remove the incentives and props. We discover how incomplete our knowledge really is. And how fallible. We realize that past assumptions, beliefs and experiences unreliably foretell future performance. And we recognize how blind we can be to naïve, maverick or self-serving behavior deep in our organization that can bushwhack us on the trail.

Etching decisions in jell is the only approach that makes sense. Carving them in stone makes no sense at all. The stone could be a gravestone.

Etching-in the "etched in jell" mindset

Make no mistake: etching decisions in jell does not license laissez-faire thinking and behavior, like doing something—anything—and hope it works out, or waiting, fingers crossed, for the situation to blow over.

On the contrary, etching decisions in jell demands responsibility and integrity. It demands that we make the best decisions up front that available input allows. Good decisions require decision makers who are clear-headed, hyper-alert, growth-minded doers who can see the forest and the trees. Sound tough? It may be. If it were easy, everyone would already be good at it. But as the boy at Dweck's blackboard said of the problem he hadn't yet solved, "I love a challenge!" Be the first on your block to rise to it and meet it. There's no first prize for second place.

To imprint the etched-in-jell mindset, we need to keep three overarching concepts in mind that, in my experience, few people entertain or apply:

- *Everything we do is a pilot test.*

That applies to an individual task or enterprise-wide overhaul, whether for the first time or the hundredth, whether deciding to act or to do nothing. The path to completion can look far different at strategic cruising altitude or when doing low-altitude flyovers than it does on the ground. It can also look different tomorrow than it does today, when ill-conceived or ossified ways of doing business suddenly break down.

- *Pilot tests are never "ends in themselves."*

They always do at least triple duty. They solve immediate problems. They point to ways to solve broader problems. And they teach problem-solving lessons that work anywhere. Problem solvers that fixate on the immediate fix miss the larger lessons because they don't know to look for them.

◆   *Forget about carving decisions and plans in stone.*

Every decision, every plan, every implementation begins a new test. Document the details and underlying assumptions up front. Look there first when things go wrong. And commit to implementing the pilot plan faithfully. If we don't, we will never know whether unforeseen problems trace to flawed assumptions, a flawed plan, or our mismanaged implementation.

ACTIVATING "ETCHED-IN-JELL"

Solving the right problems adds value.
Solving the wrong problems loots it.

The following criteria for selection come from lessons learned the hard way

◆   *Pick problems that can be solved.*

We're not trying to create world peace here. Management's impulse when besieged by problems is to solve as many as possible at the same time and for each, solve the whole problem. The bigger the company is, the stronger the gravity pulling toward big solutions. Some problems don't get fixed at all because under pressure the only fix management has patience for is the big fix—and balks at delaying it to test its wisdom and viability.

The trouble is, once big fixes gets rolling, they are hard to stop or redirect no matter how misdirected. More driven by fear and faith than facts, they invite failure after failure of the most corrosive kind—slow, expensive, maddening, etched in stone, often irreversible and fraught with unintended consequences. Nothing ever gets solved well.

Simple, strategically relevant short-term fixes may seem too little, too late. But if carefully orchestrated, they can usually solve a chunk of the problem quickly and cheaply while simultaneously pilot-testing approaches that refine and scale up into viable, comprehensive solutions. Problem solvers learn the value of a pilot test mentality and adopt it unencumbered by the burdens of doing over what they didn't do right the first time. And when the approved medium is jell, colleagues that fixate on big solutions find no granite slabs upon which to etch them.

- *Pick problems that teach and train skills for tackling more complex problems.*

Some problems—the ones we're looking for—force problem solvers into the thick of action that transcends their ability to emerge victorious on their own, demanding that they look far downrange to avoid winning a battle and losing the war. Such problems are not hard to find:

Pieces of Leadership Test problems.

These get us into the clouded world of obstacles, interactions between people and processes, infighting, misassumptions, informal processes and workarounds. Look for specific breakdowns in customer service and satisfaction, frontline implementation of management's best-laid plans, promise keeping among employees and between them and customers, plus breakdowns in communication, professionalism, performance, and overall agility. Don't forget to follow the money.

Cross-functional, multi-level problems.

That includes those that extend out to customers. We want employees to think outside their sandbox and understand the interrelatedness of everything that goes on within their organization and outside of it with the people they serve and the employees who serve them. Cross-functional workgroups quickly show how little people know, nipping counterproductive, myopic solutions to cross-functional problems in the bud.

Stepping-stone problems.

Solve specific, immediate problems that lead to solving broader, long-term problems. Choosing and solving the right problems lay steppingstones all the way to the far shore. Choose badly, and we wind up stranded on a rock to nowhere. Stepping-stone solutions advance two other objectives:

⦿ They teach us to think strategically while picking and solving problems tactically. We look at the big picture, target a landing spot on the opposite shore, plant one stone at a time and get there.

⦿ They leverage the effort and advance the larger cause instead of inadvertently erecting barriers. Solutions that focus solely on solving our own problem can create chaos elsewhere—for example, installing new software without checking if it integrates with software elsewhere in the organization. Instead, pick problems to solve that help colleagues solve theirs. Set stepping-stones that establish jumping off places needed by colleagues who have been slowed down by the lack of them.

First-domino problems.

Each domino represents a must-do event in a detailed sequence aimed at getting something done. The first domino, like a call to 911, initiates the sequence. If it falls it topples or wobbles the rest, at the patient's expense. Identifying first dominos opens our eyes to interconnected must-do events and the unintended consequences that dysfunction imposes on coworkers far down the line.

Don't opt to start by propping up wobbly dominos in the middle or end of a given problem. They may be a major pain, but we will mire down developing new workarounds to old workarounds without solving the up-line problems that wobbled our dominos in the first place.

Pick up-line problems that people know create errors, delays, dysfunction, and waste downline as one department hands off its work to another for further action. Stabilize the first domino, and it stops toppling the others.

Can we work on up-, mid- and down-line problems simultaneously? Yes, that's often unavoidable. But be careful. Problems that seem independent often aren't, not fully. They link. Solutions can conflict. We don't want one group creating round pegs while colleagues in another group create square holes. Assign an employee on each team to serve on the other's team. Get team leaders together to share progress reports. That's a quick way to spot synergies as well as potential conflicts. Sometimes one solution with minor adaptations solves two problems.

Solutions that scale up.

If conceived and pilot-tested with the enterprise as a whole in mind, then first-domino and stepping-stone solutions that work in one function or department can scale up fast to encompass broader problems. Some even emerge as "best practices" that management expands throughout the organization and out into the marketplace.

Keep alert for problems on the list that have scale-up potential. They usually stand out for the cross-functional interest they attract in solving them. They let us uncover conflicting assumptions jointly and pilot test plans, processes and components before assembling the whole. Early on, we can find and fix design defects before they cause a meltdown.

Crises will occur. The better we are at No Fail Leadership and "jell" under normal circumstances, the better equipped we will be to plan and act wisely under pressure instead of spurring recklessly into no-man's-land.

We will already know and have experienced what it means to do things right. Knowing that, we'll also know when we're on treacherous ground, mitigating risk. We may not foresee all hazards, but few surprises will surprise us. We'll already know how to spot briar patches, gullies and quicksand. And like any crack emergency response team—military, medical or other—we will be equipped to react appropriately, learn, adapt on the fly and get the job done.

Instead of muddling through virtually everything, understanding little and learning less, we see each situation more clearly, including critical gaps in knowledge that argue for even jellier-based decision making than normal.

The teacher and the taught

We teach with everything we say and do. I can't overemphasize the importance to the enterprise and its people of solving problems that can be solved and solve every one we target. People learn by doing. They can solve problems, make decisions and implement solutions well and successfully, or they can do this poorly with nothing to show for their efforts and nowhere to turn.

If you ask employees what percentage of the time the problems get solved right the first time, don't be shocked if many say, "Never." Something or many things invariably go awry that they can't make right without endless workarounds, delays, frustration and conflict. People go through their whole career with no unblemished successes they can point to with pride, just a parade of disappointments.

What does that teach? The science and art of doing things badly. When their turn comes to lead, they do what they've been taught.

97% Factors

Principle 9's objective

Learn to succeed through "etched in jell" thinking and methods, teach what success means, and establish standards for achievement from which we will not retreat.

Were Case History decisions etched in stone like dictates, or in jell, aimed at learning quickly and adapting?

Was quick implementation feedback from the front line built into the solution and plans for executing it?

Were Case History decisions made to learn and adapt while doing, or primarily to fix a problem or get something done and move on?

What was learned?

Did people blame and make excuses or did they adapt?

Did we work on the right issues?

Were problems picked that can be solved?

Were the problems among the five kinds that teach and train skills that scale up?

If not, did the solutions really solve the problems or create more?

Principle 10

Implementation is never a "no-brainer."

Anyone disagree?

Probably not. But that doesn't stop us from saying "That's a no-brainer" at times and expecting it to be true. Why do we indulge?

Are we trying to put superiors at ease about us implementing something even when we're not all that confident ourselves? Is it to elbow our way to the front with a show of bravura? Or, to put rivals on the hot seat, saddling them with an expectation of the effortless perfection we could deliver if the task were ours? Or to warn underlings that even they should be able to do a job this simple?

Implementation is never a "no-brainer"

♦   *Because the simple is never simple.*

Even the simplest implementations must be thoroughly thought through, because any ill-conceived or overlooked detail jeopardizes the effort. Glitches give naysayers an opening to trash the whole idea—and they will.

Successfully implement a simple task, and complex implementations get easier. Fail and they get harder.

* *And telling people once is never enough.*

Everyone must understand the implementation objectives and details and what's expected of them, including the need for feedback.

Missteps will occur. We cannot fix them unless we know about them, adapt, communicate and retrain. And no one will tell us unless we and our culture adamantly value a learning mindset plus no-blame, no-excuses disclosure.

Implementation assumptions, ignorance and inexperience

The act of implementation exposes all sorts of problems that planning may not foresee. Gaming implementation through in advance, step-by-step, intercepts many of them, but rarely all. That's true internally, and it is exponentially true when outsiders take part in the implementation. Think of the service and support providers, agents, middlemen, strategic allies, affiliates, and stakeholders in the value stream over whom we have limited control—plus countless customers—whose thinking, behavior and actions are hard to pigeonhole, predict, and satisfy. Furthermore, what we want and what outsiders are able and willing to provide can diverge far more than expected. The challenge compounds when the outsiders come from other countries and cultures.

Assumptions about our world

My clients have included several in the U.S. and Japan that have tried to do business across oceans. All soon discovered, along with legions of other firms, that the low-cost upsides of outsourcing had high-cost downsides.

Ellison Technologies is the largest integrator in the U.S. of advanced manufacturing technologies for fully automated production. The technologies and Ellison's customers come from all over the world. Jim Ellison, founder, summed up decades of lessons from outsourcing this way:

Producing abroad requires a leap of faith that currencies, labor costs, quality and logistics won't change. In truth, labor may cost more in the U.S. than globally today, but world labor costs keep rising.

Quality inconsistency and adulteration overseas can cost out-sourcers dearly too. The more times human beings touch a complex product, the more opportunity that exists for errors and the more errors that occur. By comparison, a well-designed, automated factory can churn out identical, flawless parts time after time, whether one-offs or in quantity. Consider the high returns tracked by *Consumer Reports* for warranty work on some high-tech consumer products produced overseas. And remember Mattel? It had to recall over 11 million toys made in China using unauthorized lead-laced paint. Pressure on foreign suppliers to cut costs and prices tempts some to cut corners, criminally at times as their government looks the other direction or not at all.

And not everything costs more. Manufacturers everywhere pay about the same for facilities, equipment, energy, and raw materials. In the machine tool industry, cutting tools, technology, and materials are usually more available here on demand and often cost less, not more.

Learning curves have often risen slower than anyone imagined, jeopardizing quality. Toyota had a very long and trying time teaching U.S. workers to take seriously The Toyota Way to defect-free quality.

Doing business across time zones and oceans delays turnaround on orders, parts and technical support issues, forcing U.S. sellers and producers to inventory product to deliver upon sale, creating customization problems, or force customers to order up front and wait months for delivery. Some, like Lenovo computers, now send customized orders to China for fulfillment and direct shipment to American customers, eliminating inventory of finished product. But warranty work takes place in the U.S., which can mean over-inventory of finished components and spare parts at great expense to keep customer facilities operating with limited downtime.

To top it off, cultural disconnects have surfaced dealing with people who react to problems and issues differently than we do.

We may not even agree on the meaning of quality, customer service, urgent, accountability and "yes."

The simple is never simple

If it's not one thing, it's another!

Implementation rarely lacks complications that must be dealt with. As Principle 1 asserts, *All problems are conflicts of belief about what's true.* Over the life of the project, conflicts arise initially from fears of loss through change and morph into fears of loss through personal and project failure. Be prepared. Sources of trouble aren't hard to find:

Blaming for the problem
Disagreement about the solution

Honest diagnosing and soul-searching about root causes can mire down in blaming and excuse making, which don't wear well. If we succeed at diagnosing the problem and coming up with a solution, then fears of individual scapegoating and radical change die down. Invoke Principles 2, 3 and 4. They can rescue us:

Principle 2: *No problem is ever what it seems.*
The truth lies elsewhere.

Principle 3: *The truth is always positive,*
even when it's painful.

Principle 4: *Make it 100% safe to tell the truth.*

Participants begin thinking collaboratively and creatively about the benefits of solving the problem and ways to do that. Some may resist and naysay, but most will get into the hunt and have more fun than doing what they usually do all day. The atmosphere warms up. Disagreements about specific solutions become discussions about solving the business problems rather than negotiations to protect status quos, turfs, and threatened egos.

Conflicts about specifics of implementation

When the stakes are high and the outcome iffy, the tension and pressure can carry over into execution, especially when implementations bog down, or make matters worse, or jeopardize someone's reputation for success.

Doubts about our will and wherewithal

Will management commit to seeing the hard-won solutions through to completion? Will leaders run interference to flatten obstacles? Realistically, do we have the time, manpower and money to succeed? Do we have the talent, knowledge and skills or must we plug gaps? Now we're into manpower, resources, timelines, scheduling and other details of getting from idea through execution. We must establish clear and realistic responsibility, accountability and authority.

Here's where implementers must commit personally, a scary moment. Some will try to beg off, citing workload and other priorities, threatening the project. Leaders must step in and referee tug-of-wars over priorities, manpower, workloads and timelines while protecting projects now underway.

Fear that it's not getting done as promised

Planning and launching does not equal finishing. Coworkers who promise but fail to deliver can infuriate employees committed to the project's success. Managers who tolerate such behavior in others and themselves make matters worse. They infect every project they touch with a virus that debilitates and spreads. And execs who change priorities or add new projects without checking can suck the manpower right out of efforts employees have been slaving to get operational, especially high-value, low profile ones. Unless someone with stature monitors progress and polices accountability, projects don't finish. Eventually, projects don't start.

Ongoing Leadership Test breakdowns

People revert to old ways. Workarounds proliferate, creating new problems that pile up unsolved. Clumsy executions time after time torpedo new, "no-brainer" projects before they leave the wharf. Management, mystified, watches them sink, and exasperated dockworkers seek safety in silence rather than be accused of not having the brains for a "no-brainer" that wasn't well thought out. Few things ever get done right. It's one mishap after another.

6 STEPS FOR IMPLEMENTING
NO FAIL SOLUTIONS

Step 1. Follow the 10 Principles. They are diagnostic, prescriptive, and predictive

◆ *Diagnostic*

If something during implementation breaks down or creates new obstacles or falls short of expectations, pull out the 10 Principles and for each one ask, "Are we applying it faithfully?" The first time through answer "yes" or "no." The common summation I hear is, "No wonder everything is so screwed up!"

Then for every "no," ask, "Why aren't we applying Principle 10? What's the result? What would things be like if we got on track or back on track? What's in our way?"

We will know why the problems are problems and, depending upon how deep the diagnosis, what to work on first.

◆ *Prescriptive*

If we want to improve, we must become realistic and honest about our underperformance and resolve to face it, learn, adapt and overcome it. How? By reasserting the Principles, retraining everyone in applying them, and persisting until they embed in individual thinking, the corporate methodologies, and the culture. Persistence is key. Remember, "The simple is never simple," and, "Telling people once is never enough." These precepts apply to implementing No Fail solutions as much as to implementing company plans.

◆ *Predictive*

Follow the Principles and we succeed. Don't, and we don't, at least not up to potential. It's as simple as that. And we can see failure coming a mile away. Business-as-usual will get us results-as-usual. If the trajectory is downward, that means worse. Even if the trend is upward, the slope cannot rise as fast or as far as it would if we had implementation down to a no-fail science.

And keep this in mind: The lack of clear standards and expectations provides wiggle room for all sorts of mischief. When a group operates from a common understanding of the Principles, someone that understands but chooses not to follow them stands out as an obstructionist with no place to hide.

Step 2. Don't assume anything about our ways or marketplace

+ *Assumptions about our ways*

BigCity Insurance Association suffered from a philosophical disconnect between its job—sell life insurance—and what it had to do to do that, namely, "sell." In fact, it was so embarrassed about "selling" anything and so unaggressive in doing so that it seriously underserved the people it was supposed to help.

BigCity had been founded as a not-for-profit association some 75+ years prior by city personnel. Objective: to make low-cost, high-value, term life insurance available to BigCity's municipal employees. Although BigCity operated apart from the city government, its board of directors consisted of career municipal executives. They liked the idea of "serving," but "selling" made them very uncomfortable.

Nonetheless, they granted BigCity exclusive worksite access to municipal employees. "Counselors" on salary, not commission, could meet quarterly with employee groups, "explain," pass out brochures, accept applications, and help members with specific problems. But they couldn't "sell." Frontline supervisors didn't want insurance people pitching or pressuring employees at work to buy something, even if they needed it.

The reticence made no sense at all. Worksites can be dangerous places. BigCity's employees really wanted to know whether they needed insurance, what kind and how much.

The counselors were unprepared to counsel. As long as they met targets for new sales and renewals "without selling," management paid little attention to how or what they presented. Insurance isn't easy to understand, even in your native language. Most of Big-City's multi-cultural employees were poorly educated. Many spoke English as a distant second language. Counselors, who were not bilingual then, presented verbally, off the cuff, with no visual aids to help bridge the language barrier. I personally witnessed Spanish speaking workers clustered intently around a coworker doing his best to simultaneously translate the counselor's rambling pitch. Listeners got no enlightenment from the brochures handed out either. They read like disclosure statements. In the interest of not selling, counselors recommended minimum amounts that had no relationship to employee needs. But supervisors were happy because they had protected workers from BigCity.

Families needed financial backup, and employees weren't going to find better insurance value anywhere else, not by a long shot. They certainly wouldn't find another insurer dedicated solely to city employees. BigCity had every right to speak up unabashedly. To do less meant to stand by while employees drifted into plans that were not in their best interest or went with no insurance at all.

That argument ultimately took hold with BigCity's leaders. I got them to stop apologizing for doing the right thing.

The sales presentation became simple, structured and visual so that all counselors told the same story and the audience could follow it, even attendees who spoke little English.

The new brochure, in English with a later companion piece in Spanish, explained whole life, universal life and term life insurance so that employees could understand where BigCity's term life fit in. Then it led employees through a simple Q&A process they could do at home with their families to decide whether they needed any insurance at all, or more and how much.

We created a heavily used video that helped thousands of Big-City's employees and government leaders understand, for the first time, BigCity's value to them personally and to the city as a whole.

We redid the post-sale processes to make sure that the promises made were kept. That meant new, improved processes plus clearer and higher standards for promise performance than before.

The old, ultra-soft-sell modus operandi yielded only a 25% share of the 40,000 captive employees. Revenue and membership had plateaued at 10,000 members for years. Once the no-selling assumption changed, so did the way of doing business. Revenue shot up 20% the first year, then another 30% the next with no price increases—just more members in total buying higher, more appropriate levels of coverage, and feeling better served.

◆   *Assumptions about our marketplace*

The mid-sized, old-school, frozen food company from the 1970s had just sold to a Fortune 500 consumer products company. A group—made up of the new marketing head (an ex-P&G product manager), two hotshot East Coast marketing consultants and I the ad agency guy—crafted a classic test-marketing plan in two cities to present to the board of directors, made up mainly of the old owners who were transitioning out of the business.

The board meeting took three hours, during which the ad agency, the consulting firm, and the new marketing team over-whelmed the old-timers with research findings, strategies, marketing and sales plans, creative work, and a plot for monitoring sales results, ad awareness and consumer attitudes. The plan was brilliantly conceived, complete with print, TV, mailed coupons offering free product, special incentives for the food broker sales force, incentives for retailers to promote the product, and a lush kickoff party to explain the program to supermarket buyers and their leaders.

By the end, two of the four board members had nodded off. One of the owners who had patiently endured all this leaned back and said, "Well, it looks like it's time for us old folks to move on and turn the business over to the youngsters." Music to our ears.

Ominously, the VP of sales, who had been there for decades and was nearing retirement, had serious concerns about the plan's viability all along. But either he couldn't finger what made him uneasy, or he didn't want to rain on his new VP Marketing's parade. To his credit, he did more than acquiesce; he pitched in and conscientiously did his part with the brokers and supermarket buyers.

Sixty days into the test markets, we couldn't figure out why the low-spending test market was outperforming the high-spending test market. The wild card, alas, was the broker. We hotshot marketing gurus were spoiled by P&G's in-house sales force that wrote the book on implementing new product test markets in the grocery business. We had never worked with independent food brokers over whom we had little control.

The broker in our successful low-spending test market followed the script we presented at the supermarket sales meetings. He insisted that the buyers have enough displays and product in stores to redeem the "One Free" coupons.

The broker in the unsuccessful high-spending test market naively took his clients aside and told them not to stock up on product. "Order once the get-one-free coupons start showing up. That's soon enough." In fact, that's way too late. What do customers do with coupons they can't redeem? They toss them.

We knew the food brokers weren't marketing savvy, but we figured that with instruction we could train them to hold up their end.

We were dead wrong. And that's what the VP of sales had tried to warn us about all along. It never occurred to us to listen. We "assumed."

Early assumptions about how much manufacturing costs could be cut by moving production west to the Far East proved rosier than reality, as recounted a couple pages ago by Jim Ellison, who witnessed the whole migration unfold. Now that some high-end work, at least, can be produced and delivered competitively from home, we have neither enough technologically skilled people left to do the work (and most are nearing retirement) nor enough young people with the quality education or interest in manufacturing to replace them. And now other nations, like booming India, have upgraded their workforce to fill our gap.

Overeagerness for change, like leaving one spouse for another, is a lousy guide in a complex, often inscrutable world—especially when the welfare of your business is at stake. Check your assumptions, not only about the world, but also about your marketplace and ways of doing business in it.

Step 3. Get problems people foresee out in the open quickly

In recent years our firm has been asked by companies that are doing well to codify the principles driving their success so that the leaders could spread and embed them more broadly and deeply and pass them on to future generations, as The Toyota Way had done for Toyota.

One of these clients was Ellison Technologies, introduced earlier. The founders were retiring, taking their valuable experience, knowledge and wisdom with them. Ellison veterans had absorbed much of it through osmosis and applying it over the decades, but the principles and practices driving success had not been documented for bequeathing to others. While some of these were well established in some offices, few were 100% in effect in any one office, let alone across the company. In addition, individual offices had developed best practices worth sharing. Ellison was a patchwork of them. And some local practices, although utilitarian, actually violated the principles that accounted for Ellison's success as a whole. The founders saw the inconsistency as unfinished business and an encumbrance for the new owners and leadership team.

Even before the Ellison Way had been finished, Jim Ellison anticipated that embedding it would take a concerted training effort and suggested creating videos to introduce the Ellison Way and each of its principles. He and CEO Tim Kilty then picked thirty, promising, mid-level managers across Ellison's eighteen territories to become local Ellison Way "mentors" and invited them to a joint training session on the Ellison Way and on mentoring it.

What happened during the training session demonstrated the importance of bringing problems people foresee out in the open quickly. Leadership assumed that the mentors would see knighthood as a vote of confidence in them as future leaders. As the reality of mentoring set in so did palpable trepidations. Mentors mostly agreed with what The Ellison Way's eight principles asserted, since they had contributed to their formulation via up-front, fact-finding interviews. But they blanched at the transformation of "things that would be nice and we ought to do" into "things we will do," followed by the realization that they would have to convincingly defend and teach the Way to the peers and employees they worked with.

Were these mentors willing and able to mentor anything? Implementation of The Ellison Way was shaping up as a bigger undertaking than envisioned.

We improvised four breakout groups during training and divided the eight Ellison Way Principles among them. The question: "What tough questions do you expect to be asked that you cannot answer?" By asking it top management preemptively invited mentors to vocalize reservations about:

- ⊚   The purpose and meaning of each principle.

- ⊚   The profound implications and practicalities of implementing them company-wide.

- ⊚   Management's commitment to invest time and resources to see this through.

Accurate answers clearly lay beyond the scope of this meeting. So we assigned each of the four groups to talk to the old guard, research and answer their own questions, and report back to the total group and to leadership.

Along the way we conferred with each group. Despite progress, the mentors discovered how much they didn't know about Ellison. That surprised them and management. Mentoring was serious business demanding a steep learning curve, effort, a management perspective, and a premium on leadership, not just manager-ship.

The whole project would have collapsed had we not found out how prevalent the fear of mentoring was, how shallow middle-management's understanding was of the principles vital to Ellison's historic and future industry leadership, and how deep the skepticism went about implementing the Ellison Way uniformly company-wide.

Mentor training by Ellison top executives had to go beyond teaching the purpose, logic and value of the principles. It had to equip mentors to deal with the most contentious questions that mentors had asked and would have to answer when mentoring their coworkers.

For example, one principle dealt with coupling national leadership with local autonomy. Mentors questioned what "autonomy" meant, how autonomously local offices could operate in practice, and how frontline employees could decide what they could and could not do—all of which were questions to which they needed good answers.

Training videos were developed, one for each principle. Each video both explained a principle and asked and answered the toughest questions head on without waiting for trainees to ask. Mentors then launched a Q&A session with trainees to get feedback, positive and negative. The tactic preempted untold speculation and naysaying by employees before they derailed the learning and the mentor, and it actually did a better job illuminating and getting buy-in to each principle than a rah-rah sales pitch.

None of this preemption would have occurred had "mentoring" not put mentors on the hot seat. The heat caused their fears about the Ellison Way to bubble up. Had their fears not surfaced, the mentors' training tools would have lacked relevance and power, and the mentors would have been sitting ducks with no ammo to shoot back.

The larger lesson:

> *We can't get problems that people foresee*
> *out in the open quickly—especially*
> *implementation problems—unless we find out*
> *what problems they actually foresee.*

We have to, as Principle 7 urges, *Get input from frontline people before making decisions they must implement, not after.* Reapply it to find out how "no-brainer" no-brainer really is. The truth is always positive, even when it's painful.

Step 4. Implement in small chunks that people can bite off

Put the 80-20 rule in action: We can solve 80 percent of a problem with 20 percent of the effort to solve the whole thing, often with miniscule investment. At one regional health insurance company, three small bites consumed three big chunks, and more.

◆ *Small Bite 1: The Quote Calculator*

The health insurer's sales agents needed a way to quote prices of health benefit packages without having to go back to its underwriters every time the employer group they courted wanted a change and a re-quote. Re-quotes had mushroomed and clients pressured competing insurers for instant turnaround. The existing process was mainly manual and unsustainable. Both Sales and Underwriting fancied a fully automated solution, but shelved that idea because of cost and manpower. And Underwriting resisted less ambitious alternatives, like empowering Sales to do quotes. Underwriters feared that they would lose rate control and that profitability would fall victim to over-eager beavers.

I gathered stakeholders and naysayers in a room, established a truce, and asked Sales to think through the absolute minimum technology needed for turning quotes around quickly. Underwriting's fears proved overblown. All Sales needed was a web based calculator with predetermined, customized rates for each employer that allowed Sales to quote on the spot.

The $20,000, 90-day project solved 80 percent of what all assumed to be a $2 million, multiyear problem. Sales and Underwriting each saved a thousand hours of time the first six months. The sales people got far more than their minimum technology. They debugged an interim solution that would have cost dearly as a $2 million solution gone awry. As a bonus, they restructured the sales process and downstream support services, eliminating untold waste and aggravation. In all, the group cut down markedly on errors, lost sales, customer dissatisfaction, and friction between Sales and Underwriting.

◆   *Small Bite 2: The enrollment form*

Employee health insurance enrollment forms made their arduous way from employee to employer to insurance agent to the insurer's sales team and finally to the enrollment group far downstream. The enrollment department could not process 40% of the forms because something was wrong or missing, and the problem was worsening. The workarounds weren't scaling up with the volume.

The enrollment people felt dumped on. They didn't create the errors on the applications; they just caught them. They fixed some of them but had to send a lot of applications back to employers and employees to fix. That triggered six figures worth of costly rework annually plus embarrassing delays for all involved. And some families that needed health care while their enrollment was being reprocessed got caught without official coverage. They found themselves stranded in the gap between the expiration of the old plan and activation of the new one. They would in fact be reimbursed later, but temporary panic isn't good medicine.

Accusations of carelessness, indifference and dereliction of duty circulated like bad money. All agreed that something had to be done, so we convened an internal group of accusers and accused to look for relief. But from what and from whom?

Fingers pointed everywhere, jabbing many, leaving people exhausted and bruised but still standing. Some participants fretted that fixing the problem would take a complete overhaul of the system plus a wholesale attitude adjustment. That wasn't going to happen anytime soon.

Out of the silence of impasse came a timid voice suggesting, "Maybe something's the matter with the form."

And there was. We checked. The form was too complicated. It was crowded with questions seeking "nice to know" answers beyond information needed to enroll. We soon learned that unfriendly, error-riddled forms posed an industry-wide problem, perpetuated by competitors plagiarizing each other's applications and then expanding them with more questions, longer paper and smaller type.

We fixed the form, not the system. Errors dropped to a handful immediately. Streamlining the questions unearthed easy opportunities to streamline the process. That illuminated new competitive advantages to exploit and intriguing paths leading to a broader, system-wide upgrade.

- *Small Bite 3: The Progress Tracker*

The problems with processing application and enrollment forms pointed out another problem. The insurance company needed a way to track the status of employer applications and employee enrollments the way UPS tracks packages. Employers and employees wanted updates. So did the sales agents, internal sales staff, enrollment people, and all the others farther downstream that had commitments to meet. The enrollment group fielded many anxious phone calls and held a lot of hands. If the sales group could follow progress, they could alert agents and employers before being asked, alleviating anxiety, call traffic, misassumptions and misinformation.

Many internal departments had a stake in solving this problem and the workgroup was large. Long term, an information technology solution seemed inevitable, upgrading data entry and reporting across departments, perhaps including ways that customers and employees could track their own "packages."

Inspired by the rate calculator's success, the group brainstormed a short-term solution. They agreed upon the smallest number of milestones and amount of data needed to keep each interested party abreast of progress. They were ready to call the head of Information Technology for counsel on programming the least ambitious solution, when chance raised its pretty hand.

The human resources director, a participant, realized that her department already had in-house software that tracked job applicants from first encounter through hiring and beyond. It also produced status reports accessible by all who needed to know. Could it be adapted for use here?

The IT people said yes and added more good news. The software could easily scale up to handle Enrollment's higher volume with no upper limit. Data entry, processing and throughput would improve dramatically. Errors would drop. The software's reporting capabilities already exceeded the workgroup's minimum requirements and could link across departments. And because the workgroup's stripped down solution laid out user requirements well, the program could, with minimal customizing, "go live" in 60-90 days.

♦ *Full without being stuffed*

Even though the rate calculator, enrollment form, and progress-tracker solutions came from workgroups focused on their independent problems, the problems intertwined. So did the solutions. The problems challenged people without exceeding their abilities. And (surprise!) the "20% solutions" quickly and cheaply solved up to 80% of problems that the groups had sidelined as too big, labor intensive and expensive to target.

Step 5. Walk through the details yourself, with leaders, then the troops: Devils lurk in the shadows

Wave a red flag in front of every implementation. Stop it at the gate until you have checked it out thoroughly and green-flagged it to proceed.

♦ *The ultimate, intimate walkthrough*

This story illustrates three points:

> *Solve a piece of the problem instead of trying to solve the whole thing.*

> *Get input from people on the front line before making decisions that they must implement, Principle 7 again.*

> *Keep the solution simple, because per Principle 10, implementation is never a no-brainer.*

External interviews, echoed by internal interviews, revealed that levels of professionalism in this paramedic operation were lacking across the board, but most visibly in the field—to the dismay of most everyone. A small, but powerful "professionalism" workgroup, including the CEO, was formed to address the problem. For the sake of patients of the outside professionals that paramedics served daily—and the sake of their own integrity—they viewed anything less than 100% professionalism as unacceptable.

They quickly found that the problem was too multifaceted and the number of facets too large to polish all of them. Someone finally observed that the ambulances themselves were billboards to the community. "If we could just keep them looking clean like fire engines, we'd have a start." The more ambitious souls wanted more ambitious efforts, but they reluctantly agreed to go along.

As participants explored the details, the number of problems and fixes expanded from one to five:

1. Be clean on the outside for image reasons.

2. Be clean in the patient compartment for the health of both patients and medics.

3. Be clean in the front where the paramedics sit, because no one wants to contend with an off-going crew's trash.

4. Keep the rig fully stocked with meds and equipment. Incompletely stocked rigs can be life threatening. They tempt crews to cannibalize other rigs. And they increase downtime to restock, preventing crews from taking 911 calls and jeopardizing area coverage overall.

5. Top off the crankcase with oil. Rigs go through oil fast without going through miles because they idle on station for hours in summer keeping meds and people cool, and hours in winter keep meds and people warm.

Before issuing a dictate demanding compliance, the workgroup had the good sense to ask the rest of the paramedics whether they thought that all this was worth doing, also known as "getting input from the front line." The issues turned out hotter than the workgroup expected, particularly among the female paramedics, who considered the lack of cleanliness downright abusive, along with the expectation that they would clean house.

One of the supervisors came up with an inventive idea: a Promissory Shift-change Check Sheet with a top half and bottom half with identical checklists requiring yes-no answers. The off-going, two-person crew fills the out the top half certifying that the rig is road-ready in all five areas, or ready in some and not ready in others. The oncoming crew inspects the rig, verifies the accuracy of the off-going report, checks the yes-no boxes on the bottom half of the sheet, notes exceptions, and signs off. The report then goes to the supervisor, who reviews deficiencies, corrects them and reports weekly to all crewmembers, at the same time seeking no-blame feedback on what works, what doesn't and what needs to be adjusted.

"Great idea," I said. "Now, how do we get word to the medics that have to execute it?"

One of the supervisors in the workgroup literally said, "That's a no-brainer," then proposed that the CEO send out a cover letter with the check sheet and instructions, then follow up with an email, saying, "You will! Or else."

"Your own internal surveys," I countered, "say that no one reads memos or emails until they have seen them five times, even on issues like health insurance that directly affect their wellbeing. Let's pretend that implementing this little project perfectly spells the difference between this organization succeeding or collapsing. You're going to send out a memo and an email!"

"We'll have a group meeting," said a supervisor.

"You're kidding! That's never worked."

"You don't mean that you expect us to talk to each crew member individually, do you?"

"When that's potentially the difference between success and failure, what's the option? Send a memo? Put it on the agenda of a weekly meeting?"

With that settled, we moved on. I stood up and wandered around with a blank piece of paper in hand. "Pretend I'm an off-going crew member. I'm supposed to fill out this check list. Where do I find it?"

"It's up front where the medics ride."

"Who can find anything up front where the medics ride?"

Their solution: Screw a holder to the dashboard with a slot for blank checklists and a slot for the lists filled out by the off-going crew, which the oncoming crew would be looking for.

Someone then asked, "What if the off-going crew didn't have time at the end of its shift to do all the cleaning and other tasks?"

Their solution, unpopular among offenders: The oncoming crew does not have to accept the rig—and usually didn't—until the off-going crew completed its tasks. The new crew can volunteer to do the work itself, but it cannot take calls until all tasks are done.

"So," I continued, "I'm the off-going crew. What do I do with the form I just filled out?"

"Put it on the supervisor's desk in the station," someone suggested.

"Supervisor's desk? There's no supervisor's desk, just an everybody's desk. What do I do with this checklist so that it gets where it's supposed to go?"

Solution: They built a mail box for depositing completed checklists.

"What happens to them? Where are they supposed to go and how do they get there?"

Solution: The off-going supervisor picks them up and takes them to headquarters. And gives them to whom? The CEO chimed in, "I want to see them first, so hand them to me or put them on my chair." Then what? The CEO gives them to an associate to tabulate and …

You get the picture. The "what thens" continued through the tiniest detail.

Importantly, the three supervisors figured out a way to talk to each paramedic individually over the next week for 15 minutes to explain the plan. They covered the problem, the solution, its importance, the frontline enthusiasm for the project, the individual's role and responsibilities, what management expects and the value of flawless implementation.

What happened? Compliance was unheard of: 100% from the go-live date and was still 100% three months after.

The CEO then floated the idea that since compliance was so high, maybe the checklist could be incorporated into other "pre-flight" checklists the medics filled out. He got shot down. The consensus was, to quote one paramedic, "This is the first time we've ever got anything right. Don't screw it up!"

If I have gone into this story with more detail than the reader has patience for, then good! The time you have spent immersed in the details is meant to give you an appreciation of the time that, when it comes to implementation, you need to spend immersed in the details.

Step 6. Measure what counts, qualitatively as well as quantitatively, as we go and retrospectively

◆ *Not everything we can measure deserves measuring.*

It can be tempting, for example, to measure handoffs from A to B to C and cheer about how few errors show up. That's only 3% of what matters. The 97% that really matters encompasses all the chaos and scrambling going on in A, B and C to get a perfect score. It also encompasses all the rest of the obstacles the Leadership Test unearths that people leave buried or tiptoe around because they're too … human … to disturb. Too personally or professionally threatening or too politically incorrect to mention.

◆ *The quantitative 3%.*

When trying to measure pilot test solutions to bite-sized chunks of problems, take bite-sized measurements. We want to know if our solution accomplished its primary purpose by a wide enough margin that taking it further makes good sense.

Start with a clear definition of success—as simple as, "How will we know if we've succeeded?"—and a simple way to measure it, such as the paramedics' yes-no report on ambulance readiness that showed 100% compliance from day one. Look also for information we capture routinely—like specific missing information on an enrollment form—that has never been recruited for tracking, but could reflect the effects of pilot tests we try. Knowing what's missing or incorrect, we can have enrollment people track how long they spend getting answers, before and after.

Don't forget that quantitative measurements require "quantities" of data to return statistically significant results. That can take a long time. We don't need peer-reviewed, scientific data. We need the quick, actionable implementation feedback to make course corrections that can multiply successes or rescue us from miscalculations.

- ◆   *The qualitative 97% that matters.*

Deming's 3% may exaggerate the importance of everything else, but take his warning seriously. Researchers can inundate us with comforting methods for tracking progress quantitatively on transactions, errors, defects, delays, throughput and other data-driven variables. And whole industries exist to quantify shifts in human usage, attitudes, opinions, intent, choices and action among sizeable groups of people that we employ, serve or depend upon.

But all the attention given the 3% diverts attention from the importance of the other 97% and undervalues it. "97% problems" don't respond much to Lean Six Sigma and other production-bred treatments. Trying to achieve less than six defects per million opportunities is a quixotic quest when only ten or a hundred transactions occur per year. And all involve human or human-process interactions, replete with surprises, nuances, exceptions and judgment calls.

You'll find that the deeper you dig into the 97%, the more you'll find that's worth measuring, but not necessarily what you expected up front or in the usual ways. Preplanned research makes good sense, but preset routines can miss what counts while counters are diligently counting.

So, how do we get actionable answers to hard-to-measure questions in the 97%? First, identify the crucial, hard-to-measure problems, then craft the right questions, and then innovate ways to get answers. You have already been using two tools for exposing critical problems and asking good questions. Bring both to bear:

Do and redo the Leadership Test.

Establish a "dysfunction" baseline before settling on the specific, "97%" problems to address. Give the Leadership Test to all top managers plus supervisors and frontline employees immersed in the action. Do this up front. Ask them to elaborate on whichever breakdowns and obstacles they checked as problematic. Use their answers to target and prioritize problems to work on. The finalists are legitimate problems that people will want to solve, securing buy-in from the outset.

Repeat the test after the first round of problem solving and implementation to find out what has gotten better or worse. Retest people directly involved in the project, plus others who contributed importantly along the way or had a stake in the outcomes. Again, ask them to elaborate on Leadership Test problems they now see that prompted "yes" answers this time around.

Compare the "before" and "after," not just the yes-no stats, but also the verbal and written responses. Have barriers to performance begun to weaken? Which ones and in what ways? Which barriers triggered new problems? Managers that manage by numbers may not consider the results statistically significant, but visible improvement in Leadership Test assessments can point to future productivity gains beyond measureable progress solving specific problems.

Apply your personal case history questions to other problems stalled in Leadership Test territory.

The questions dig deep into what works, what doesn't, how far you've come, how far you have yet to go, and what's likely to get you there. Answers will raise other questions that may never have been asked. If Lean Six Sigma analysis can help shed light, go for it. But don't bog down narrowing statistical probabilities when directional answers tell enough of the story to convince people that the status quo is indefensible or that an implementation is on the right track.

Better yet, involve others. Talk to colleagues and to witnesses on the front line. You can only solve Leadership Test problems by dismantling them and rebuilding solutions jointly anyway. Lead the expedition. The discoveries will prove diagnostic, prescriptive and predictive of success—or the lack thereof—whether staying the course or venturing in new directions. You'll find yourselves moving far beyond the 3% you can measure into the eye-opening 97% that truly counts, strategically as well as tactically. Successes here ultimately change the culture. And you too, not only into a better problem solver and implementer, but into a growth-mindset, No Fail leader.

97% Factors

Implementation evaluation

Did leaders walk through the details of implementation, or did they stop with the plan and task list?

Did participants measure the 97% as well as the 3%, assessing implementation process and dynamics, breakdowns and things to do more of?

Implementation pilot test

Pick a routine implementation plan in progress or starting. Ask implementers: "Suppose the survival of our enterprise rested upon flawlessly executing this seemingly minor plan. What would we do differently during implementation?"

Note initial reactions, positive and negative, to the what-if idea of setting higher expectations that could require more work.

Together, walk through the implementation details, beginning to end, in search of anything that could fail.

List the risks and decide what, if anything, deserves to be fixed.

How close was the original plan to a No Fail plan, and if it fell short, where?

LOOKING AHEAD

HERE ARE SOME OF THE MOST COMMON LESSONS that people have learned from No Fail Leadership, most of them not foreseen:

The power of the 97% that matters

Employees have been conditioned to believe that the 3% management measures is what matters above all else. So employees focus their efforts there, even though personal experience tells them that what happens in the other 97% matters more, despite lacking the metrics to prove it.

The Leadership Test focuses on the 97% and makes it abundantly clear to the metric minded—and securing grudging acknowledgement—that Lean Six Sigma, et al, don't solve the people-driven problems rampant in the 97% or they would have already solved them. Further, the 10 Principles in theory and application make it abundantly clear that what happens in the 97% drives success or failure in the 3% far more than the reverse.

That arms 97-percenters, often for the first time, with the ammunition to hold their own against the 3-percenters. The purpose isn't to make enemies, but to unhorse the high riders and introduce them to the muck of everyday battle in the 97%. Once baptized and welcomed, many 3-percenters I've witnesses begin tapping their ingenuity and knowledge to help 97-percenters monitor their hard-to-measure efforts. And the partnerships work.

The power of 3-percenters to make major contributions

When you try to make sense of everything from business strategies to tactical workarounds, do not be surprised if the data you wish you had in order to figure out what worked, what didn't, and why, simply isn't available because no one foresaw the need to collect it. This is especially true for 97% Factors and Leadership Test problems. You may need tracking and other diagnostic tools customized to your task.

This offers an opportunity to move 3-percenters into 97% Territory. In my experience, they have come up with elegantly simple, information gathering solutions that cost virtually nothing, sometimes coopting existing in-house technology. They can also help develop tracking plans for upcoming pilot tests that scale up if needed, and much more. Their contributions add credibility with management to the projects they work on, and they seem to have as much fun in 97% Territory as everyone else.

If they're willing, count them in.

The power of the Leadership Test and 10 Principles to:

⊚ Diagnose the causes and effects of problems in the 97%

⊚ Prescribe what to fix and how

⊚ Predict the outcome based upon how faithfully the 10 Principles are honored

Simply asking which Leadership Test problems remain unsolved provides a sobering snapshot of dysfunction that's hard to deny. Then, for each problem, asking which of the 10 Principles we have not honored is an eye popper that cuts through any lingering denial. The answers open windows to why—as an organization—things aren't going as expected, from flawed input and assumptions up front, through flawed decisions and plans, to flawed implementations down the line. The answers also point to what systemic as well as immediate problems to fix first.

Further, the 10 Principles don't just prescribe and run. They provide a practical, collaborative, ground-up-top-down methodology for fixing pieces of each problem successfully, accumulating successes, and scaling up what works.

Importantly, through these successes, No Fail Leadership teaches employees at all levels to lead others in solving problems and executing solutions.

You can't do it alone

If you answered the 97% Factors questions along the way, you may now know more about the Leadership Test problem you chose to examine than anyone else in your organization. Even if you only thought about the questions or simply read them, you may still be ahead of the pack.

But you may also have discovered, a bit unsettlingly, that you didn't have the answers needed to solve the problem and implement the solution. Not even close. That recognition takes you a huge first step into the land of leadership. You will know far more clearly what you don't know, where to go for critical input, and how to get it. More strides forward.

Above all, you will know that when you're in the Leadership Test's 97% territory, you can't do it alone. What's "it?" Lead. Deliver exceptional performance.

Leadership is not an "I" endeavor, not once you get off the paved road into the 97% that matters. Here, top-notch leaders need top-notch followers to trek new territory successfully as much as top followers need top leaders. The problems aren't "I" problems, the solutions aren't "I" solutions, and the implementations aren't "I" implementations. They are we, we, and we.

The power of doing something right

Employees at every level, the ones that care the most, lament how seldom anything gets solved right; a downer they can't shake off. What's remarkable is how experiencing start-to-finish successes (including well-executed pilot tests that teach us what to improve) so reinvigorates them that they welcome more challenges and set standards for excellence—on their own—from which they do not want to retreat, a near miracle that can rattle the status quo. The awakened drive for excellence deserves to be applauded and nurtured as a prerequisite mindset for transforming followers into leaders. It also has immediate value:

The best training for succeeding in a crisis
is learning to succeed when there isn't one.

Instill the habit of doing things as right as possible the first time and adapting based on timely, quality feedback. Then, in a crisis, you will be hyper aware of the shortcuts and risks taken by acting quickly without complete information. Knowing that, you will also be hyper alert to signs of trouble in areas of calculated risk and be trained to respond quickly enough to mitigate threatening consequences.

The power unleashed when leadership commits to action, honesty and safety

Action:

It's amazing how fearlessly and productively work sessions move ahead when top leaders make two unexpected commitments up front:

- ⊚   "The status quo is not an option." And leaders means it.

- ⊚   "If it takes a few grand to fix a problem, we'll spend it."

Employees aren't used to hearing these promises. They may need repeating along the way to overcome the disbelief. But the whole problem-solving dynamic changes. Participants take their liberation seriously. They look at everything the big program in question tries to accomplish, then, knowing that "a few grand" can't tackle everything, strip the search for a solution down to the few objectives that matter most, then find truly ingenious, low-cost ways to achieve them.

And, I have never witnessed participants abusing management's vote of confidence.

Honesty and safety:

Leaders cannot overcome the problems in the people-stressed 97% by applying extra coats of the status quo. The truth must surface, which means that leaders must agree that the truth is not only positive but essential in tackling these tough problems. Leaders must also insist that employees open up, which will happen only with two other firm assurances:

◎   *Here it's 100% safe to tell the truth* (Principle 4).

◎   *No blaming and no excuses allowed* (Principle 5).

These last two preconditions dismantle the main obstacles to sessions where serious work of extraordinary value gets done. People actually start talking to one another, comparing notes about unclear objectives and expectations, the details of how they do their job, what they need and aren't getting from each other, what they don't need and are getting too much of, what daily-to-unusual predicaments create roadblocks to achieving mutual ends, and the wastefulness of the whole scramble.

Out of honestly shared agonies come honestly workable solutions that people want to succeed.

The power of the pilot test mindset

"Everything we do in life is a pilot test.
Even doing nothing."

Thus far I have encountered few who have thought of life's choices—and workplace choices—this way, even though people instantly recognize the statement's validity. They quickly see and accept the huge difference between striding blindly through life and embracing each important venture as an experience that, like any good pilot test, can teach us lessons that "just do it" can't. "Just doing it" leaves no trail. Not knowing where we've been, we can't really know what we did that accounts for where we're at.

At work, astute pilot-testers document the going-in premises, plan, and expected outcomes before launch so that progress can be monitored. They borrow techniques from the 3% and apply them in the 97% that matters, not in search of Lean Six Sigma certainty but to detect early warnings of implementation problems to sidestep, plus develop opportunities to exploit. They accumulate knowledge from each experience, learning lessons others miss, adapting and growing and succeeding against odds that stymie others—basic training for leadership.

And, per Principle 9, they *etch all decisions in jell*. Etching them in jell automatically rejects finality in favor of agility based upon a stream of lessons learned during execution. We not only up the odds of success as we go, but we also get better at learning lessons and at applying them promptly to works in progress and to future implementations.

The power of upstream, cross-functional ignorance and errors to sabotage other departments downstream

Some employees may think that just getting their job done one way or another is two jobs—their job, plus all the unfinished business others keep sending their way. In fact, as workforces grow in size and complexity, employees typically know less and less about how each department interconnects and goes about its job and how severe the downstream consequences can be of upstream errors and delays that seem incidental to those who create them and who are also just trying to get their work done.

Everyone thinks that everyone else is the problem, a problem that finger pointing and excuses don't solve. The truth gets caught in the crossfire, shredded from both sides, at which point I call a truth truce by invoking Principle 2, *Nothing is ever what it seems. The truth lies elsewhere*, which I assume, rightly, will turn out to be accurate.

The revelations soon turn up a mutual problem so gnawing that everyone involved wants it solved. Employees discover they have virtually no concept of what others do, how and why. Acts that seem reasonable and necessary to the doers turn out to create devastating unintended consequences up and down the line. I've seen doers become appalled by the harm they've done, confessing, "I can't believe I didn't see this."

The power of tactical solutions to first domino problems to solve major chunks of strategically big problems

Admittedly, some big challenges, like integrating medical records across hospitals, insurers, medical practitioners and patients, argue for big solutions. But the specifics of most Leadership Test waste and dysfunction are singular to the organization looking for relief.

In such circumstances, look for the first wobbly domino in a sequence of must-do events for getting something done. Gluing down that first domino is often quite manageable and can have profoundly positive stabilizing effects on dominos down the line. Usually, gluing down a few solves much or most of the big problem at a fraction of the cost and aggravation of big solutions. Furthermore, first-domino solutions pretest new processes and other changes, allowing critical adjustments before venturing into a wholesale solution that touches every domino, even those that don't need gluing, creating new problems where there weren't any before.

The insurance company in Principle 10, *Implementation is never a "no-brainer,"* was a case history in point. Enrollment forms emanating from the sales department cascaded into the enrollment department with high percentages of errors and omissions that the enrollment people had to rectify before medical providers considered enrollees truly insured. Employees were doing their job as faithfully as possible, but keeping up with the rework created huge waste. Talk of a total process overhaul dominated the thinking. Its objective: to micromanage each step in the process so that no error could slip through. Finally, someone asked if the complicated enrollment form—the first domino—was the culprit, and it was. And it was simplified. And the existing process and system then worked fine for the most part. Could it be tinkered with to handle increased volume error free? Sure, and the IT people now knew exactly what to tinker with—not "overhaul."

Surprises like this one pop up routinely. People-process and people-to-people interactions at specific points can be the problem from the outset. Such problems often require focused, rather than big, solutions and investments, with results often exceeding expectations at minimal time and cost. Bite-sized solutions to big problems present lessons from the front line that management bent on big solutions would be wise to listen to. They also teach enterprising employees that, through small successes, they too can experience what it's like to lead.

The misuse of accountability

When a manager delegates accountability without the seven prerequisites for achieving it, he or she sets up the project and the responsible person for failure. Employees who have felt the sting of such failures suddenly see how unnecessary those failures really were.

I have witnessed this phenomenon at every rung on the management ladder. Some employees on lower rungs were new to leadership and naïve in delegating accountability effectively. At the other extreme, some managers at higher levels deliberately offloaded accountability and risk to deflect responsibility from themselves, maybe even to engineer an underling's failure. But most managers simply assigned accountability—as they were taught—to make sure employees understood who was primarily responsible for what task and what outcome. When expectations were not met, a smog of attacks and counterattacks polluted the air.

Was there something fundamentally flawed, I asked myself, about the whole idea and practice of "accountability?" Out of the quest came the seven prerequisites and the realization that without them in place, management undermines the accountability it seeks. That realization comes as a shock to delegators—until they think about the time and resources they waste overcoming accountability breakdowns.

The fix isn't all that mysterious: pause up front to assess whether whoever is accountable has all seven prerequisite in place and if not, shore up any weaknesses before moving ahead. Then be realistic about what can't be shored up, especially the gap due to limited authority over others. The gaps leave you faced with several options:

- ⊚ Identify holes and plug them as a team and organization before proceeding—the most successful way.

- ⊚ Plug the biggest holes, live with the rest, and plug the rest of them on the fly if needed—a viable way if closely monitored and backed by a rapid response team (but if holes remain unplugged, the risk of failure can rise fast).

- ⊚ Adjust the scope or nature or deadline of the project to align expectations with what's possible, or scrap the project in favor of better use of resources—an unpopular call with project advocates but one that keeps active, priority projects on schedule and stops cannibalizing the enterprise's scarce time and resources in favor of new projects that jeopardize those in progress.

All of these options decisively trump the business-as-usual way: namely, ignore the prerequisites, assign accountability, and plunge ahead. Think of the No Fail alternative as an accountability risk assessment. Do it and you end up making not a business-as-usual decision but an informed business decision—namely, "What level of risk do we want to accept?" You decide. You accept.

You delegate knowing you shouldered the risk. Accountability assigners like you may not appreciate having to adjust the accountability and expectations they load on whoever they want to hold responsible. But in the end, the risks will be better understood by all, along with the individual responsibilities and accountability of those making unique contributions. More will get done with buy-in, on time, with fewer resources, and done right.

No Fail Leadership isn't always easy. If it were, everyone would already be doing it, blunting its competitive edge.

Start small. Word of No Fail Leadership's success solving nagging problems will spread quickly, and so will interest, especially since so many Leadership Test problems engage cross-functional problem solvers. As the pool of No Fail veterans grows, so will camaraderie, and an expectation of accomplishment. And so will a culture shift, for that's the ultimate achievement, a No Fail culture. As you well know, culture change of any kind is a tall order, because, as Machiavelli cautioned in 1512, "The innovator has for enemies all those who have done well under the old conditions and lukewarm defenders in those who might do well under the new."

Don't get impatient with yourself or others when experimenting with No Fail Leadership. Bring newcomers up to date with the No Fail process as you have used it, so that you incorporate them into the experiment.

When you hit a roadblock in the middle of solving a problem the No Fail way, don't panic. Simply go back to Principle 1 on conflicts of beliefs and work your way forward again. Chances are the conflict simply hadn't surfaced the first round, emerging only after extended discussion laid it bare or after people got past their fears of speaking up. Keep trying.

And keep learning. Each success teaches how to succeed more efficiently the next time. And each improvement in your enterprise's performance puts you incrementally ahead of competitors, who fall farther behind. Eventually you may find that the culture and standards come close to your own.

ACKNOWLEDGMENTS

Some books "take longer." This was one of them, its manuscript caught up in a Darwinian flux. A broadening base of clients put No Fail Leadership's principles through fitness tests, with survival lessons worth incorporating. The pace of evolution eventually settled down, until I turned the manuscript over to Heather Lee Shaw, editor and book designer. Her astute questions challenged me to rethink assumptions and ideas, leading to clearer ones, better stated, that cast my net over an audience beyond the businesspeople I initially targeted. For that, her professionalism, and faith in the value of the book, I offer my sincerest thanks.

To Jim Ellison, retired president of Ellison Technologies, mentor and friend of fifty years and the embodiment of a No Fail leader. Over the decades he challenged me with some of the most broadening assignments of my career.

To Rod Jones, Senior Advisor at DMG / *Mori Seiki* USA and renowned expert in the machine tool industry, who immersed me in Japanese management thinking and high-tech manufacturing practices.

To Frank Morsman, a friend whose ongoing encouragement and suggestions coupled with his encyclopedic knowledge of history and philosophy helped anchor my understanding of the present.

To Jan Carlzon, President of Scandinavian Airlines in the 1980s, and his frontline employees, who showed me how they aligned their entire operation and workforce to keep a powerful promise of performance to their customers.

To Dr. Leonard Bertain, consultant and early colleague, who shared his methods of solving problems from the front lines all the way back to the production lines.

To Diana Deming Cahill, daughter of Dr. W. Edwards Deming, who helped track down the origin of her father's warning to business leaders that the 3% they can measure misses the 97% that matters, the leadership problem this book seeks to overcome.

To Stanford University psychologist Carol Dweck, whose book *Mindset: The New Psychology of Success* shed bright light on the dynamics of leadership success and failure. Thanks for meeting with me.

To Dr. Dan McDougall, founder of Bizedquest, business educator, trainer and author who critiqued early versions of the manuscript.

And to Brad Istnick, the talented, imaginative designer who created a cover for *The 97% Factor* that captured its thrust and spirit with power and class.

Most of all I want to acknowledge the contributions of members of my talented, accomplished family. My wonderful wife Valerie tops the list, for her love, friendship, good instincts and judgment, and unwavering support. Her studies in the human spirit outside the business world helped me understand its power within it and the power of the 10 Principles. Daughter Tracy, who's love, work ethic and achievements have inspired family and friends. Daughter-in-law Valerie (yep, another Valerie), and son Jeff, an active duty Army colonel, both in advanced leadership positions, dug deep into the manuscript to ensure the relevance of the No Fail Leadership principles and practices in their business consulting and military settings. Daughter Hilerie, a professional singer and small business entrepreneur dealing with her overflowing voice studio, scoured every line of text to make sure that eager newcomers to the world of business and leadership understand every word and idea. Son Tyler, a creative team lead and lifetime disciple of the No Fail Leadership way, whose devotion and passion helped carry the book across the finish line. And finally, thanks go to our eight grandchildren, especially the younger ones, whose mere presence helped bare the roots of workplace behavior.

INDEX

The 8th Habit: From Effectiveness to Greatness, 299
10 Principles of No Fail Leadership, 18, 43

Ajax, 56
accountability, 216–223, 234–241, 285, 358
Alphas, 195, 197–199, 201, 229
American Consumer Satisfaction Index, 280
assumptions, 52–68, 228–229, 330–334
Avis, 46

Bad Leadership, 196, 308
Baker, Edward M., 38
The Beast in the Jungle, 144–145
belief, 85–107, 127–128, 203, 237
Bertain, Leonard, 45, 52, 361
blame, 215–241, 326
Bold, 56
Bonabeau, Eric, 97
bullies, 114–115, 160–161, 195, 203

Cahill, Diana Deming, 362
Cavanaugh, Roland, 35
Carlzon, Jan, 187–188, 197–199, 280, 295–297, 361
China, 325
Chrysler, 310
Churchill, 90
Claus Fornell International Group, 280
Clorox, 55–56
Cold War, 144
competition, 55–56, 65
complexity, 139–141
conflict, 119, 158–159, 161–163, 327
Consumer Reports, 148, 325
Continuous Quality Improvement, 37
control freaks, 186

Copernicus, 94
Corporate Culture and Performance, 130, 143
Covey, Stephen, 299–300
customers, 278–282, 286–289

decision-making, 261–274, 305–322
Deming Award, 48
Deming, W. Edwards, 37–38, 76, 98, 247
denial, 174–175
design, 73–76, 79–80
The Design of Everyday Things, 74
Detroit Big Three, 37
Disney, 36, 290
distrust, 77–78
DMG / Mori Seiki USA, 361
Doyle Dane Bernbach Advertising, 46, 369
Drucker, Peter, 261, 272, 289
Dweck, Carol S., 308–311, 362

Einstein, 98
Ellison, Jim, 324–326, 334–336, 361
Ellison Technologies, 324–326, 334–336, 361
Ellison Way, 334–336
enterprise, 65–67
Erlandson, Eddie, 195

failure, 33–35, 208–212
fear, 109–128, 159–160, 203, 227, 327
Ford, Henry, 90
Ford Motor Company, 38
Fortune 500, 35

Galileo, 94
Gandhi, 90
Gates, Bill, 90
General Electric, 90, 310–311
Gerstner, Lou, 310–311
Google, 75

Harvard Business School, 59
Harvard Business Review, 59
Heskett, James, 130–132, 143
Holmes, Oliver Wendell, 139, 216, 258
honesty in advertising, 47
Human Computer Interaction, 75, 78

IBM, 310–311
implementation, 323–349
improvisation, 72
In Search of Excellence, 187
intimidation, 234–236, 238
Iacocca, Lee, 310

James, Henry, 144–145
Janitor in a Drum, 56
Japanese manufacturing, 37
Jones, Daniel, 93, 154
Jones, Rod, 361

Kardes, Frank R., 88, 147, 255
Kellerman, Barbara, 196, 199, 205, 308, 311
Kilty, Tim, 334–336
Kotter, John, 130–132, 143

Lean Six Sigma, 36, 41, 45, 48, 75, 246–247, 292, 345, 351
Lean Thinking, 93, 154
learning to lead, 33
Lenovo, 325
Lestoil, 56
Levitt, Theodore, 59–60
Liker, Jeffrey, 41
Lincoln, 90
Ludeman, Kate, 195

Machiavelli, 35–36, 95, 99
Managing for the Future, 261, 272
manufacturing, 174

Marceau, Marcel, 74
Marcher, John, 144–145
Maslow, 116–117
Mass Casualty Incident, 12–16, 19–23, 27, 173, 245–246
Mattel, 325
McDougall, Dan, 362
McEnroe, John, 310–311
McManus, George, 255–256
Microsoft, 75, 90
Mindset: the New Psychology of Success, 308, 362
mission, 34, 293–303
Moments of Truth, 187
Mr. Clean, 56
Mulcahy, Anne, 310–311
myopia, 152–157

Nakao, Chihiro, 93–94
NASA, 75, 282, 297–298
Neuman, Robert, 35
The New Economics, 38
The New Turnaround, 45
The No Asshole Rule, 114, 308
No Fail Leadership Test, 30
Norman, Don, 74–75
neutrality, 92–93, 101

opinions, 250–260
Our Lady Hospital, 12–16, 20–23, 245–246

Pande, Peter, 35
Pandora's Box, 263
paradox of strong beliefs, 100, 105
performance, 58
People Process Interaction, 78
personal problems, 142
Peters, Tom, 187
philanthropy, 57
Poirot, Hercule, 111

Porsche, 93–94
processes, 69–81
Procter & Gamble, 45, 53, 185–186, 363
product, 51–62, 279
    intangibility, 59–62
    marketing, 55–56, 60
    naming, 55–56, 60
    packaging, 56, 60
promises, 277–303

quality control, 61, 325, 340–341

Rely, 185–186

Sanbonmatsu, David M., 88, 147, 255
safety in numbers, 38–39
Saul's epiphany, 91
Scandinavian Airlines System, 186–188, 197–199, 280, 295–298, 361
Scientific Management, 186
setbacks, 34
service, 60
ServiceMaster, 289
simplicity, 139–141
Six Sigma, 35, 36, 37, 41, 45, 48, 78, 89, 104, 149–150
Snowy Bleach, 56
Stardust, 55–56
statistical process control, 37
Sutton, Robert, 114, 308, 311

Taylor, Frederick Winslow, 186
Top Job, 56
Total Quality Management, 37, 45, 48, 89
Toyota, 325, 334
The Toyota Way, 41, 325, 334
Toxic Shock Syndrome, 186
truth, 96–99, 133–170, 175–213, 248

U.S. Army, 294, 297–298
U.S. Constitution, 139

value, 288–289
victims, 115–118, 160–161, 203
Volkswagen ads, 46

waste, 38–40, 77
Welch, Jack, 90, 310–311
West Point, 176–177, 184
Wiedeking, Wendelin, 93
Womack, James, 93, 154
Work Ethic, 195

Xerox, 310–311

ABOUT THE AUTHOR

NIEL K KLEIN'S CAREER BEGAN IN MARKETING at Procter & Gamble and advertising at Doyle Dane Bernbach, winning national and international awards for his work after founding his own firm. Attracting business to a client's door was challenging, but the bigger challenge was helping clients keep it and grow it. That triggered a venture into the realm of internal dysfunction and how to overcome it, especially in service, support and customer-intensive activities where production-bred methodologies that focus on processes and metrics work least well. Out of that immersion evolved the 10 Principles of No Fail Leadership.

Klein's clients have spanned service, distribution, manufacturing and not-for profit organizations, with major assignments in the healthcare, financial, airline and machine tool industries, in consumer and business-to-business products and services, and in media, education and culture. Klein earned a B.A. from Stanford University and an M.A. from UCLA. He and his wife live in Traverse City, Michigan.

Contact the author at nklein@nkkbooks.com.